MYTHOLOGIES OF MIGRATION, VOCABULARIES
OF INDENTURE: NOVELS OF THE SOUTH ASIAN DIASPORA
IN AFRICA, THE CARIBBEAN, AND ASIA-PACIFIC

MARIAM PIRBHAI

Mythologies of Migration, Vocabularies of Indenture:

Novels of the South Asian Diaspora in Africa, the Caribbean, and Asia-Pacific

UNIVERSITY OF TORONTO PRESS
Toronto   Buffalo   London

© University of Toronto Press Incorporated 2009
Toronto   Buffalo   London
www.utppublishing.com
Printed in Canada

ISBN 978-0-8020-9964-8 (cloth)

Printed on acid-free, 100% post-consumer recycled paper with vegetable-based inks.

Library and Archives Canada Cataloguing in Publication

Pirbhai, Mariam, 1970–
    Mythologies of migration, vocabularies of indenture: novels of the South Asian
    diaspora in Africa, the Caribbean and Asia-Pacific / Mariam Pirbhai.

    Includes bibliographical references and index.

    ISBN 978-0-8020-9964-8

    1. English fiction – South Asian authors – History and criticism.   2. English
    fiction – 20th century – History and criticism.   3. Indentured servants in
    literature.   4. South Asian diaspora in literature.   5. South Asians in literature.
    6. Great Britain – Colonies – In literature.   I. Title.

    PR9080.5.P57 2009   823'.914093553   C2009-901846-2

University of Toronto Press acknowledges the financial assistance to its
publishing program of the Canada Council for the Arts and the Ontario
Arts Council.

University of Toronto Press acknowledges the financial support for its publishing activities of the Government of Canada through the Book Publishing
Industry Development Program (BPIDP).

In loving memory of my mother,
Qamar Iqbal
(your story is my legacy)

Contents

Acknowledgments

Drs Amaryll Chanady, Frank Birbalsingh and Ty are owed a special thanks for seeing in this work something of value, even at its fledgling state.

Dr David Docherty, the Dean of Faculty of Arts, and the Research Office of Wilfrid Laurier University, must be thanked for funding this project at various stages of its production. My colleagues at the Department of English and Film Studies have helped me see this project through with much professional guidance and support. I am also greatly appreciative of the efforts made on my behalf by Daniel Quinlan, Associate Editor at University of Toronto Press, and to copy-editor Dr Miriam Skey, for her meticulous work on the manuscript.

Author Cyril Dabydeen's poetic insights into the Caribbean have greatly enriched my reading of this special part of the world. Similarly, my conversations with Priti Sharma and Chamika Kalupahana about South Asian immigrant identities are an indelible part of this book.

No endeavour is ever complete without the intellectual input and nurturing guidance of my siblings, Dr Reza Pirbhai and Nooreen Pirbhai; and a heartfelt thanks to my parents for having had the courage to show us the world through the eyes of the diaspora.

My husband, Ronaldo Garcia, is owed my deepest gratitude for always believing, for always listening, for always inspiring ...

PART ONE

The South Asian Diaspora

1 The Multiple Voices of Indenture History: An Introduction

Indenture: A 'New System of Slavery'

The movement and migration of South Asian peoples predates European colonial history, and can be traced back to several millennia of intellectual exchange, inter-cultural contact, and vigorous trade that is most tellingly manifested in the imprint of Hindu, Buddhist, and, later, Islamic civilizations across the Asian continent. However, the largest dispersal of South Asian peoples within a finite historical period occurred under the auspices of the British colonial administration in a post-emancipation economy. There was a burgeoning demand for manual labour on sugar, rubber, tea, and coffee plantations in the island colonies; for the construction and policing of such projects as the East Africa Railway; and for administrators, servicemen/women, merchants, and traders to the far posts of the Empire. This not only put into effect an unprecedented impetus for individual and en masse migration, but also gave rise to a new diaspora of cross-continental range and global reach. No continent was left untouched by South Asian migration, which spanned the greater part of the nineteenth and early twentieth century, and brought with it the panoply of languages, knowledge systems, religious beliefs, social mores, and cultural traditions of the diverse peoples of the Indian subcontinent.

The principal recipients of South Asian immigrants in unprecedented numbers were East and South Africa, the Caribbean region, South-East Asia, Mauritius, and Fiji. The Indian subcontinent was also indelibly altered by the push and pull of migration at this time, the most significant example being Ceylon (present-day Sri Lanka), which received a staggering one million and a half immigrants of largely Tamil origins.[1] While it was still a settler colony, Canada[2] also saw an influx of mainly Punjabi immigrants around the turn of the twentieth century, but this population remained negligible until the mid-twentieth century. In fact, shortly after the earliest influx of Chinese and South Asian peoples to North America, Asian immigration was prohibited or severely curtailed up until the post–Second World War era. In the United States, for example, antimiscegenation and anti-immigration laws culminated in the implementation of the Oriental Exclusion Act in 1924, which banned immigration from Asian countries; similarly, South Asians were denied entry into Canada by 1908 and immigration remained strictly controlled as late as the 1970s.[3]

Even though the South Asian presence in the western hemisphere emerged alongside European imperial expansion,[4] South Asian immigration to North America, Europe, and Britain's settler colonies mainly brings to view a second major wave of migration of which the initial catalysts were the interrelated factors of the world wars and the decolonization of the British Empire. For instance, the period between the 1960s and 1980s witnessed a substantial increase in South Asian migration as a response to Europe and North America's shortage of industrial, skilled, and professional labour, resulting in the subsequent lifting of their racially discriminatory immigration policies. During this period, the Middle East oil boom also created a demand for South Asian labour in Gulf Arab states, which has since created another important axis of the South Asian diaspora. Suffice it to say, en masse South Asian migration to the western hemisphere, and western Asia in particular, should be regarded as a more recent, ongoing phenomenon driven by the political economy of a post-colonial era and globalizing forces.

The bulk of immigration to the Caribbean region, South-East Asia, East and South Africa, and the islands of Mauritius and Fiji, took place within a finite period between the 1830s and 1920s. The very sizeable presence of migrant populations in the British colonies necessitated various kinds of professional, administrative, commercial, and domestic services. The ever-expanding Empire turned to its colonial subjects in the Indian subcontinent[5] to help meet its increasing bureaucratic and other demands. For example, colonial functionaries in East Africa often regarded Goans (people from the former Portuguese colony of Goa along the southern Malabar coast of the Indian subcontinent), as ideal clerics and administrators, given their English-language skills. In contrast, wholesalers and traders from the northwestern state of Gujarat populated the commercial centres of East and South Africa as well as South-East Asia, continuing a centuries-old tradition of mercantilism.

Together, such migrants were referred to as 'free passengers' or, in some colonies, as *khula* (open)[6] since they were not bound to the contractual obligation of indentured labour, and since their arrival, settlement, and return to their point of origin was, at least in theory, a matter of independent choice and means.

The majority of peoples who migrated during the colonial era, however, did so for the purposes of contractual work, which came to be known as indentured labour. Indenture was the British Empire's solution to an urgent shortage of manual labour, primarily in the plantation colonies, after the abolition of slavery. Indenture is defined as 'a formal agreement, contract, or list ... binding an apprentice to a master.' During the colonial era, indenture referred to the agreement signed by a person 'to work for a set period for a colonial landowner in exchange for passage to the colony.'[7] Thus, the major difference between the free passenger and indentured migrant was as follows: the former was generally an autonomous agent (albeit circumscribed by a colonial infrastructure) while the latter was bound by a written contract (covering a period of two to five years), which dictated everything from the terms and conditions of labour to the accommodations and freedom of movement (or lack thereof) in the colony.

The severely restrictive terms to which the indentured labourer consciously or unwittingly agreed resulted in his/her appellation as *girmit-wallah/girmitiya* or the 'agreement people.' Historian Hugh Tinker notes that '[i]n folk-art, the indentured Indian was always portrayed with his hands bound together, and shoulders hunched: for he was now a tied creature, a bondsman.'[8] In other words, the labourer was no longer a free agent but a doubly bonded entity as a colonial subject and as a contracted worker, headed for conditions that have been described as little better than slavery. Subsequently, several stereotypes formed around the indentured labourer (as they did for the African slave), condemning him/her to images of servility and bondage.

Indeed, the use and abuse of indentured labourers grew out of the legacy of slavery and, at least in its earliest stages, bore an unsettling resemblance to its historical precursor. Prior to 1842, the exportation of labour from the northern and southern regions of the Indian subcontinent was an unregulated trade which neither the local nor colonial authorities cared to monitor or police.[9] In fact, the first group of indentured labourers to arrive in Mauritius ended up joining an older community of South Asian slaves who had served the French plantocracy as early as the 1700s. As the first colony to receive contracted workers from the Indian subcontinent in unprecedented numbers, however, Mauritius became the blueprint from which a more regulated system of indenture developed, as much in the interest of Indo-British relations as in the upkeep of agricultural productivity.

The push for migration during the colonial era was often driven by the dire conditions prevalent in the ancestral homeland. Historians now speak of the disruptive effects of colonial rule as a catalyst for migration, particularly for the peasantry whose lives and livelihoods were devastated by the exploitative taxation system of the British Raj. In his third novel, Trinidadian author Sharlow Mohammed provides a scathing indictment of colonial practices and the internal forms of displacement they produced for the local Indian civilian. In a novel aptly titled *The Promise,* which alludes to the false promise of an *el dorado* often used to entice prospective migrants, Sharlow traces the disruption of a peaceful pastoral Indian village.[10] The arrival of the British tax-collector is strategically followed by the appearance of the *arkatiyas* (or recruiters for overseas labour) to offer the promise of rescue for those facing ruin in the implementation of the new land tax. For the character of Mahadeo, then, the refusal to 'pay taxes for our own property' results in not only his removal from his family's land but also a six-month jail term under the new 'land-laws' of the colonial taxation system.[11]

The Indian Rebellion of 1857[12] has also been identified as a major push for migration, given the increased militarization and policing of the subcontinent, and the fear of persecution for those suspected of anticolonial activity.[13] As will be seen in chapter 3 on Mauritius, Deepchand Beeharry's foundational indenture narrative *That Others Might Live* – a fictionalized historical account of the labourers' plight – exposes several of the catalysts for migration as they were created by the destructive presence of the British Raj itself, particularly in the post-mutiny era.[14] As more examples of the indenture narrative emerge alongside revisionist historiography and increased archival research on this aspect of British colonial history, writers seem to be turning a more critical eye not only on the deployment of criminal elements in the business of recruitment (the emphasis on trickery and coercion finding its way into many of these stories), but also on the general atmosphere of political repression, social unrest, and economic exploitation created by the British Raj, which often made conceivable the otherwise unthinkable prospect of leaving the homeland. Again, in Sharlow's *The Promise* the following lines capture a sentiment that is echoed by various characters who find themselves making the journey to the colonies: '"Leave India?" Rati whispered again. India was her home, the only world. It was not possible to think of leaving the holy land. Here it was all the gods lived: in the fields and in the air, and in the rivers.'[15]

The main ports of embarkation were Madras and Karikal on the Indian subcontinent's southern coast, and Calcutta on the northern coast. These ports of embarkation drew a largely rural, Hindu-dominated populace from the surrounding southern Malabar, Coramandel, Tamil, and Telugu districts, and the northern regions of Bihar, Bengal, and Uttar Pradesh. Historical records and archival data indicate that Hindus constituted the overwhelming majority of indentured labourers (86 per cent) who ventured overseas. Muslims comprised the minority (14 per cent) of indentured labourers, though they generally made up the larger body of free passenger migrants who made the voyage to Africa, South-East Asia, and Fiji as merchants and traders. Punjabis who also went to the colonies as free passengers usually did so in their occupational capacity as policemen or as military officers rather than as agricultural labourers. However, Punjabis were the first South Asians to have emigrated to the United States (as early as the 1820s) and to Canada (by the turn of the twentieth century), where they found employment as agricultural labourers and have since come to constitute the first generation of diasporic South Asians in North America.

Colonial records also indicate that the majority of indentured labourers (both male and female) were lower caste Hindus (including 'untouchables'), while '16 percent belonged to upper castes, 32 percent to agricultural castes.'[16] The high percentage of lower caste Hindus has led historians to speculate that emigration may have presented itself as an opportunity to escape the rigid hierarchies and occupational structures of the caste system. It is further suggested that many of the single women (particularly those of lower castes) who emigrated during this time did so to escape the sexual and other abuses of the *zamindari* (the local feudal system), or to elude the punitive consequences of acts deemed by the Hindu orthodoxy as sexually or socially transgressive. As Subramani affirms with regard to the Fijian context, indenture 'was the first stage in the transformation of the feudal Indian into an individual.'[17]

However, historians are equally quick to point out that the female migrant's position as a conspicuous Oriental minority in a predominantly male demographic of migrant workers, together with the grossly exploitative conditions of plantation life and colonial rule, often subjected her to even harsher forms of abuse than those she might have sought to escape. But here, too, generalizations should be avoided. As indenture historian Brij V. Lal suggests, indenture also provided women the means to escape various forms of bondage, including child marriages, and caste discrimination. Since this early generation of female migrants 'were employed as individuals in their own right,' they could exercise some level of economic independence once in the colonies.[18] However, the material conditions of indenture (lower wages for women, for one) as well as the inescapable fact of gender disparity, which rendered these women a doubly marginalized entity within an already oppressive system (further circumscribed by patriarchal attitudes and structures) immediately put these women in a vulnerable position, which left them open to sexual assault, concubinage, prostitution, and even uxoricide. In this regard, historian Verene A. Shepherd refers to the experience of migrant women on the plantation as one of 'ultra-exploitability.'[19]

On the one hand, the systemization of labour resulted in a more strictly legislated and principled administration of an otherwise haphazard trade; on the other hand, it merely facilitated in greater numbers the supply of workers who continued to be regarded as 'units of production.'[20] Like slavery, the indenture system was eventually dissolved, coming to an official end in 1922, after three generations of labour at a very low cost to the European plantocracy and British administration.[21] Like the African slaves, too, the vast majority of labourers had little choice but to settle permanently in their diasporic location, thereby creating multigenerational communities whose mythic and historic beginnings continue to be traced to the moment of their ancestors' arrival in the colonies, thousands of miles from home.[22]

The 'Old' South Asian Diaspora: A Sociohistorical Overview

There are approximately seven million South Asians who constitute what Indo-Fijian scholar Vijay Mishra refers to as the 'old Indian Diaspora'; that is, the descendants of people who first crossed the Indian, Pacific, and Atlantic Oceans to arrive in Britain's numerous outposts and plantation colonies across the imperial century. In *Literature of the Indian Diaspora*, a study of diasporic writing from both the western and non-western hemispheres, Mishra makes the significant distinction between 'old' and 'new' diasporas from the Indian subcontinent:

> To explore the narrative of the Indian diaspora critically, we may want to read it as two relatively autonomous archives designated by the terms 'old' and 'new.' The old (that is, early modern, classic capitalist or, more

specifically, nineteenth-century indenture) and the new (that is, late modern or late capitalist) traverse two quite different kinds of topography. The subjects of the old ... occupy spaces in which they interact by and large with other colonized peoples with whom they have a complex relationship of power and privilege.[23]

Mishra's distinction is one that is central to my own discussion of these writers and contexts, for the material and historical factors that have given rise to these two vectors of migration are central signifiers in the mapping of a diasporic body of writing. However, I also take Mishra's circumscribed reading of the 'old Indian Diaspora' as my point of departure on a number of levels, more of which will be said in chapter 2, in the section entitled 'Theorizing the South Asian Diaspora.' For the purposes of delineating the major historical, material, and geopolitical differences between the en masse migration that took place in the two periods marked as 'classic capitalist' and 'late capitalist,' however, Mishra offers a useful point of clarification.

Given the centrality of religious identification throughout the history of South Asian civilizations, religious delineations were not only carried over in the process of migration but were often determining factors in the process of resettlement and acculturation overseas. In fact, rooted as the majority of indentured peoples are in religious tenets and customs, their literatures are often grounded in a distinctly Hindu ethos. By extension, the South Asian diaspora can itself be examined in terms of its multiple sites of religious identification, primarily those of Hinduism, Islam, and Sikhism. Even though religious identification is a distinctive feature of South Asian diasporic communities as a whole, the diaspora itself should not be classified in the traditional or biblical sense of a religiously allied group undergoing persecution or exile. Rather, as the continued centrality of religious identification might suggest, the South Asian diaspora affirms a strong collective identity that is rarely articulated in the semantics of a detribalized, decentred, or deterritorialized consciousness. On the contrary, diasporic South Asians generally form tight-knit ethnic and religious enclaves with strong social structures, endogamous relations, and cultural traditions that help preserve a deeply rooted sense of community. These communities should not be mistaken, in turn, as unified or homogeneous; they are dynamic, highly stratified, and often contentious alliances, internally divided by such factors as religion, caste, class, language, gender differences, generational differences, political ideology, nationalistic feeling, and orientation to the host society itself.

It is also important to keep in mind that the first wave of South Asian diasporic peoples has undergone a major historical shift in the transition from a colonial to a post-colonial era. As all of the regions under study will reveal, the era of decolonization drastically reconfigured the diasporic community's positioning within nascent post-colonial states. Where indigenous communities were present, South Asian peoples often found themselves precariously positioned between anticolonial and nativist discourses. The en masse expulsion of South Asians from Uganda in 1972 under the notorious edict of then President Idi Amin Dada is the most overt manifestation of such internal racial and political tensions.[24] Similarly, the 1987 coup which ousted Fiji's first multiracial government, though not accompanied by a clear policy of ethnic apartheid, has compounded the poetics of exile that already permeated the Indo-Fijian psyche. For the Indo-Fijian, like his/her counterpart in Uganda, diasporic experience is prefigured as a series of multiple displacements, or exile-as-continuum, rather than as a completed pattern of transplantation and resettlement. Indeed, the radical diminishment of South Asian diasporic populations in the entire East African region in a post-independence era,[25] and the continuing emigration outward of Indo-Fijians since the 1987 coup[26] also underscores the volatile position of diasporic populations in the process of nation building.

Each of the contexts considered herein indicates that a pattern of interrelation has emerged in the post-independence and, in the case of South Africa, the post-apartheid era. Diasporic South Asians in the non-western hemisphere fall into three possible axes of interrelation: dyadic, triadic, and quadratic. The dyadic axis consists of indigenous populations living alongside the diasporic group, or it consists of two diasporic groups, of virtually equal size, coexisting. East African countries and Fiji account for the former configuration, while the Caribbean context, specifically Trinidad and Guyana, account for the latter configuration. The triadic axis has particular resonance in the former settler colony of South Africa where diasporic South Asians and indigenous Africans live alongside the European settler. The triadic axis is also applicable to Malaysia, where native Malays, Sino-Malaysians, and diasporic South Asians form the bulk of the population, though we might also speak of the triadic axis as one of the principle features of the colonies, where Europeans lived alongside several diasporic and indigenous groups. Finally, the quadratic axis is unique to Singapore's vibrant multiethnic state, which is home to peoples of Chinese, European, and South Asian origin, as well as to indigenous Malays. The particular axis along which diasporic subjectivity is formed is implicitly addressed through conflict, character, and theme in the novels under discussion.

In the island communities of the Caribbean and Mascarene archipelagos, demographics have played a major role in nationalist formations. The Indo-Mauritian population, the largest ethnic group in the island, has not been at the political helm since the country's independence. In contrast, where Afro-Caribbean and Indo-Caribbean populations are almost equal in number, as is the case in Guyana and Trinidad, racial polarization still holds political sway. Finally, where South Asian diasporic populations constitute a minority or are part of a minority position with other ethnically delineated groups, they are usually politically subordinate to the dominant culture. This seems particularly true where political power is racially hierarchized. This seems equally true of minority communities in the western hemisphere. However, a diasporic community's economic clout, political zeal, and other points of identification beyond those of ethnicity or race create a very different kind of political dynamic within a given national context. For instance, Malaysia's Muslim-South Asian community has secured its place within the Malay-dominated Islamic Republic with far less cultural anxiety than its Hindu counterpart. And in the neighbouring pluricultural context of Singapore, the Tamil community is afforded linguistic, religious, and cultural autonomy albeit within a highly policed state governed by a largely Sino-Singaporean majority.

Given the ongoing economic and political instability of many postcolonial states, it stands to reason that diasporic experience has often resulted in subsequent migrations to other destinations, particularly to the western hemisphere. In fact, since the mid-twentieth century, the descendants of this older diaspora can be said to have merged with the new diaspora (the second major wave of South Asian migration of the mid to late twentieth century). Today, then, South Asian diasporic peoples might migrate from and to any number of diasporic locations worldwide. When they do so, they migrate not only as Sri Lankans or Bangladeshis but also as Trinidadians or Tanzanians (to name only a few examples).

Mira Nair's film *Mississippi Masala* is a wonderful example of this trend.[27] Here, a Ugandan of South Asian origin living out his exile in the United States yearns to reclaim his 'home' in his beloved Uganda, a theme that is echoed in exiled Ugandan author Peter Nazareth's novels. South Asian writers living in Britain also reveal the diasporic subject's transnational frame of reference. This can be seen in Meera Syal's novel *Life Isn't All Ha Ha Hee Hee*, a story of friendship among three South Asian women negotiating their cultural identities alongside the universal pressures felt by a new breed of urban, thirty-something professionals juggling mother-hood, romantic relationships, and careers. The most traditional member of the triad, Chila, is a Punjabi from East Africa, whose '*desi*-ness' is con-figured differently from that of her second-generation London-born peers, and she is further misunderstood by an education system that misdiagnoses her cultural malaise as a learning disability.

Even for those who are not forcibly exiled from their homelands, the subsequent migration westward (be it temporary or permanent) is shown to be an unfortunate economic, political, and/or social necessity rather than a much-anticipated journey to the Western metropolis. Thus, dias-poric peoples can be seen to occupy multiple territorial and national spaces in which the very concept of origins and home/homeland be-comes a highly individuated process of association and affiliation that is predicated on personal as well as collective history. Ironically, then, for the second or third generation diasporic subject living in the West, the mother country signifies the historic country of settlement rather than the originary culture (that is, the Indian subcontinent). Subsequently, South Asian diasporic writers identify the site of return not as the origin-ary culture but as the country of settlement most recently left behind. Whether they have remained in their countries of birth or engaged in subsequent migrations to the western hemisphere, however, the des-cendants of this early wave of migration continue to manifest the quint-essential characteristics of a diaspora and a concomitant 'diasporic consciousness' that is grounded in a cross-cultural and transhistorical network of identification.

This brings us to another subset within the old South Asian diaspora, namely, those who left the colony (the initial point of migration) to join the new diaspora in Europe, Australia, or North America. The latter group will be referred to throughout this study as the 'double diaspora.' I believe this label captures the simultaneous and multifold historical, geographical, and cultural realities that these migrants experience. For one, the double diaspora connotes the second catalyst for migration along an individual's personal migration history; it also signifies the complex subject position of straddling not just two cultures, to borrow Rushdie's phraseology,[28] but two diasporic trajectories simultaneously (namely, the old and new South Asian diasporas in the non-western and western hemispheres). In leaving out the national and geographic point of origin, the term 'double diaspora' implicitly draws attention to the extent to which diasporic subjectivity and interrelation is individually mapped for those whose cultural and geographic frames of reference are as multiple as they are varied.

When we speak of diasporic South Asians today, we are referring to people – be they descendants of the oldest diasporic communities or part of more recent migrations – who now occupy a common position away from the Indian subcontinent, a distance that is experienced, to differing degrees, in geographic, national, linguistic, political, socio-economic, ethnocultural, religious, and gendered terms. Of course, the diversity and complexity of South Asian identity can be traced to the Indian subcontinent itself, a densely populated region whose cultural fabric is as ancient as it is changing, and as cohesive as it is fragmented. On the other hand, South Asian identity continues to be shaped within the equally complex framework of multiple cultural and national affiliations that stretch from East to South Africa, West to South-East Asia, the Caribbean region, North America, Europe, Australia, New Zealand, and the islands of the Indian Ocean and the Pacific Rim.

2 New Approaches to an Old Diaspora: Theorizing Texts and Contexts

Theorizing the South Asian Diaspora

The ethnicity of South Asian migrants has historically been classified by British colonial administrators as 'Indian' in most locations of the diaspora. This is also a culturally expedient label of self-identification to refer to an otherwise diverse collective. Though the present-day countries of Pakistan, India, Bangladesh, Sri Lanka, Bhutan, Nepal, and the Maldives comprise the Indian subcontinent, India, as the largest of these nations, holds greater political and cultural currency on the international stage. Divorced from its geographic designation, therefore, the use of the term 'Indian' is all too often identified with the national entity, thereby imposing a monolithic ethnic and cultural identity on peoples who, prior to 1947 (the year of independence and the partitioning of the subcontinent) thought of themselves in regional, ethnic, and religious terms, i.e., as Punjabis, Tamils, and Biharis, or as Muslims, Hindus, and Sikhs, to name only a few examples. This would certainly have been the case for our early migrants who left their ancestral homeland one hundred years prior to Indian independence. For Goans, occupied by the Portuguese centuries before British colonization of the surrounding region began and decades after it ended, cultural and political distinctness is a necessary condition that renders the term 'Indian' meaningless in anything other than a geographic or statist sense.

Most theoretical, historical, and literary studies to date nevertheless continue to refer to this diaspora as Indian,[1] even though the authors are aware that the term 'Indian' often incurs accusations of 'historical inaccuracy and nationalist chauvinism.'[2] Indeed, Indian peoples themselves 'do not always interpret the term "Indian diaspora" in the same way.'[3] I have opted to refer to the peoples of the diaspora as 'South Asian' rather than 'Indian' so as to capture the historical and geopolitical breadth and complexity of a region which has undergone multiple reconfigurations, not only since European colonization but over a period of five thousand years. The term 'South Asian,' as a regional designate, offers a more accurate reflection of the vast geographic area of the Indian subcontinent, and highlights the positioning of these peoples within the greater Asian continent, itself an ancient arena of cross-cultural exchange.

South Asian peoples warrant their classification as a diaspora, not in the sense of the term's traditional association with the religious persecution of Jewish peoples, but rather with the broader understanding of diasporas as migrant communities with a shared set of interdependent historical, ethnic, religious, or other attributes. As all of the major diasporas illustrate, such as those of Jewish, African, Palestinian, Armenian, and Chinese peoples, a diasporic consciousness arises out of vastly different historical circumstances and should thus be viewed in polythetic terms rather than through a singular taxonomical lens.

The South Asian diaspora, in its demographic scale alone, suggests that there are many kinds of diasporic peoples within the larger phenomenon of South Asian migration during the nineteenth and early twentieth centuries. For instance, those who emigrated as free passengers come closest to our present-day conception of migration as an independent choice made possible by individual will and means. The indentured labourer of course may seem easily classified as a labour diaspora. However, historian David Northrup's suggestion that the push for migration from the Indian subcontinent had as much to do with the disruptive effects of British colonial rule there as with the prospect of material opportunities overseas complicates this assertion. As I have suggested, recruitment itself was often a coercive process that included false promises of 'lands where the streets were paved with gold'[4] or simply the exploitation of those at their weakest and most vulnerable state. Even as a labour diaspora, then, we might think of the various motivations and circumstances (voluntary and involuntary) that would compel an individual to leave his/her cherished homeland. These include the desire for adventure and fortune seeking, escape from political, social, or other forms of persecution, or internal dispossession and displacement.

Anthropologists have traditionally viewed diasporic identity as an oppositional tension between an authentic past and an inauthentic present. In other words, the homeland is branded as a static, monolithic, and ahistorical entity while the diasporic location is thought of as the site of ontological fracture and instability. This vision of diaspora has since been refuted, given its obvious deference to a totalizing view of cultures and cultural identity. Anthropologists Smadar Lavie and Ted Swedenburg correctly suggest that 'diasporic populations frequently occupy no singular cultural space but are enmeshed in circuits of social, economic, and cultural ties encompassing both the mother country and the country of settlement.'[5] Such critical reevaluations owe much to post-structuralist critique. In exposing the discursive and infinitely open-ended nature of signification, deconstructive methods expose any such fixed and essentialist cultural codes as constructs that serve as potentially hegemonic acts of self-legitimization.

However, post-structuralism alone cannot account for the complex processes of diasporic identity formation. This is because diasporas give way to a politics of identity which is perhaps most acutely and self-consciously subject to the interplay between rupture and continuity, similarity and difference, and de- and reterritorialization. Consequently, diasporas tend to reconstitute themselves in the critical juncture between ontological ambivalence and an essentializing politics of identity. In other words, diasporas are both passive and active agents in the politics of location and identity.[6] The post-structuralist method does not account for the impulse of the diasporic subject not only to deconstruct and interrogate fixed notions of identity but also to engage in a self-conscious restructuring of identity in self-affirming and often militant terms, particularly when posited against discriminatory practices, racial hierarchies, and other forms of oppression.

As far back as W.E.B. Du Bois's conceptualization of black diasporic identity as having produced a 'double consciousness,'[7] it has become de rigeur to speak of diasporic displacement in the semantics of a hyphenated or split identity. This is an ironic attribute for a cultural phenomenon that is also seen to internally displace any such binary model.[8] Nevertheless, diasporas undeniably inhabit a time frame that brings to view the reality of 'here' with the memories and resonances of a necessary 'elsewhere' (particularly in the early stages of resettlement and for first-generation migrants). In turn, this is shown to create a sense of disorientation (an intellectual and cultural ambivalence) to the systems in which they find themselves.

The diasporic subject pivots around what I call a 'multiply positioned identity,' which is further undercut and transected by such factors as gender, class, ethnicity, religion, generational differences, and sexual orientations, all of which necessarily alter the dynamics of diasporic experience and identity. Moreover, as 'already hybridized'[9] entities, the 'here' and 'elsewhere' do not necessarily prefigure oppositional, hierarchical, or mutually exclusive spheres, but are often dynamic systems of cross-cultural influence and exchange.

To date, theorizations of the African diaspora have offered the most widely applicable hermeneutics of diasporic consciousness and experience. This is particularly true of its applicability to the South Asian diaspora, considering each group's inextricable relationship to the plantation economy. However, the African diaspora should not become a master trope (even for those diasporas which grew out of or intersected its historical vector) for the diasporas created under the historical catalyst of European imperialism. Indeed, the South Asian diaspora and its imaginative landscape must be mapped along the course of its own particular trajectories. Caribbean theorist Edouard Glissant makes this distinction explicit in his classification of the African diaspora as a 'transferred diaspora' and other émigrés in the Caribbean as 'transplanted' diasporas, to underscore the difference between the forced dislocation meted out by the slave trade and other forms of migration that facilitated the direct transplantation of the familial, verbal, and physical cues that ensure communal wholeness.[10]

In his model of the 'old Indian diaspora,' Vijay Mishra marks an important shift away from the overreliance of the Middle Passage and African diaspora to explain those diasporic formations born out of plantation history. The Middle Passage, the term used to refer to the Atlantic slave trade, connotes the trauma of forced removal, enslavement, and exile for the millions of Africans transported from Africa to the New World. The Middle Passage has powerful echoes for indentured labourers who made a similarly treacherous oceanic journey from the Indian subcontinent. Much in the same way that the crossing of the Atlantic ocean has come to convey the profound sense of displacement, rupture, and inestimable loss of life created by the Atlantic slave trade, the oceans that carried the indentured labourers far from their homes are poetically referred to as the dark or black waters, the *kala pani*, the symbol of the diasporic subject's separation from the sacred homeland.

Offering the first sustained theorization of the old South Asian diaspora, Mishra's emphasis on its historical and material genealogy undercuts the post-modern conceptualization of diasporas as an all-encompassing symbol of late modernity. Moreover, Mishra's suggestion that the 'old Indian diaspora' reconstituted itself as sites of 'exclusivism'[11] also confirms James Clifford's notion that diasporas often retreat within a self-protective space in response to the discriminatory, assimilationist, or essentializing gaze of the 'other.' It further points to Stuart Hall's concept of the diasporic imaginary as the projection of the past through the realm of representation and symbolism – an act of 'desire, memory, myth, search, discovery'[12] – given the impossibility of an actual 'return.' Indeed, loss and the incumbent methods of cultural and material survival in a foreign and often hostile environment are part and parcel of the diasporic text's thematic concerns, particularly for writers of the old diaspora. This is predicated on Mishra's concept of *girmitiya* ideology – the emphasis on the *girmit* or contractual 'agreement' drawn up by imperial administrators – which functions as the diaspora's raison d'être in the colony. For *girmitiya*, or agreement people, the original terms of agreement and the respective degrees to which they are experienced as sites of trauma, betrayal, abuse, and, to a lesser extent, individual and spiritual triumph, serve as the teleological basis for the birth of a new cultural and historical consciousness.[13]

However, it is important to note that Mishra turns to the Indo-Fijian diaspora as the definitive template of diasporic experience, and he restricts his theorization of the particular kind of 'imaginary' produced by this diaspora to its predominantly Hindu population and spiritual beliefs. In this sense, Vedic traditions come to typify the doctrinal and other belief systems of the diaspora at the expense of cultural and religious diversity, locational specificity, and temporal determinants. Not only does this erase the vast canvas of historical, national, and regional differences that make up the diasporic collective as a global phenomenon, but it also erases gender, religious, and other differences while homogenizing the motivations, conditions, and experiences of migration and settlement across the nineteenth and early twentieth centuries. Indo-Fijian author/scholar Sudesh Mishra has also come to perceive the limitations of Mishra's paradigm. Though he rightly points out the fact that Vijay Mishra is 'not oblivious to such crossovers and fusions,' he goes on to conclude that 'within the historically divided framework of shared nomination, the old diasporas represent – and V.S Naipaul's oeuvre is a worrying source for much of this representation – largely self-enclosed or internally "continuous" societies.'[14]

In other words, Vijay Mishra tends to overemphasize the 'traumatic' and uniform underpinnings of the South Asian diaspora insofar as this precludes the diverse factors that gave rise to South Asian migration during the colonial era, including the element of choice for indentured labourers and free passengers alike. Similarly, in his emphasis on the diaspora's ethnocentrism as a compensatory drive to transplant and recuperate the motherland (the object of loss), Mishra also glosses over the local expressions of national and cultural belonging or the complex processes of syncretism, creolization, and indigenization that are evident in multigenerational communities in the Caribbean and other locations. Moreover, as Sudesh Mishra critically underscores, Vijay Mishra's model of 'communal cohesion' is largely predicated on 'an almost monotheistic concern with a single sacred text, the *Tulsidas's Ramayana*.'[15] As will be seen throughout this book, the *Ramayana*, as the epic tale of exile, combat, and return, reappears as a metatext in the literary and spiritual life of Hindu diasporic subjects. Often, the trope of Rama's exile is employed as a literary conceit designed to elevate the diasporic subject's condition from degradation and disillusionment to self-aggrandizement and heroism. However, references and allusions to the *Ramayana* are often quite polemically broached. As a distinctly patriarchal narrative that positions Rama's wife, Sita, in a distinctly subordinate position, while brandishing an ethnocentric world view of Aryan ascendancy, the *Ramayana*, like the Hindu ethos itself, must be seen as an expression of one particular group within the diaspora rather than as emblematic of the old diaspora and its descendants writ large.

In this light, I would suggest that the poetics of exile is particularly resonant among early migrants for whom the possibility of return was written into the contractual agreement of indenture itself, suggesting that life abroad would be a temporary investment of blood, sweat, and tears. Where such returns became impossible, the feeling of betrayal and exile has assumed the epic proportions of Rama's travail. However, for those who chose to stay in the new land or never imagined the return journey, as well as for subsequent generations born in the diaspora, Rama's epic circular journey might also be seen as a self-defeating rather than a redemptive metaphor that is not entirely commensurate with the diverse and ever-changing realities and configurations of 'home' in the diaspora.

Mythologies of Migration, Vocabularies of Indenture

With the rise of this diaspora came the concomitant development of a body of writing which responded, be it through oral testimony, cultural history, folklore, or lived experience, to the particularities of migration, transplantation, and resettlement in Britain's numerous plantation, interventionist, or, in the case of South Africa, settler colonies. This book specifically examines the writing of those South Asian migrants and their descendants, whose historical genesis is either directly or indirectly related to the phenomenon of indentured labour or to inter-related patterns of en masse migration and labour history under British imperial rule. Most of the regions under study, except the Caribbean, received both kinds of migrants – that is, the bonded labourer and the free passenger – while plantation colonies received the highest number of indentured labourers. The Caribbean alone received over 750,000 migrants during 1838–1917, the official period of indenture.[16]

Literary works that have emerged from peoples whose migration history can be traced back to the era of indentured labour accordingly warrant an appreciation and awareness of the British 'imperial century.' This is a loosely interconnected body of writing bound by repeated evocations of a collective consciousness that is anchored in colonial history and the vocabulary of indenture. This involves the semiotic and mythic nomenclature of indenture history as a shared experience of travel, transplantation, and resettlement in plantation estate 'logies,' or the makeshift housing of the plantation colony; the quotidian rites and rituals of cultural and material survival within the restrictive boundaries of the plantation economy; the poetics of survival embedded in 'immigrant success stories' for those whose migrations were opportunities for personal and spiritual growth or upward social mobility; individual and familial negotiations with castehood as it is symbolized by the crossing of the *kala pani* (black water, so named for its Hindu signification of caste contamination, mainly for Brahmins, once away from the sacred Gangetic plain); the turbulence of anticolonial uprisings and national independence struggles as they impact diasporic communities; and the ongoing catalysts for migration and diasporic reconfiguration in a post-colonial era or at the behest of globalizing forces.

The vocabulary of indenture refers to a cluster of terms that came to be defined both by colonial administrators and South Asian peoples themselves in the management of and emergent mythology about the experience of bonded labour, migration, and transplantation as Britain's colonial subjects. These terms include the Hindi or Urdu words *girmitiya* (agreement people, to refer to the contractual nature of bonded labour); coolie (a derogatory term to disparage those engaged in manual labour, and then redeployed by the British colonial administration as a racial slur); *khula* (meaning 'open' to refer to the free passenger or passenger

Indian who travelled voluntarily or by independent means); and *jahaji-bhai* or *-bhain* (ship brothers / sisters, a term of spiritual fraternity initiated by the traumatic and perilous journey across the *kala pani*). These terms become the linguistic, cultural, and metaphysical markers of a shared migration history, which has set in motion a distinct imaginary found across the body of South Asian diasporic writing.

Given the varied but largely intersecting histories of the labourers, freed labourers (those who carried out the terms of their contract to its completion and became permanent settlers in the colonies), or free passengers under the aegis of European colonial rule, the kinds of stories produced by this diaspora usually foreground individual experience through the lens of collective memory and communal interrelation. Moreover, even for those novelists who have been comfortably settled, across several generations, within the adoptive homeland, the diasporic novel soon reveals that an individual's migration history and genealogy of settlement within the colony is at the forefront of the diasporic imagination. This is where the distinction between the old and new diaspora becomes crucial. Unlike the first- or second-generation perspective of the new diaspora, the immigrant experience for the old diaspora is usually captured in the context of a multigenerational saga, where grandmothers and grandfathers or great-grandmothers and great-grandfathers carry the weight of transplantation and rupture, and are mythologized as heroic individuals in family lore, since it was these forefathers who took the historic leap of faith across the *kala pani* or transported their dreams for a better life across the far-flung outposts of the British Empire.

Though one might imagine that the first novelists to tell the tale of their ancestors' journey would be drawn to the genre of historical fiction, this has not been the case. In fact, Deepchand Beeharry's *That Others Might Live* is the earliest example (in English) of what I have classified as an indenture narrative. The indenture narrative is a story that functions as a revisionist reading of the initial impetus for and experience of emigration in the colonial period, with particular emphasis on the day-to-day vicissitudes of bonded labour and life in the colonies under indentureship. The indenture narrative might also be referred to as the *kala pani* narrative when emphasis is placed on the recruiting methods of the *arkatis* (the Hindi term for recruiters) and other functionaries of the British Raj, and on the rewriting of the Middle Passage paradigm in the depiction of similar degradations and fatalities for South Asian migrants on-board colonial ships. The indenture narrative made its earlier appearance in short fiction. A marvellous example of this is South Africa's

Agnes Sam's 'And They Christened It Indenture.' Here, the entire process of indentureship is synthesized in three short pages, a parodic inversion of a Christian parable, though the moral of the tale is projected at the multifaith community of South Africa's citizenry:

> And when they survived cholera, dysentry and typhoid, and after they resisted the impulse to throw themselves into the Indian Ocean, and they finally arrived at their destination, to be given in bondage to a master of indentureship – only then they understood, as clearly as they could not write their names, that although they belonged to a master, and could not move anywhere without the master's permission, they certainly were not slaves. For slavery had been abolished. And a bond is a man's word.[17]

Since the collective migration history of colonized peoples has been a mere footnote in the official annals of imperial history, these novels are dotted (through direct reference or allusion) with the historic markers of its epic journey. For example, the names of the passenger ships that would have transported the early migrants to their colonial destinations are often commemorated: the *Leonidas*, the *Fatel Rozack*, the *Syria*, the *Shah Allum*, and others. Here, K.S. Maniam's *The Return*, Satendra Nandan's *The Wounded Sea*, and Lakshmi Persaud's *Butterfly in the Wind* stand out, for they either eulogize the losses incurred in the perilous ship voyage, or celebrate the heroism of past generations who took the initiative to emigrate and prevailed, usually in the absence of family and community and against seemingly insurmountable odds, in the colonial outpost. Indeed, many of these novels, irrespective of their settings within contemporary post-colonial societies, incorporate some aspect of indenture history in their characters' mental, physical, spiritual, and cultural cartographies of being. In this regard, one of the main features of the indenture narrative – the description of recruitment in the subcontinent and the historic ship voyage westward across the Atlantic or eastward to South-East Asia or the Pacific Rim – appears in the form of a subplot or flashback which memorializes ancestral struggle in the formation of character and his or her advancement of communal unity and cultural self-preservation.

The descendants of indentured labourers have not been the only ones to see, in the experience of indenture and its considerable demographic, cultural, and socioeconomic impact on life in the colonies, the creative material for novel writing. As a literary endeavour that seeks to

imaginatively record life on the plantation under indentureship, the indenture narrative can be said to have begun in the 1877 work, *Lutchmee
and Dilloo: A Study of West Indian Life*, by the Indian-born British barrister
Edward Jenkins, whose personal history as an advocate for the indentured labourer in colonial Guyana culminated in the earliest study of
Indo-Guyanese life. Similarly, Trinidadian-born A.R.F. Webber's *Those
That Be in Bondage: A Tale of Indian Indentures and Sunlit Western Waters*
(1917) was unique insofar as it provided a study of plantation life from
a white Creole perspective (and here I use 'Creole' as it was understood
in the colonial period to refer to those of European ancestry born in
the Caribbean). Later, the post-indentureship period of the 1920s
and the subsequent movement for labour reform that became the cornerstone of anticolonial struggle in the early part of the twentieth century
ushered in the publication of Edgar Mittelholzer's *Corentyne Thunder*
(1941). Mittelholzer's own life in the small coastal towns of Guyana during the early twentieth century might have given him the occasion to
observe the daily routines, speech, and interactions of the peasantry, not
only in the drudgery of plantation labour, but also in the personal, human-
izing realm of the individual as a fallible though complex being. These
are perhaps the best known novel-length studies of indenture experience
and plantation life by those who are not part of the old diaspora.

The relative dearth of indenture narratives penned by this early generation of diasporic novelists might be accounted for in socio-political
terms. Since these novelists emerged in the era of decolonization, during the 1950s and 1960s, their attention was focused on the increasing
expression of ethnonationalism or the racialized politics of the emergent post-colonial state. In almost all of the locations under study, the
post-colonial moment has quite often radically altered the trajectory of
diasporic peoples. It is this volatile destiny that many early writers sought
to capture through various modes, including satire, the post-colonial
dystopia, social or documentary realism, the post-colonial Bildungsroman,
and elegiac prose. For instance, those novels set in Guyana, East Africa,
South Africa, and Fiji focus on the tumultuous present rather than the
ancestral past.

This brings us to the 'narratives of native paramountcy,' stories that
describe the dyadic axis of the diaspora and the indigene, where the
latter is still reeling from the material and ideological fall-out of colonial occupation and dominance, and the former's lingering presence
on native soil becomes a symbol of past injustices. Uganda and Fiji are,

of course, the most obvious examples of the tenuous position of the diaspora in the move toward the nation-state. Each location has thematized the phenomenon of 'native paramountcy,' or the strategic favouring of the 'native' on the part of the outgoing colonial regime, as it applies to the African and Polynesian indigene respectively. Peter Nazareth's *In a Brown Mantle* and Satendra Nandan's *The Wounded Sea* are significant examples of this genre. Narmala Shewcharan's *Tomorrow Is Another Day*, which depicts the racially divisive government of Forbes Burnham (Guyana's first president), provides a different model of native paramountcy. While no indigenous population is favoured by the outgoing colonial regime, the South Asian diaspora finds its political aspirations eclipsed by the African diaspora's territorial claim on the former colony in the wake of the colonizer's departure. These are stories which quite overtly foreground an exilic perspective and subject-position in the persona of the 'bastard sons' of Mother Empire, created and then abandoned by their surrogate imperial guardian at the birth of the nation.

Here, one might also speak of the 'narrative of exile-as-continuum,' which comes out of the moment of decolonization, and its subsequent recasting of citizenship and belonging in ethnonational terms. It is also the catalyst for subsequent migrations from the adoptive homeland, and the resultant commingling of peoples of the old and new diasporas in the western hemisphere. Exile-as-continuum also evokes the internal forms of displacement that the diasporic subject has come to experience beyond the post-colonial moment, either as an internally felt condition of outsidership or at the level of *real politik* (be it under racialized policies and systems of representation, minority politics, or other forms of cultural and political disenfranchisement).

Fortunately, life in the diaspora has not always produced such a bleak picture. Indeed, the 'narrative of upward mobility,' a story of individual and collective empowerment through financial gain, access to education, professional achievement, and cultural autonomy, is as much a part of the mythology and actuality of the old South Asian diaspora as its narratives of dispossession and exile. The immigrant success story as another feature of the collective saga of the indentured labourer and his/her descendants also considerably rewrites the poetics of victimhood associated with the image of bondage and servitude. This suggests that both the free passenger and the indentured labourer might well have seen and realized, to differing degrees, horizons for self-betterment in the cartography of empire. The thriving communities of Trinidad,

Singapore, and Mauritius, and the ever-growing community of South Africa are telling examples of this phenomenon at the collective level. Indo-African author M.G. Vassanji poetically underscores the labourers' Odyssean spirit of adventure in suggesting that something greater than material forces propels the individual to leave behind all that is familiar: 'For Indians abroad in Africa it has been said that it was poverty at home that pushed them across the ocean. That may be true, but surely there's that wanderlust first, that itch in the sole, that hankering in the soul that puffs out the sails for a journey into the totally unknown.'[18]

As James Clifford asserts, 'Diasporic experiences are always gendered.'[19] The gendered experiences of migration are particularly poignant where the drive for upward mobility is not merely a material struggle but also an intellectual and spiritual struggle directed by a feminist or at least a female-centred consciousness that strives for self-determination against communal, colonial, and national structures of subordination and exclusion. The fact that diasporic writing has been a traditionally male-dominated activity reminds us that women have often found themselves silenced by the limiting parameters of old and new patriarchies, that is, a double patriarchy consisting, on the one hand, of colonial structures and, on the other hand, of the religious doctrines and sociocultural norms transplanted to the new land by diasporic peoples themselves. In one of the most vitriolic critiques of the distinctly male-dominated Fijian literary tradition, Shaista Shameem denounces the Indo-Fijian writer for imposing the same obstacles to publication and representation on the female writer that the male writer had to fight in terms of Western-imposed aesthetic and cultural standards.[20]

As the largest populations of the diaspora in the non-western hemisphere, the Caribbean and South Africa have afforded a 'gendered' reading of South Asian diasporic literature for a longer period than other regions. For example, the steady appearance of several new Indo-Caribbean women novelists over the past two decades (for example, Ramabai Espinet, Joy Mahabir, Ryhaan Shah, Niala Maharaj) is as indicative of a break in what began as a distinctly male-dominated literary tradition, spearheaded by the likes of Samuel Selvon and V.S. Naipaul, as it is of the increasing marketability of female writers over the last few decades since the emergence of feminist interrogations of Caribbean and postcolonial identity. Similarly, women novelists have come to form a considerable voice in African literature, both within the continent and in its satellite island society of Mauritius.

This is a truly significant turning point in the development of the South Asian diasporic novel on a number of levels. First, these female authors offer a gender-specific reading of migration history and experience for the descendants of the old South Asian diaspora (here, I prefer the term gender-specific to feminist, because the former does not ipso facto produce the latter, nor is the latter exclusive to women-authored texts). Second, they bring to the genre various stylistic, aesthetic, and thematic innovations, such as the female Bildungsroman or women-centred family sagas variously structured around the matrilinear chain. Third, and perhaps most significant, they challenge the dominant poetics, tropes, and archetypes that have been accepted, at face value, as the definitive features of female diasporic subjectivity. In particular, the Rama-Sita paradigm, which presupposes female devotion and self-sacrifice for the exclusive insurance of male integrity and ascendancy, is quite often challenged or overturned by women writers whose communities have come to revere the stories of the *Ramayana* (and Rama's distinctly male plight of suffering, exile, and heroism) as the spiritual corrollary to diasporic experience.

Perhaps the most striking challenge to the male-dominated tradition of novel writing by this diaspora is the feminist and historiographic shift in emphasis from the perspective of the *jahaji-bhai* to that of the *jahaji-bhain* (from ship-brotherhood to ship-sisterhood). This is a direct response to the historic erasure of indentured women's lives in the male writer's psyche and in official colonial records. Lakshmi Persaud's *Butterfly in the Wind*, Farida Karodia's *Daughters of the Twilight*, and Rooplall Monar's *Janjhat* foreground the female perspective in the struggle for individual and collective self-empowerment, while K.S. Maniam's *The Return*, Deepchand Beeharry's *That Others Might Live*, Narmala Shewcharan's *Tomorrow Is Another Day*, and Sharlow's *The Elect* thematize this struggle in the form of minor or subsidiary female characters.

In all of the diasporic regions under study, novel production has proved to lag behind other genres, appearing as the final frontier for literary production after the short story, poetry, and drama. Each region of the South Asian diaspora has brought to bear on the diasporic writer its own set of publishing opportunities, expectations, and constraints. For instance, the paucity of English-language novel production in Mauritius or Malaysia has as much to do with the designated status and politics of the English language in Mauritius's dominant French/Creole environment or among Malaysia's indigenous Malay-speaking population as it does with the numerous challenges of publishing. Conversely, the initial popularity of drama and poetry across the diaspora attests to the indelible influence of South Asia's ancient literary traditions and the rich textual, aesthetic, and artistic traditions of Hinduism and Islam on diasporic cultural production. This influence is poignantly captured in the fact that the extravagant and colourful dramatization of the Hindu epics, the *Ramayana* and *Mahabharata*, are still a common sight in regions as far-flung as Trinidad and Singapore, and they continue to be a common source for allusion, imagery, and theme in diasporic writing.

Though the novel is an inherited genre, the recent emergence of the novel in many of these diasporic contexts has less to do with a group's versatility with the genre than it does with other socio-economic factors. For the descendants of indentured labourers, for instance, English-language literacy itself came about in the late nineteenth century with the granting of access to missionary schools. Moreover, the technical and financial obstacles of publishing in small literary communities as well as the greater expense and risk that novel publication necessarily incurs, particularly if it is to survive reprint or reach an international audience, continues to be a factor that curtails novel production across the ethnic and linguistic communities of many of these regions. It is not surprising to find that many of the authors under study who write across genre (namely, Peter Nazareth, Deepchand Beeharry, Gopal Baratham, K.S. Maniam, Rooplall Monar, Sharlow Mohammed, and Farida Karodia) first garnered attention for their short fiction, poetry, or plays before they turned their attention to novel writing.

With the era of decolonization several decades behind them, and with a greater sense of a shared stake in the national culture, younger writers, alongside researchers and publishers, are turning their attention and resources to the excavation of the diaspora's buried histories. Access to archival data, to old colonial records, to the documentation of oral history and testimony, and modestly increasing government support for such activity is ironically producing a generation of writers who, in spite of their distance from the historic moment of arrival, are better equipped to narrativize the historical genesis of the diaspora. This phenomenon applies most readily to the Caribbean and South African contexts where there has been a much longer tradition of novel writing, at least in the sense that it is a genre that has found expression across several generations. A younger generation of writers is increasingly concerned with migration history, not merely to come to terms with the experience of dislocation or transplantation, but to partake in the wider cultural conversation as 'citizens' who are now firmly rooted in the new land, and whose racial memory forms an indelible part of national consciousness. Here, 'the *kala pani* narrative' functions as a focused attempt to fill in historical gaps not only in family and community lore but also in national lore, by describing the kind of degradations and fatalities on-board colonial ships and as 'units of labour' that African slaves had once endured. Since writing their first novels, several of these writers have gone on to write indenture narratives or at least to write historical fictions that encompass not only the characters' immediate past in the diaspora but also the ancestral past in the originary homeland. Sharlow's *The Promise* (1995) and Lakshmi Persaud's *Raise the Lanterns High* (2007) are two such examples.

The Locational Politics of Author and Text

Mirroring these patterns of migration, most of the writers under study identify themselves as the descendants of indentured labourers, with the exception of Peter Nazareth, Farida Karodia, and Gopal Baratham (whose ancestors made the journey as free passengers). This is indicative of the differences to be found across the colonies, as South Africa, East Africa, and Singapore were popular destinations for voluntary migration for those seeking commercial opportunities or civil service positions. Fiji and Malaysia also received a more diversified migrant body, though indentured peoples formed the larger and older communities in these locations. Those who directly or indirectly call attention to their migration history as the descendants of free passengers nonetheless reveal a shared experience of diasporic subjectivity under the intertwined social, cultural, and economic fabric of the British colony. Their personal and communal destinies are often shown to be enmeshed in the greater imperial machinery that governs colonial migration and settlement.

In all cases, these writers are second- or third-generation descendants of the peoples who comprised the first major historical wave of migration between the 1830s and the 1920s, which, to date, has received little attention as a distinct historical and cultural phenomenon. This period calls for a model of inquiry and a set of reading practices that are necessarily different from those applied to writing by and about more recent post-war, post-colonial waves of South Asian émigrés. As subjects of the British Empire, the majority of the descendants of indentured labourers and free passengers alike would have received a colonial education – hence the proliferation of English language literature by South Asian diasporic peoples and its intersection with many of the themes and tropes of post-colonial writing. It should be noted, however, that South Asian diasporic peoples continue to produce literature in their own ancestral languages, such as Hindi, Urdu, Bhojpuri, Tamil, and Punjabi, not to mention more recent contributions to French and Creole literary production in such areas as the Mascarene and Caribbean archipelagos.[21]

The majority of writers under study – namely, Mauritius's Deepchand Beeharry, Malaysia's K.S. Maniam, Singapore's Gopal Baratham, Guyana's Rooplall Monar, and Trinidad's Sharlow Mohammed – never left their countries of birth, establishing their literary careers therein. As such, they offer a rare and important glimpse into contemporary diasporic experience from the perspective of the descendants of South Asian immigrants who are now several generations removed from the originary homeland and who constitute a near-bicentennial presence in their respective diasporic locations. Moreover, they are all among the first generation of English-language novelists in their own regions; they are also among a handful of novelists of South Asian origin who hold a prominent place in the production and canonization of anglophone writing. Maniam and the recently deceased Baratham (who passed away in 2003), for instance, have been leading literary and academic figures in South-East Asia. Not only does Beeharry occupy a similar position in his native Mauritius but this prolific author also stands out in his classification as the first Indo-Mauritian novelist, if not the first English-language novelist to emerge from this vibrant polylingual and creolized context.

This book provides a critical analysis of non-Western contexts which, though necessarily engaged in and influenced by the literature and literary developments beyond their borders, are also centres of literary production and activity in their own right. My decision to search out authors who have remained 'at home' in their diasporic locations is not meant to confer on these writers a passport of authenticity reminiscent of the anthropologist's 'native informant,' one which ipso facto precludes the possibility of imaginative representation of the homeland from the perspective of the exile or émigré. Rather, it is intended as a gesture of inclusion of those texts and contexts that constitute the centres of literary production and their accompanying schools of literary criticism outside the Western metropolis. As scholars of South Asian literature Arun Mukherjee and Aijaz Ahmed have suggested from their own migrant vantage points in Canada and England, the 'valorization' of 'the deterritorialized, border-crossing sensibility as the possessor of a special kind of truth'[22] is not only a custom-made straightjacket designed to fit all manner of South Asian writers living in the West but also serves to desensitize us to the 'difference between documents produced within the non-Western countries and those others which were produced by the immigrants at metropolitan locations. With the passage of time, the writings of immigrants were to become greatly privileged and were declared, in some extreme but also very influential formulations, to be the only authentic documents of resistance in our time.'[23] Of course, this calls for the re-orientation of our own perspectives as readers and scholars, for it invites us to reconsider those conservatively held 'peripheries' of English literary production as individual satellites or 'centres,' each of which inhabits its own axis of cultural, national, and diasporic interrelation. A cross-continental body of writing whose centre can be said to be both imaginary and multifold further decentralizes, if not democratizes, our perspective as readers and scholars.

My focus on the locational politics of author and text admittedly emerges in response to the persistent eclipsing of South Asian diasporic writers who have either not made the journey westward or do not fall into the canon of those writers whose residency in the Western metropolis has, at least in more recent years, provided a comfortable niche of teachable and marketable texts. The formidable reputation of V.S. Naipaul at the expense of other diasporic writers of his generation offers perhaps the most recognizable case in point. Naipaul is conspicuously absent from this study, even though Vijay Mishra has suggested that his early novels laid the structural and aesthetic cornerstone, in the Caribbean context, of a diasporic poetics that is grounded in indenture history. Considering the sheer volume of criticism already available on Naipaul's estimable literary career, as well as Mishra's extensive theorization of Naipaul's 'diasporic poetics,' I have opted instead to draw on a selection of Naipaul's paradigmatic insights into the old diaspora as a referential tool for comparative analysis rather than as an authoritative or definitive statement on indenture experience or diasporic poetics.

In Mauritius and the Caribbean, diasporic experience does not always readily capitulate into the semantics of cultural dislocation that pervades Naipaul's world view.[24] Though the quintessential motifs of exile and transnationalism found in Naipaul's oeuvre are echoed in some of the texts under study – particularly those by Indo-Fijian male writers – these motifs are usually counterpoised by a desire to belong to the new land, if not by a sense of self-proclaimed rootedness therein. Moreover, a younger generation of writers reconceptualizes Naipaul's diasporic poetics of dislocation, cosmopolitan wandering, and colonial angst by turning their gaze inward to the diasporic community's own discourses of exclusion and sites of oppression – such as caste, class, and gender differences – while simultaneously articulating a politics of identification with the wider multi-ethnic body of the post-colonial state.

All the authors discussed in this book have been selected on the basis of their particular contributions to the development of anglophone novel production in regions and ethnonational configurations that have only recently come to the attention of a wider international readership. In a few cases they are the first novelists of South Asian origin to have had their works published locally. Thus they shed critical light on the literary history and development of South Asian diasporic writing in these regions. Though many of them do not receive the critical or commercial attention that ensures their works' longevity in the literary marketplace, it is my premise that were scholars to only chart the careers of the few authors who, for whatever reason, are ensured international marketability, literary criticism would not only be at the service of commercial interests, it would also be unduly confined to a geocentric vision of global literary production. Therefore, my criteria for selection, as well as my methodological approach in this study, is motivated by the desire to provide an alternative critical resource that helps chart the chronological development of diasporic writing within its national or regional contexts where foundational texts or literary 'firsts' (be it in terms of gendered authorship, thematic innovation, or chronological development) are difficult to trace in the Western academy because they have never made it to commercial bookshelves or classroom curricula, and have all too quickly fallen out of print.

I have also tailored author selection to reflect, wherever possible, the author's contribution to, or subsequent impact on, the local literary tradition. Here, Farida Karodia (one of the first female novelists of South Asian origin in apartheid South Africa) offers an important case in point. Karodia has since returned to her place of birth in the post-apartheid era. This return has ushered in a continued output of novels of increasing length and significance to the local literary and academic community. As Rajendra Chetty notes, 'Karodia is a hot publishing property, like many female writers in South Africa, due to the marginalisation and exclusion of women's writing by the academe and the androcentric publishing houses.'[25] However, if we were to judge Karodia's contributions and significance to post-colonial writing generally, and South African literature specifically, on the basis of the print value of her oeuvre, the short-lived life cycle of each of her texts, including the 2000 Penguin edition of her second last novel to date, *Other Secrets*, would render her

oeuvre a mere blip on the screen of Western and international scholarship. In other words, the publication history of a particular writer in the
international arena should not be seen as either an unqualified validation or a discrediting of that author's place in local canon formations or
literary lore. In some cases, I have also gone against the grain in terms of
local literary choices, foregrounding authors who might also be under-
valued for the same reasons identified above. I believe these authors
nonetheless speak to the development of the diasporic novel in a given
national context. Sharlow Mohammed provides an interesting example
of a writer whose career has been largely dependent on self-publication
in his native Trinidad. While this has necessarily limited his readership,
it does not detract from the important gaps in our understanding of the
locally and nationally centred interests and developments that his writing exposes and seeks to fill.

I have also generally restricted my reading to first novels with the pur-
pose of situating these writers' individual literary careers within the wider
framework of the history of novel production in a particular region. Too
often, studies ascribing to the label of diasporic writing pay little attention to local practices and processes of literary production and dissemination or the historical trajectories along which they arise, examining
texts solely on the basis of their particular thematic resonance or theoretical applications within transnational modalities. While such approaches offer insight into paradigmatic shifts, contextual particularities are
usually subordinated or glossed over in the interest of a study's a priori
focus. In this study, I work in reverse order by first offering an overview
of context; I examine historical and cultural backdrops in order to consider the exigencies, opportunities, and spheres of influence particular
localities have come to produce for the writer, and to provide some insight into the local critical machinery that often helps shape reader and
author sensibility. In this way, these texts are offered not merely as imaginative windows into localities but also as artefacts of that locality's literary history or documents of its unfolding literary identity.

A Note on the Authors

The oldest member of this group of writers, Deepchand Beeharry, has
produced the first historical novel in English to systematically chart the
development of indentured labour, from the moment of recruitment
in the Indian subcontinent to the administration of an otherwise ill-
regulated trade across Britain's colonies. In fact, in Beeharry's *That Others*

Might Live (1976), the documentary realism with which the author approaches subaltern agency in the reformation of living and working conditions that were 'little better than slavery' is indicative of the author's own lifetime achievement as a political advocate for Indo-Mauritians and the greater African community of which they are so indelibly a part. As noted earlier, the innovation of this novel lies in its depiction of the key features of an indenture narrative, including its historical veracity, its revisionist impulse, and its faithful description of the experience of indentureship.

Guyana's Rooplall Monar is now receiving the critical attention he deserves, particularly as the first Indo-Guyanese writer to set his works exclusively in the Guyanese interior's Lusignan Plantation Estate, one of the major sugar plantation estates of the old colony. Home to several generations of indentured labourers and their descendants, these estate dwellings became centres of an ethnic and cultural community which subsequently came under threat in the dismantling of the colonial plantation structure and the increasing urbanization of the Guyanese interior. Moreover, Monar's use of a Hindi-and Bhojpuri-based Creole adds a new lexical texture to the body of Creole writing in the Caribbean that is quite revolutionary.

Like Monar, Sharlow Mohammed is one among a rare breed of Caribbean writers whose writing life has been entirely lived in the diasporic location of his birth. His status as a largely self-published though no less prolific literary figure is itself a telling reflection of the obstacles to publication in a small literary community.[26] The author's dedication to channelling his pen into biting satirical portraits of contemporary Indo-Trinidadian life and culture is brought out in the novel included here. *The Elect* exposes local and imported forms of religious charlatanism, particularly American evangelicalism, which have consumed the devout Hindu populations of the Indo-Trinidadian enclave. Indeed, as a satirist Sharlow partakes in the tradition of the self-critical gaze championed by his contemporary V.S. Naipaul, while also offering a more redeeming portrait of Caribbean society, if only in his obvious celebration of its resilience when pitted against the often nefarious guises of neoimperialism. Indeed, as Sharlow continues to self-publish in his native Trinidad, he remains one of the most prolific figures in the local literary and cultural community. His studies of Indo-Trinidadian life as well as his more ambitious texts, such as *When Gods Were Slaves* (1993) – a fictionalization of the African slavers, the Middle Passage, and a detailed portrait of the slave plantation economy in Trinidad in the century before emancipation – mark his vigorous engagement with the broader onto-logical underpinnings of Caribbean society.

Uganda's Peter Nazareth, Guyana's Narmala Shewcharan, Trinidad's Lakshmi Persaud, and South Africa's Farida Karodia can be said to have joined, for personal, professional, or political reasons, the second major wave of South Asian migration to the United States (Peter Nazareth), Britain (Narmala Shewcharan and Lakshmi Persaud), or Canada (Farida Karodia), though Karodia has since returned to South Africa. These writ-ers can now speak of a double diasporic identity as the descendants of the first major wave of migration who now form part of the newer dias-pora in the western hemisphere.

Peter Nazareth has, since his exile in the United States, turned his atten-tion away from novel writing. As Professor of African Literature at the University of Iowa, Nazareth has contributed extensively to the body of criticism on East African literature, both as scholar and as director of the International Writing Program. With the exception of Jameela Siddiqi's *The Feast of the Nine Virgins* (2001),[27] Peter Nazareth's novels *In a Brown Mantle* (1972) and *The General Is Up* (1991) are the only extant texts to offer an insider's view of the historic expulsion of South Asian peoples, both the descendants of indentured labourers and free passengers, from Uganda in 1972. Penned a year before this momentous and, most would argue, tragic shift in political destiny for African-born South Asians, Nazareth's first novel eerily prophesies the event prior to the author's own expulsion. Though the 2003 publication of M.G. Vassanji's *The In-Between World of Vikram Lall* offers what may be characterized as the most detailed fictionalization of Indian-African relations, Nazareth's novel is one of the only such portraits to capture the dire consequences of ethnonationalism for diasporic South Asians, and thus constitutes a foundational text in Ugandan and, more specifically, Indo-African writing.

Laskshmi Persaud's inclusion in this book, a writer who continues to garner greater critical attention in England where she resides, is made all the more significant given her status as the first female Indo-Trinidadian novelist. Persaud holds an estimable place in Caribbean literature, bearing as she does the significant achievement of penning what is arguably the first 'full-length work' to be published by an Indo-Caribbean woman,[28] and continuing with a steady output of novels (all of which are set in the Caribbean and thus rarely betray the author's resi-dency in Britain) since the publication of *The Butterfly in the Wind.*[29] Much like Jamaica Kincaid, Maryse Condé, and other Afro-Caribbean women writers, Persaud has set the stage for other Caribbean women writers of

colour to break out of the straitjacket of a male-dominated literary tradition so as to widen the critical lens through which Caribbean history and
experience is witnessed and imagined. Narmala Shewcharan is one such
writer of a younger generation of Indo-Caribbean women. She is also the
youngest writer in this study and thus affords a cross-generational view of
Indo-Caribbean writing in particular. Set entirely in the Guyanese capital,
Georgetown, Shewcharan's first novel, *Tomorrow Is Another Day* (1994),
breaks narrative ground in its realistic indictment of the economically
crippling Forbes Burnham dictatorship in 1960s Guyana from the perspective of a 'male' Indo-Guyanese protagonist. Her strongest characters, however, are the Afro-and Indo-Caribbean women who are united
by the shared memory of the indignities of plantation labour regardless
of class, race, or gender differences.

South Africa's Farida Karodia brings a unique perspective to this study,
first, as a South African of Muslim-Indian origin, and second, as a strong
political voice whose life in exile mirrors that of many of her literary
peers. Her oeuvre offers a new point of entry into the developing archival research on representations of female agency in antiapartheid
activism. Her Bildungsroman, *Daughters of the Twilight* (1986), captures a
young Muslim girl's political awakening as a response to her family's dispossession by the Group Areas Act of 1950.[30] The Group Areas Act was
one of the first apartheid policies to rob 'Coloureds' and 'Asians' of their
properties and businesses, and it commenced the practice of relocating
them into separate racial homelands. The ensuing sense of displacement
and loss is all the more resonant for a girl whose father's history as part
of the South Asian labour force in South Africa's colonial outposts is a
recent memory of constant upheaval and economic uncertainty.

Karodia's migration history also makes evident the fact that diasporic
experience is continually unfolding, for she has since made the journey
back to South Africa. Between the publication of *Daughters of the Twilight*
in 1986 and the post-apartheid era, Karodia has been a lone star among
a male-dominated community of writers of South Asian origin. For this
reason, I believe she warrants special consideration as a pioneering voice
in the South African context. Since the contributions of Achmat Dangor[31]
and Farida Karodia to the novel genre from the 1980s onward, a new
generation of writers of South Asian origin has marked the turn to
the new millennium: Imraan Coovadia's *The Wedding* (2001), Neela
Govender's francophone text *Acacia Thorn in My Heart* (2001), and Aziz
Hassim's *The Lotus People* (2002) are three works that underscore the
multicultural make-up of South African identity and hint at the changing

frontiers of its literary landscape. This recent spurt of novel production not only signals the growing inclusiveness of South African cultural policy in the post-apartheid state, but also attests to the significance of Karodia's earlier contribution to antiapartheid literature. Her depiction of life under the regime as it is experienced by a multiracial caste of South Africa's disenfranchised outsiders becomes all the more compelling for having been imagined by an author who was herself in the throes of antiapartheid activism during the regime's heyday.

The seasoned literary careers of Gopal Baratham and K.S. Maniam are evident in their anthologized works and many contributions to the field of South-East Asian anglophone writing. Their inclusion in this book is a modest attempt at bringing their formidable reputations to light outside the academic circles of Singapore and Malaysia respectively. Gopal Baratham's witty *Kunstlerroman*, *A Candle or the Sun*, is an unflinching critique of the interrelated processes of self-censorship and state censorship in contemporary Singapore. Baratham's oeuvre, which includes detective fiction, also illustrates that diasporic fiction is not limited to its focus on migration history but also participates in the development and innovation that defines a national literary community. K.S. Maniam's *The Return*, on the other hand, overtly narrativizes indenture history in the form of the post-colonial Bildungsroman, giving voice to the *pendatang* (a pejorative Malay term for the immigrant or outsider) as he has been circumscribed by the 'coolie stereotype' of the common labourer still shackled to the destiny and bidding of Empire. Both authors reveal the rarely considered perspective of minorities or immigrants within the Asian hemisphere, whose histories are not only traceable to the period of migration and labour under the auspices of the British Empire but are also situated within an ancient arena of cross-cultural exchange between Islamic, Hindu, and Buddhist societies.

It is only fitting to conclude this book with a look at Fiji's first English-language novelist, Satendra Nandan, who is also one of the island's most recognizable figures, given his public life as a cabinet minister under the first multiracial government headed by Timoci Bavadra in 1987. Fiji was the last colony to receive indentured labourers, but the enduring legacy of indenture experience is nowhere more evident and perhaps has nowhere been more eulogized as the source of trauma and loss than it is in theorizations and creative representations of Indo-Fijian identity. Boasting one of the largest communities of the old South Asian diaspora, Indo-Fijians have an active literary community in Hindi, English, and more recently, Fijian Hindi. Not surprisingly, Satendra Nandan, a poet and scholar of national repute, penned and published the first full-length novel in English by an Indo-Fijian, *The Wounded Sea* (1991). A decade later, a considerable gender gap in Indo-Fijian literature was filled by Satya Colpani's *Veiled Honour* (2002), a portrait of the daughter of a conservative bourgeois Indo-Fijian family whose unquestioning acceptance of custom is put to the test in an emotionally unsatisfying arranged marriage and in the growing awareness, through a younger generation of women, that self-determination is not an exclusivly male birthright. Though these are not the first novel-length descriptions of Indo-Fijian life, they are the first contributions to the novel genre in English from the island. Nandan's novel brings this study full circle, starting as it does with Beeharry's foundational narrative of indenture as a story of survival and spiritual triumph in the first colony to receive indentured labourers, and ending, in the last colony to receive indentured labourers, with Nandan's distinctly elegiac lament of the volatile post-colonial destiny awaiting the descendants of these early colonial migrants.

This book makes numerous important inroads in South Asian diaspora criticism generally and South Asian diasporic literature specifically. First, it insists on the historical and material basis of the old diaspora, which simultaneously captures the diversity of colonial and post-colonial experience, in the formation of a diasporic consciousness and imaginary. Second, my focus on the non-Western hemisphere reorients the reader's gaze to consider movement and migration between non-Western societies and non-Western cultures rather than the largely unchallenged paradigm of the south to north or east to west trajectory of formerly colonized peoples, a pattern of migration that typically culminates in the Western metropolis. Third, this is the first monograph of its kind to draw cross-continental connections between Asia, Africa, and the island cultures of the Mascarene, Pacific, and Caribbean archipelagos, while also paying attention to local, national, and regional specificities. And, finally, these specificities are revealed not only in an author's individualized portrait of the diaspora, but also in terms of the local or national literary life out of which he or she emerges. As such, each chapter provides a national or regional literary map which features minor authors alongside those who have come to be regarded as prominent figures in either national or international circles, so as to situate these texts within a literary tradition – particularly in terms of the novel genre – in development.

Though Emmanuel S. Nelson's *Reworlding: Literature of the Indian Diaspora* (1992), Jasbir Jain's *Writers of the Indian Diaspora* (1998), Rajendra

Chetty and Pier Paolo Piciucco's *Indias Abroad* (2004), and Vijay Mishra's *The Literature of the Indian Diaspora* (2007) reveal the critics' increasing desire to expand our understanding of diasporic experience, both in terms of non-Western contexts and non-canonical authors (here Chetty and Piciucco's study stands out), the brush with which the diaspora is painted is still rather broad and unruly. In edited collections, South Asian diasporic writing is understandably approached as a disparate, globalized phenomenon or, in the converse desire to avert this 'imperative ambiguity,' as a highly localized phenomenon.[32] I believe a better medium can be struck between the open-endedness of diasporic experience (in light of the diaspora's ever-changing local or national spheres of influence) and its rootedness within a shared historical genealogy and cultural point of origin.

The writers included in this study accordingly speak from a multiply positioned identity that foregrounds the dialogic relationship between individual and collective memory, and between the individual and the ethnos, nation, and global community to which he or she belongs. This book is a modest attempt at filling the considerable gap in scholarship that currently exists on anglophone literary production by the old South Asian diaspora. Its focus on non-Western contexts as centres rather than peripheries of literary activity strives to offer a way into heretofore undiscovered or little-known material, and to foreground the unexpected connections that can be charted between diasporic, cultural, and national literatures that are otherwise oceans apart, in the hope that we might better attune ourselves to the contrapuntal dialogues in which these writers are engaged across the local and global contours of the diasporic imagination.

PART TWO

Africa

3 The Indenture Narrative of Mauritius: Deepchand Beeharry's *That Others Might Live*

'Abandoned Imperial Barracoon' or Originary Site?

As a post-colonial island nation that continues to produce the bulk of its literature in French, Mauritius occupies an ambiguous position in a study devoted to South Asian diasporic literature in English.[1] However, as the first sugar colony to receive a large number of South Asian immigrants in a post-emancipation era, Mauritius stands at the epicentre of indenture history. This history permeates the imaginative landscape of the majority of South Asian diasporic peoples.[2] Consequently, Indo-Mauritian history reveals the central tropes of the old South Asian diaspora: the recruitment for labour; the ship voyage across the *kala pani*; the process of transplantation and settlement; the dehumanizing conditions of indentured labour; plantation estate existence and the formation of *jahaji*-hood or an ethnocentric community; the oppositional currents of creolization and cultural exclusivism; anticolonial resistance and the post-colonial state; the push and pull of subsequent migrations; and the multiply positioned identity of the diasporic subject.

The other regions under study here to have received a similar flood of indentured labourers – namely, South East Asia, the Caribbean, and the Pacific Rim – have necessarily borne witness to all of the above phenomena. Indeed, many of the theoretical paradigms that pertain to the Caribbean archipelago are strikingly applicable to the Mascarene islands, given these regions' imperial history as plantation economies that relied exclusively on the enforced and voluntary labour of colonial subjects. Yet Mauritius occupies a unique position in the history of Britain's former colonies, not merely as the progenitor of indenture history, but also because the island was uninhabited prior to colonization. It is itself a creation of those historical forces which first brought continental Africans and South Asian peoples to its pristine shores. It is impossible to imagine Britain's rapid accumulation of overseas wealth in a post-emancipation economy without the blood, sweat, and tears of the South Asian and Chinese labour force alike. As Britain's first major sugar colony, one might say that Mauritius's natural and human resources literally and figuratively sweetened the Englishman's tea.

As Hugh Tinker states, 'The main movement of indentured emigration took place in the years before 1880. Mauritius was the great consumer, and by 1871, the population was composed of 216,258 Indians and 99,784 Creoles, mainly of African origin.'[3] A 2007 census puts Mauritius's population at approximately 1.2 million inhabitants. Prior to the influx of South Asian labour from 1835 onwards, slaves from continental Africa constituted the majority of the island-colony's population. By 1861 the South Asian population became the majority, constituting two thirds of the general population. Mauritius today is made up of Franco-Mauritians (French descent), Creoles (mixed European and African or South Asian ancestry); Indo-Mauritians (South Asian ancestry) and Sino-Mauritians (Chinese ancestry). Thus, it forms a unique demographic configuration that includes a modest minority of European settlers, the dominant South Asian and smaller Chinese diasporas, and a creolized African population that is not indigenous to the island. Indeed, there is no record of indigenous peoples on the island prior to the series of seafaring encounters which began with Arab and later Portuguese and Dutch navigators. The Dutch attempted settlement in 1638; however, France established its first major settlement, colonizing the island from 1721 until the British takeover in 1810, though the British did not settle the island in large numbers.

Prior to 1842, the exportation of labour mainly from the northern and southern regions of the subcontinent was an unregulated trade that bore an unsettling resemblance to slavery.[4] But as 'the first of the plantation colonies to import contract workers from India' in unprecedented numbers,[5] Mauritius soon became the primary site in which the labourers' working and living conditions necessitated reform, as much in the interest of India-British relations as in the upkeep of agricultural productivity. On the one hand, the systemization of labour resulted in a more strictly legislated and principled administration of an otherwise haphazard trade; on the other hand, it merely facilitated in greater numbers the supply of workers who continued to be regarded as 'units of production, not people.'[6] Mauritius nevertheless constituted an originary site, for it furnished a systematic blueprint for plantation societies in the Caribbean, the Pacific Rim, and the African continent. However, as Deepchand C. Beeharry illustrates in *That Others Might Live* (1979),[7] a sociohistorical novel that retells this history from the perspective of the indentured labourer, the indenture system should not be seen as a preconceived imperial model superimposed on Mauritian soil, but as one which emerged out of the experience of active struggle and resistance on the part of diasporic peoples themselves.

Mauritius has figuratively functioned as a geographical tabula rasa, etched and reetched with the ebb and flow of human history. Conversely, the image of the island has been distorted by the imperialistic or touristic gaze. Mauritius has been written into being by passers-by who witnessed in the island little more than a relic of seafaring or plantation history. This is typified by the popular *Paul et Virginie*,[8] written by the eighteenth-century writer/philosopher Jacques Henri Bernardin de Saint Pierre, a romanticized account of a legendary shipwreck off the island's coast. Several hundred years later, V.S. Naipaul recorded his impressions of the then fledgling post-colonial state not as a place of character and substance but as a vacuous site of 'disaster': 'an agricultural colony, *created by empire in an empty island* and always meant to be part of something larger, now given a thing called independence and set adrift, an *abandoned imperial barracoon*, incapable of economic or cultural economy.'[9]

Naipaul's metaphor of the 'abandoned imperial barracoon' evokes Mauritius's muted past prior to its three-hundred-odd years of French and British occupation. However, Naipaul's view of the island's significance as little more than a vestige of empire warrants scrutiny insofar as it reinscribes a tradition of European travel writing which sought to 'encode and legitimate' the hegemonic imperatives of European expansion.[10] Naipaul's reading of Mauritius thus adopts a hierarchical, Eurocentric dialectic that 'blinds itself to the way in which the periphery determines the metropolis'[11] or, in a post-colonial context, denies the possibility of self-determination. At worst, such a reading of island societies is formulated in tropes of isolationism and premodernity. At best, it revisits these societies 'as "museums" for tourism, anthropological inquiry, or sociological praxis.'[12]

In other words, though Naipaul paints a credible portrait of the island's growing overpopulation and underemployment, this is nevertheless an unredeeming account of a purportedly helpless people who are perceived as not only the victims of history but of their own inescapable deficiencies as secluded island dwellers, disconnected from the pulse of industry and progress. While Naipaul admirably desists from succumbing to Edenic projections of a tropical island-paradise, he perpetuates instead a dystopic paradigm of post-colonial island societies as squalid, deficient replicas of their imperial founders. Mauritius accordingly becomes an 'empty' signifier or 'repeating island'[13] of a lifeless, obsolete system, that is, 'the politics of the powerless' prostrate before the 'sugar cane and sugar cane, ending in the sea.'[14]

In a 1984 lecture on spatial dynamics, Foucault describes the colony as 'an extreme type of heterotopia' in its creation of an illusory or compensatory 'space that is other, another real space, as perfect, as meticulous, as well arranged as ours is messy, ill constructed and jumbled.'[15] According to Foucault, the heterotopia functions as an alternate space that is self-contained where 'all the other real sites within the culture, are simultaneously represented, contested, and inverted.'[16] As is made evident in Naipual's metaphor, Mauritius has invariably been conceived as an archetypal heterotopia; as a static and peripheral entity that 'can only signify as such when it is constructed in binary opposition to the history and geography of its continental visitors.'[17] However, as a primary or originary site which exerted a profound influence on the workings of the imperial machinery, Mauritius can be said to have altered the course of British history rather than to have merely served as a controlled extension of the metropolis. Mauritian writing therefore echoes that of other island societies in articulating an 'I-land' subjectivity[18] that rejects the colonial mapping of such geopolitical spaces as ahistorical and atemporal. As such, Mauritius can be said to metaphorically function as a counterheterotopia in revealing the extent to which island immigration, interethnic contact, and the collective agency of its creolized inhabitants have transformed the periphery into a virtual epicentre of historical change.

Even in more contemporary terms, then, Naipaul casts an ill-suited metaphor over a nation which, since its independence in 1968, has carved itself a singular niche in the world. As an officially heteroglossic and relatively harmonious multiethnic community, Mauritius has charted an identity that is distinct from that of its sister island, Réunion, and its neighbouring African countries. In Françoise Lionnet's comparison of Réunion and Mauritius, the Mascarenes' two major island societies, the former's status as a department of France accounts in part for its continued deference to a monolithic and 'dominant symbolic system – metropolitan French culture.'[19] In contrast, Lionnet clearly credits Mauritius for its 'cultural and political autonomy.' Because of its institutionalization of multiracial policies to accommodate its diverse population, Lionnet describes Mauritius as a '"model" post-colonial state, one that is even being hailed as a superb example of successful mediations of the uncertain relationship between nationhood and ethnic diversity.'[20]

The island's multicultural heritage is, of course, attributable as much to a number of unusual sociohistorical factors as to present conditions. For one, the island has been subject to a curiously sustained double imperial legacy. Indeed, unlike the palimpsestic succession of colonial entities during the era of European expansion, France's cession of Mauritius to Britain in 1810 led not to the usurpation of the island by Britain but to Britain's presence as a 'temporary resident' therein.[21] For the most part the British formally administered the island but left the older French plantocracy to dominate its sociocultural infrastructure with relatively little or no interruption. Thus, one cannot really speak of an 'English' community in Mauritius in the way it is possible to speak of the 'Anglicization' of many Caribbean islands, for Mauritius belongs as much to the *francophonie* as to the British Commonwealth. Having said this, it is equally significant that Mauritius's population has been dominated by its formerly indentured peoples (since the earliest stages of their arrival), a demographic which has in turn made the subcontinent the third sociocultural and political axis around which a relatively Indianized community operates.

English Literature: The Vernacular of the Indo-Mauritian Writer

It is necessary to consider further these historical and cultural influences if one is to appreciate the complexity of the island-nation's literary trends. This Franco-Anglo-Indo triad has understandably produced a multilingual community in an otherwise relatively small but increasingly growing nation of approximately 1.2 million residents. In fact, there is nothing simple about Mauritian identity. The majority of its citizens migrated from the subcontinent; among its oldest residents are the descendants of slaves from Madagascar and Mozambique and, to a lesser extent, southern India.[22] The traditional elite are by and large of French origin. The new body politic consists of a select group of Indo-Mauritians, Franco-Mauritians, and Creoles.[23] Daily life is conducted in Kreol, the island's lingua franca, while the language of officialdom is English.

As Larry Bowman states, Mauritians 'alone of all the fifty-plus African states have a citizenry that is fluent in both French and English,'[24] and the average citizen might be able to communicate in up to three or more languages. Each language in turn bears a particular sociohistorical register:

for example, French has been generally associated with the cultural elite, whereas Kreol and South Asian vernaculars are markers of ethnic identification. As such, many politicized writers of the left or of non-European origins have been known to reject French on 'ideological ... grounds,'[25] adopting English as the more neutral of the two imperial idioms. In contrast, Kreol is fast becoming the symbol of national culture, although there exists a counterbalancing impulse to officially maintain English, French, and Hindi or Bhojpuri in the interest of socio-economic exchange with Asia and the West. Bhojpuri is itself a creolized Hindi spoken in the region known as Bihar, in present-day India. Since the majority of Indo-Mauritians are from the region of Bihar, Bhojpuri is the dominant South Asian vernacular in the island as well. As Danielle Quet suggests, Kreol and Bhojpuri vie for acceptance as national idioms in Mauritius.[26]

The English-language writer might well be faced with additional complications in a country where, as late as 1972, only 0.3 per cent of the population identified English as their primary language of communication.[27] In addition, the marketability of texts in a small economic community severely curtails the opportunity for publication, irrespective of one's linguistic preferences. English-language writing in Mauritius occupies a curious if not paradoxical position in Mauritian literary production. On the one hand, it is perceived as a 'political statement in favour of cultural nationalism';[28] on the other hand, it is least reflective of local parlance. However, as a literary medium, English produces a complex dynamic of seeming contradictions which is most readily apparent in the deployment of the language as a political statement. In other words, though the English language often serves those who are opposed to the cultural elite, it betrays an inherently European literary tradition that overshadows Kreol or the numerous South Asian vernaculars that colour the island's cultural heritage.

English-language writing also has its own set of ethnic or racial markers. As Nandini Bhautoo-Dewnarain suggests, the emergence of English-language publication prior to independence was greatly 'motivated by the desire to carve a place within the establishment of literature for the *non-white* Mauritian.'[29] Indeed, the Indo-Mauritian community is the principal proponent of English-language writing. Though this phenomenon is best left to sociolinguistic and historical inquiry, it is worth noting that the Indo-Mauritian's exposure to English would have preceded his/her arrival in the Mascarenes, while any anti-imperial resistance to the language has been muted by an overriding reaction to French. Add to this equation the erosion of South Asian vernaculars and it is not difficult to see why the Indo-Mauritian might be drawn to English-language publication, despite its relative disadvantages in a community where the majority speak French. Finally, the practical appeal of English in an international literary marketplace cannot be underestimated (as is the case for all of the regions under study).

The few scholars who have accorded this body of literature critical attention[30] concur with Angela Smith's (1984) conclusion that the 'Indo-Mauritian writer's attitude to English is that of a borrower. He can speak English and write English – but his culture must find tones of adjustment with the language he uses to write literature.'[31] Smith correctly points to the numerous obstacles which impede the quality and production of Mauritian literature in English, such as limited distribution, readership, and criticism, not to mention the minority position of the English language itself in a predominantly French-Kreol environment. As Smith and others have noted, these constraints have resulted in a long tradition of self-publication. As Bhautoo-Dewnarain's more recent survey of English-language writing reveals, a younger generation of Mauritian writers (of various ethnic backgrounds) has undergone a metamorphosis since the 1990s, exploring in 'new overtones of irony and detachment the complexities of island existence.'[32] In other words, a growing investment, on the part of British and local cultural organizations, in anthologies, literary competitions, and publishing ventures might reshape the local English literary landscape.

However, the same can be said about the growth of francophone writing in recent years. In fact, given that many, if not most, of the post-millennium novels authored by and about the Indo-Mauritian community are written in French, it would appear that the francophone novel is winning out over its anglophone counterpart. Perhaps this might also partly account for the dearth of criticism on earlier figures such as Beeharry in studies of the development of the Mauritian novel. Indeed, one must turn to francophone studies to gauge the direction and development of recent Mauritian writing. In a 2005 survey, 'Le roman mauricien d'aujourd'hui,' Kumari Issur refers exclusively to francophone or Kreol works. Issur mentions several developments, including the shift from historical fiction to more experimental and post-modern forms, as well as the honest assessment of the various ills besieging contemporary Mauritian society (including social inequality, the environmental and social impact of the tourist industry, political corruption, and interracial tensions). It is clear that Indo-Mauritian writers are equally represented among a new generation of novelists who, according to

Issur, dare expose the bankruptcy of the system and give voice to the desires and aspirations of individuals: 'La nouvelle génération de romanciers change complètement de ton, renouvelle la thématique et, loin de perpétuer des stéréotypes ou d'exprimer un espoir démesuré dans la jeune nation, osera pointer du doigt les défaillances du système et donner voix aux désirs et aspirations des individus.'[33] Another important trend that Issur's survey reveals is the predominance of women writers among this new generation, particularly since 2000. Ananda Devi is hailed as having established the feminist Mauritian novel with the publication of *Rue la poudrière* (1989), a study of prostitution and other taboo themes such as incest and sexual abuse. Despite its English title, *Indian Tango*, her second novel to date, is also a French-language work, published by Gamillard in 2007.

While it is perhaps just a matter of time before these works appear in translation, the other post-millennium Indo-Mauritian novelists that Issur identifies, such as Shenaz Patel, Natacha Appanah, Barlen Pyamootoo, and Nanda Bodho, confirm the linguistic direction that contemporary Mauritian literature seems to have taken. The range of linguistic choices available to Indo-Mauritian writers certainly makes it harder to trace the thematic and other developments emerging across the body of Indo-Mauritian writing. However, Natacha Appanah's *Les rochers de poudre d'or* (2003), a historical novel about the arrival of labourers during the indenture period, or Barlen Pyamootoo's *Benares* (1999), a study of Indo-Mauritian village life, confirms that for the younger generation, the originary homeland – be it through the echo of names, ancestral ties, cultural practices, or the shared historical consciousness created by indenture experience – still infuses discussions of contemporary Mauritian society with the diasporic sensibility articulated, albeit with greater anxiety, by their literary forebears.

Deepchand Beeharry's Epic Imaginary

Deepchand Beeharry belongs to the first generation of English-language writers. His works surfaced well before this cultural resurgence. As one of the first writers to set his fiction within both the historical and contemporary context of his native island, Beeharry himself repeatedly laments (in several of the forewords of his own works) both the material and wider cultural implications of publishing constraints on the aspiring writer: 'The difficulties the writer has to grapple with over here to get his books published are too well-known to bear repetition ... The cost of producing a book is still high enough to compel writers to stow away their manuscripts somewhere in their drawers. And this is the pity. For, in these hours of darkness, the presence and voice of the writer have become more than ever indispensable.'[34] Beeharry's oeuvre nonetheless stands as a testament to the complex multilingual context of his island identity and as a triumph over the numerous 'financial and technical obstacles' which impede publication.

Born in Floreal, Mauritius, in 1927, Beeharry studied classical languages before earning an MA in English from Viswa Bharati (a University in India founded by Rabindranath Tagore). His literary output includes English, French, and Hindi works, many of which are further interlaced with Bhojpuri and Kreol. His active professional life includes his contributions as a journalist, teacher, member of the bar, government official, and independent political candidate (upon his resignation from the Labour Party). Beeharry's lifetime commitment to public service is underscored in his repeated claim that the ideal writer should combine the need for self-expression with his role as a social critic and activist.

In fact, those thematic concerns which are closest to his homebase – themes such as the mobilization of labour movements, interethnic relations, and individual agency – are indicative of an oeuvre that was conceived over a twenty-year period and straddled the ideological and political upheavals of a pre- and post-independence Mauritius. Recalling other African contemporaries such as Chinua Achebe, Ngũgĩ wa Thiong'o, Sembene Ousmane, and Peter Nazareth, whose literary careers are intellectually driven by the era of decolonization, Beeharry states: 'In newly independent or under-developed countries, the writer has a special duty or care ... He is mostly against systems which ride roughshod on the dignity of the individual, and make it possible for inequality and iniquity, corruption and favouritism to dig their feet in the ground.'[35]

Over the course of his literary career, Beeharry has produced five novels, several short story collections, and a short play. He has also been the recipient of a British Council literary award. In their literary surveys,[36] Michel Fabre and Danielle Quet generally agree that Beeharry is the best Mauritian novelist in English.[37] In spite of the author's extensive literary output, not to mention his singular position as his nation's first major English-language novelist, Beeharry has won little international recognition or critical attention, even in India where he has published several of his works. This is primarily attributable, once again, to the virtual inaccessibility of his writings both on and off his native island's shores, given the aforementioned hurdles confronting aspiring and established Mauritian literary figures alike.

Beeharry's novel *That Others Might Live* challenges Vijay Mishra's claim that Naipaul stands at the epicentre of a diasporic poetics borne out of the experience of indenture history. Beeharry's novel offers a compelling narrativization of the struggles and triumphs of indenture history as the structural and psychological cornerstone of his characters' lives. Though sometimes compromised by the shortcomings of poor editorship and shoddy printing, his novelistic career is nonetheless enlivened by exciting new subject matter. The Hindi novel *Lal Pasina* (1977) by Beeharry's Indo-Mauritian contemporary, Abhimanyu Unnuth, fictionalizes the historic plight of Indian labourers during the nineteenth century, and Beeharry's *That Others Might Live* foregrounds new thematic concerns in the Indo-Mauritian anglophone novel. His linguistic and cultural influences, which include French, British, and Indian literary works, together with a rich oral Creole tradition, have combined to produce the distinct multiply positioned diasporic identity so evident throughout his oeuvre.

The post-modern reader might see Beeharry as a technically and stylistically conservative writer who faithfully adheres to his classical training, but in fact Beeharry ventures into wholly uncharted novelistic terrain: he fictionalizes the earliest stages of indenture history, beginning with the impetus for migration and the sea voyage to the colonies (with its echoes of the Middle Passage) and ending in the dehumanizing conditions of plantation labour and existence; and he configures the diasporic subject as an agent for transgressive and transformative action who is caught in an uneasy tension between cross-cultural collaboration and an instinct for self-preservation in essentialist or purist terms; and he catalogues and animates the vocabulary of indenture, using terms such as *girmitiya*, *kala pani*, and *jahaji-bhai* that are specific to indentured peoples and their descendants.

According to Vijay Mishra, *girmitiya* forms the cornerstone of indenture experience since it marks both the symbolically and legally binding terms that the individual recruited for labour accepts when he/she enters into the 'agreement' to honour the two- to five-year labour contract. The indentured labourers were thus often referred to as the *girmit-wallahs*, *girmitiyas*, or 'agreement people.' *Kala pani* is translated as 'black water,' so named for the 'strict caste injunctions' which forbade travel 'beyond the Indus to the west, and the Brahmaputra to the east'[38] in the fear of caste contamination and other impurities. *Jahaji-bhai* is literally translated as 'ship brothers.' Together, these terms combine to produce the main vocabulary of indenture, symbolizing the circumscribed life of bondage that the colonial contract represented, the traumatic journey away from the motherland on colonial ships, and the shift from a personal plight to a collective consciousness and ethos underscored by the experience of indenture.[39] As will be seen in chapter 8 on Fiji, *girmitiya* becomes the basis of an ideology that has particular resonance for those who experienced indenture recruitment and labour, and for those descendants of indentured labourers who find themselves disenfranchised in the new homeland.

In *That Others Might Live* (1976), Beeharry catalogues his ancestors' historic journey across the *kala pani* or black water and their subsequent struggle for fair and humane treatment under British colonial rule, animating Mishra's concept of *girmit* ideology. This novel captures the conflicting impulses with which the diasporic subject must contend, namely, the move toward a pluralistic sensibility grounded in the ethics of anti-imperial struggle and conversely the retreat behind an ethnocentric ethos in the interest of communal stability. Though Beeharry's didacticism often overdetermines character and plot, he consistently aims to strike a critical balance by exposing the inequities of both colonial and Indian power structures. This can be seen in the comparison of the subaltern's exploitation under both an inherited feudalistic, caste-bound society and an imposed imperial infrastructure: '"We have not gained much, I am afraid. There it was the bondage of [the] zamindar system; here it is [the] servitude of indentured labour," he mumbled to himself.'[40]

Before focusing attention on the novel at hand, however, I would like to provide a brief overview of Beeharry's oeuvre, because each of his novels writes against the poetics of loss in a manner that is echoed across the old South Asian diaspora. For instance, even though *Never Goodbye* (1965) leaves something to be desired in terms of artistic flourish, its protagonist is convincingly constructed as a diasporic subject who is no longer bound to an atavistic longing for the past; instead he is socially and spiritually fuelled by a love for the new land, even as the temptation to escape to the West is tangible if not realizable: 'For months he had been busy contacting the Canadian authorities, for months he had been looking forward to the day when he would be offered a job somewhere in Montreal or Ontario. But now that the offer was there beckoning him to a new world, his mind went blank.'[41]

Beeharry's first two novels, *Never Goodbye* and *A Touch of Happiness* (1966), comprise thematic sequels insofar as they chart an Indo-Mauritian's

emerging social and political consciousness in an ailing post-war economy. Here, Beeharry faintly recalls his Barbadian counterpart, George
Lamming, in exposing the effects of the world wars on the lives of seemingly far-removed island colonies.[42] Beeharry's first two novels also depict
the post-colonial archetype of 'colonial alienation'[43] brought about
through the imposition of a colonial education and the non-European
subject's journey 'westward' as a requisite vehicle for upward social mobility. Here, one immediately thinks of Naipaul's *Mimic Men*, though it is an
archetype that is also repeated in the works of a more recent generation
of diasporic writers such as Lakshmi Persaud and K.S. Maniam.[44]

Although their settings diverge by a century, Beeharry's fourth novel
Three Women and a President (1979) mirrors *That Others Might Live* insofar
as it fictionalizes another turning point in Mauritian annals. Here,
Beeharry reconstructs the events of the OAU (Organization of African
Unity) Conference held in Mauritius in 1976.[45] The novel highlights the
Mauritian government's attempt to forge stronger alliances with its
African neighbours while trying to maintain its antiapartheid stance
against its major trading partner, South Africa. Structuring these events
around an Indian secret agent's mission to subvert a plot to assassinate
the conference's most controversial delegate, Ugandan President Idi
Amin, Beeharry simultaneously reveals his sympathies for the exiled
Ugandan-South Asian and what he perceives to be India's moral obligation to involve itself in African politics.[46]

The novel is a departure from the author's usual brand of social realism in its ribald portrayal of the secret agent's voracious sexual appetite.
However, Agent 'XXX 13' comes across as a puerile version of James
Bond rather than as a solid character. Beeharry's protagonist (however
comically intended) sadly compromises a novel that otherwise wrestles
itself free of sexist stereotypes in the unselfconscious foregrounding
(hence the title) of three female characters – an African, an Indian and
a European – who function as key operatives in the goings-on of political
espionage, intelligence gathering, and revolutionary activity. In fact,
most of Beeharry's female protagonists combine to create a feminist
ethos that envisions women (regardless of their ethnicity or race) as political, cultural, and intellectual agents of change.

In *Heart and Soul* (1983), Beeharry's last and most philosophical novel,
he attempts to break out of the stylistic straitjacket of his former novels.
Here one finds the recurring motif of cultural alienation in the Western
metropolis that is so often addressed in 'immigrant novels.' Set in
London during the years preceding Mauritian independence, the novel

critiques neocolonial practices, in terms of both British-Mauritius relations and the racialized minority in Britain. Beeharry attacks, with unflinching candour, the exploitation of foreign workers abroad and the pervasive suspicion directed at people of colour. Yet, with a characteristically even hand, he dismantles racial barriers in his portraits of a German au pair with whom the protagonist Rishi falls in love, and a Madagascarian journalist/activist of French ancestry. Together, these characters, in their intellectual, political, and spiritual solidarity, form an interracial alliance. Though characterization is often driven by sentimental idealism, this is a moving and redeeming culmination of the author's deeply committed role as a social and political advocate.

Though there is much to commend all of Beeharry's works, *That Others Might Live* clearly stands out as his most compelling for it is here that the author breaks narrative ground. As Vijay Mishra writes, in his theorization of the Indian diaspora, there is 'no subaltern Marlow who has recounted the first encounter with these outposts of Empire, even though scattered and oral accounts of the indentured labourers have survived in folk stories and songs. All that remained was the memory of the passage and a loss that could only be sustained through the categories of myth.'[47] Mishra's suggestion that the history of indentured labour, particularly at its earliest stages, does not seem to exist beyond scant archival data, oral transmission, and collective memory lends considerable weight to *That Others Might Live*, a historical novel that tells the story of the material and spiritual genesis of a new diaspora under the indenture system.

As I will show in subsequent chapters, indenture history is encoded in a narrative perspective that is now several generations removed from the initial crossing overseas. As such, it is filtered through individual and collective memory, but it is rarely the prime mover of character and plot. In contrast, *That Others Might Live* attempts to realistically chronicle the 'tale of the tribe.'[48] Indeed, the author seeks to capture, with documentary realism, the emergence of a new way of life for a community of displaced peoples. Though Arthur Pollard suggests that this is a sociohistorical novel in the classic sense,[49] I believe that Beeharry invests at least the potential for heroic depth in his characters and a touch of mythic resonance in place and events. In fact, the epic intent is clear in the didactic drift of the title: this is, in fact, a story that 'must' be told not only to ensure the survival of the people but also to reclaim their pivotal role in history.

As an Indo-Mauritian writer who has dedicated his literary career to telling the tale of this first and oldest community of indentured labourers,

Beeharry expresses his own literary ambitions in terms reflecting Rudyard Kipling's persona as the 'bard of empire.' Having said this, it is important to note that Beeharry's undertaking reverberates as much with his Hindu upbringing as with his Western classical training. Indeed, the epic tales of the *Ramayana* and *Mahabharata* surface through each of his novels, connecting even his most existential protagonists to a primordial past, one that is imbued with the spirits of Hindu gods and goddesses, and the ancient rituals, practices, and beliefs invoked in their ubiquitous presence. For Beeharry, therefore, there is little dissonance between the realistic, material rendition of the tale and the endowment of character, place, and theme with 'the common aspirations, ethical beliefs and unifying myths of a people.'[50]

In *That Others Might Live*, the documentation of human deeds naturally inspires an expression of the values they generate. This heretofore undocumented tale is infused with the language and sentiment of an odyssey, for it traces the diaspora's emergence as a figurative and literal journey, motifs that reflect the migrants' radically changing physical, material, political, and cultural circumstances. In depicting the indentured labourers' historic beginnings, Beeharry also commemorates the emergence of a new collective consciousness which sets forth the common destiny of a people who seek to spiritually or materially transcend past and present limitations. Moreover, he faithfully records those aspects of the odyssey that spawned a shared mythology of migration and settlement, including the ship voyage across the *kala pani*; the makeshift accommodations at the ports of embarkation and disembarkation as dehumanizing sites; the plantation as a system of bondage; the stirrings of rebellion; the subaltern woman's double colonization by patriarchal and colonial hegemonies; the (re)formation of community among a variously stratified group; the simultaneous preservation and creolization of cultural artefacts and values, languages, and ideas; the (re)conception of old and new mythologies as a gesture of 'settlement' in an otherwise alien landscape; the migrant's physical and psychic displacement; and, finally, the real and imagined journeys 'home.'

To highlight the protean nature of diasporic experience, the novel is constructed as a circular narrative which symbolically begins and ends in the liminal space of the ship, one of the unifying symbols of indenture history:

> The ship had left Calcutta late in the evening, the day before, with a cargo of cattle, rice and *some three hundred immigrants of whom more than half were*

men. The rest were women and children ... They were a *motley crowd* of workers, who still carried in their eyes the dreams of a *land of milk, honey and gold,* promised to them by the recruiting agents ...; a life of privations, mingled with a sense of adventure, had thrown them together on the transport ship, the *Ganges,* on its way to Mauritius.[51]

In these opening pages, Beeharry underlines both the conditions and motivations of indenture experience: the migrants are valued as little more than the cattle whose cargo space they share, while their reasons for migration are as varied and complex as their backgrounds. Moreover, the symbolically named ship, the *Ganges,* introduces the mythic proportions of the act of faith that such a journey across the *kala pani* and into the unknown surely must have entailed. As the journey signalled caste contamination for many of its Hindu passengers, the ship's name symbolically alleviates their anxiety of separation from all that is sacred, recasting the voyage not in terms of loss and rupture but of continuity and spiritual redemption.

Though indentureship is often defined as a 'new system of slavery,'[52] the South Asian and African diasporas should not be categorically conflated. On the one hand, the voluntary nature of the labourer's journey, together with the eventual allowance for family emigration, necessarily differs from the excruciating and violent dislocation of the African slave. Moreover, in their collective 'transplantation' – one which facilitated the mobility of values, customs, traditions, and goods in the process of resettlement – the labourers together formed large enough ethnic, cultural, and religious entities to counteract the assimilative forces of life overseas, far from the protective veil of their ancient homeland. On the other hand, it is interesting to note how the ship serves as a unifying symbol for indentured peoples just as it did for those who endured the Middle Passage. Indeed, the ship voyage would have brought South Asians of different backgrounds together in unprecedented proximity, as it did for African slaves.

The impetus for the labourers' journey, however, not only speaks of the horrors of upheaval, servitude, and bondage, but also recalls colonial quest narratives, such as the search for *el dorado* (the mythical city of gold). This is because the labourer's journey is as fuelled by personal ambition and desire as it was for the colonizer or imperial adventurer. In this sense, the mass exodus is likened to religious or pioneer narratives, as the allusion to the promised land ('the land of milk and honey') suggests. The quest motif applies as much to the sentiments of the colonized passengers as to the crew, while the illusory or deceptive nature of the voyage, at least during the earliest stages of indenture, is exposed as an apparatus of mismanagement, commercial self-interest, and corruption. As Beeharry illustrates, many of the initial shiploads of migrants had been coerced or tricked into undertaking a potentially fatal voyage riddled with the dangers of malnutrition, disease, and overcrowding, a voyage that was designed to facilitate the en masse recruitment of people to work under appalling conditions.

The symbolic import of the ship, the water, and the sea as sites not only of flux but also of a counterdiscourse of cultural and political reconfiguration is mirrored in the literary and theoretical works of Afro-Caribbean peoples.[53] However, post-modernists such as Antonio Benitez-Rojo tend to overstate the extent to which cultural hybridity somehow 'sublimate[s] [the] violence' of plantation history.[54] Though Benitez-Rojo and other Caribbean theorists offer a widely applicable hermeneutics of the sea as a metaphor for the process of transculturation, one must resist a simplistic reading of oceanic space as symbolic of syncretic processes that undermine the hegemonic narrative of imperialism. On the contrary, the interrelated tropes of the ship, the water, and the sea embody a paradoxical poetics that at once prefigures paradigms of syncretism and flux and serves as a permanent signifier of the legacies of bondage, uprooting, and loss inherent in the journey 'across.'

In the South Asian diasporic text, therefore, water/sea has a specifically symbolic role to play in its atavistic association with the *Ganges*, in its circular, fluid link between past and present, or in its spiritual potency as a purifying element. Indeed, in the daily activities of these characters' lives, it rarely arises as a metaphor for cultural or ethnic hybridity (as it does in so many Afro-Caribbean texts). For instance, in *Never Goodbye*, the protagonist Ashim's eventual emigration to Montreal is counterpoised by a premigratory pilgrimage to a secluded lake. Ashim's pilgrimage to a body of water is meant to ensure his spiritual and cultural connection to his island community. In other words, water/fluidity indicates an implicit tension (as the contrast between an open sea and an enclosed lake reveals) between the chaotic nature of an identity in flux and the steady continuum of deeply rooted beliefs that are 'carried across' in the process of migration.

In *That Others Might Live* the tension between two seemingly oppositional currents – those of continuity and change – is made evident in the 'passage' toward the unknown. True to historical record, Beeharry describes the cramped spaces of the lower decks, where the majority of passengers were forced to stay, irrespective of their caste and gender differences:

After the strenuous preliminaries of embarkation ... they were caught between the gauntlet of customs officials and the iron glove of a weather-
beaten crew. They just managed to creep up the gangway to the lower deck
where charpoys or wooden beds had been placed so close to one another
that they had to jump over to reach them. The beds were some two feet
high and had neither mattress nor bed-stead.[55]

On the one hand, therefore, the voyage is portrayed as a liminal space in
which a diverse group undergoes considerable disruption. On the other
hand, these passengers are transported 'into another state or place'[56]
through a new ethos of identification in which linguistic, ethnic, religious, caste, and other differences and rivalries are at least momentarily
suspended in a new kind of commonality. While the individual's sense of
identity is destabilized, both in the process of transplantation and the
moment of contact, there is a counterimpulse toward a transcendent
spiritual fraternity.

The ship and, by extension, the sea nonetheless serve as the primary
arena for the reconfiguration of identity. Hence, not only does the ship
contain the 'motley crowd' – which is representative of the subcontinent's ethnic and religious diversity – it also disturbs the highly stratified
patterns of the caste system. Though the impetus for the voyage is largely
self-propelled by individual choice and circumstance, the passengers are
shown to almost instinctively reconfigure themselves as a newly allied
body or collective unit. This is made all the more understandable in the
perception of the imperial machinery as carrying a greater threat than
the elemental nature of the journey itself: 'The waves and the winds outside were not just the elements, they were the combined forces of a
powerful enemy which had to be resisted, cornered as the immigrants
were.'[57] This interreligious, interethnic, and interlinguistic fraternity is
deftly represented in the bond formed at sea between the three young
protagonists, Manish, Dhiren, and Thomas, upon their first encounter:

'My name is Manish Atwar. And what is yours?'
'Dhiren Das.'
'And yours, our friend from the South?'
'Thomas Sivaramen Pillay.'
'Good. Now we know each other's names. We are brothers.
Jahajea bhai, as we say in Dharharra. Being brothers we speak our language.
We speak no English except with *Feringhees,* all right? We swear, all three, to
help each other even at the cost of our lives, if necessary. Agreed?'[58]

The phenomenon of regroupment and affiliation that the protagonists represent solicits the vocabulary of indenture. *Jahajea bhai* – translated as 'ship brothers' or, more figuratively, the 'bondage of brotherhood'[59] – is central to a diasporic consciousness in its evocation of the labourers' shared histories of migration across the Atlantic, Indian, or Pacific Oceans. Though the journey gives rise to a more heterogeneously (re)configured group, the bond also reconstitutes essentialist identities and gender hierarchies, patterns of being that will be transposed in the new land. However, once the labourers find themselves in the colonies, where their individual and collective hopes and desires are devoured by the dehumanizing machinery of the plantation, this sense of 'common bondage' becomes the basis for a newfound ethics of personal and cultural survival:

> The idea of the clan or community which was, momentarily smothered by powerful economic forces resurfaced to uphold cultural and religious unity ... Individual differences or dissensions, however, gave way to mutual aid and assistance ... In short, the individual sense of self-preservation sublimated into collective participation.[60]

In keeping with the epic imaginary, therefore, the bulk of the novel is dedicated not to what divides but to what unites the *jahaji-bhai*, that is, the shared experience of being racial subordinates twice removed from the homeland, the drudgery of indentureship, and the feeling of isolation and alienation as linguistic, racial, and cultural others. This is not to suggest that Beeharry subsumes the individual histories of his characters' lives in the interest of romanticizing communal ties. To the contrary, the novel emphasizes the individualized nature of diasporic experience, as is made evident in the contrasting stories of Manish, Dhiren, and Thomas. For instance, Thomas's Christian faith affords certain privileges, for he is immediately put in the service of the church. He is quickly engaged as a priest's cook. Manish's knowledge of English wins him the favour of the ship's captain, who uses him as a translator for the benefit of his crew. Escaping the indignities of physical labour, Manish and Thomas illustrate how forms of cultural assimilation are rewarded (and, conversely, resistance to colonial indoctrination is treated in harshly punitive terms), be it through better wages or preferential treatment by those in positions of power.

Beeharry is equally insistent that the reasons for migration were often as contingent upon the increasingly hegemonic rule of the British Raj in the subcontinent as upon the migrant's personal circumstances or ambitions. In this respect, the novel brings to view a rarely glimpsed aspect of indenture history, namely, the correlation between the push for migration and the fall-out ensuing the 1857 Indian Rebellion. As indenture historian David Northrup confirms, the eruption of violence on both sides of the colonial divide had telling effects on migratory patterns:

> Even if people's decisions were determined largely by their personal circumstances and conditions in their locality, the influence of the Raj was certainly pervasive. The strongest case for British rule pushing people to emigrate can be seen in the correspondence between the peak in migration overseas at the end of the 1850s and the widespread disruptions associated with the Indian Rebellion of 1857 and its suppression.[61]

Tinker confirms Northrup's assertion in suggesting that emigration peaked in the years between 1858 and 1859, not only for those seeking to flee persecution but also for those who suffered the loss of land and livelihood in the aftermath of the Rebellion.

Manish's story reveals the inextricable link between the disruptive effects of colonial rule and subsequent patterns of migration.[62] His migration is shown to be part of an ongoing quest to find his father, a suspected mutineer who saw in the prospect of overseas labour a means for escaping his imminent arrest by colonial authorities. By the time Manish locates his father overseas, however, the extent to which the Rebellion has cemented distrust between colonizer and colonized becomes abundantly clear. Realizing that Douglas Wallace, his childhood companion, has been assigned the task of locating mutineers in the far reaches of the colonies, Manish's hope that their earlier friendship might kindle the latter's sympathy for his father's case is sadly thwarted. Beeharry makes an even stronger indictment against the punitive measures taken to curb the Rebellion in suggesting that the unduly severe treatment of the indentured labourer abroad sprang 'from a spirit of vengeance against them and their fellow countrymen in India for having mutineered against British rule there.'[63]

Each character serves to individualize the labourers' motivations for and experience of emigration. As we have seen, Manish brings to view the push for migration that was directly linked to the political and social unrest created by anticolonial resistance in the subcontinent itself. On the other hand, Dhiren sees in the colony a fecund new land to be cultivated and possessed, and so his aspirations loosely recall those of early

American settlers. Moreover, although Thomas's narrative cautiously affirms that the colony might hold the opportunity for self-betterment, his example stands in ironic contrast to the majority for whom any such improvement is a gradual, hard-won, and often cross-generational struggle that comes at great personal cost.

Beeharry debunks two central myths regarding indentured peoples: first, that this was a homogenous, identity-less group of people with common goals, aspirations, attitudes, backgrounds, and experiences; second, that emigration was an apparatus which categorically ameliorated the migrant's material conditions or social standing (particularly in its purported dissolution of caste consciousness and gender inequalities). In their obvious differences, Beeharry's characters reveal that *jahaji*-hood is first and foremost driven by the abject material conditions of plantation life. *Jahaji*-hood thus transforms the dehumanization of the subaltern migrant as a homogenous labour force (or 'unit of labour') into a spiritually united group.

To bring home this point, Beeharry sets his novel in the turbulent period of the 1870s, approximately forty years after the first migrant would have arrived on Mauritian soil. Indenture historian Marina Carter states, 'The year 1874 ... represented a watershed in the history of indenture in Mauritius because it marked a formal recognition of the discrimination suffered by Indians and the beginning of a slow retreat and reform.'[64] The narrative thus pivots around the mobilization of collective action against the apartheid-like Pass System, or Ordinance 31, which reinstated the planter with 'proprietorial rights reminiscent of the pre-emancipation period.'[65] Beeharry foregrounds, in countless examples, the excessive stronghold of Ordinance 31 in restricting not only the labourers' movements both on and off the plantation, but also those of the women and children who lived and worked among them. The penalties were immediate, humiliating, and severe, as is demonstrated by Manish's and Dhiren's prolonged incarcerations without recourse to the law. In her analysis of the indenture system, Carter suggests that Ordinance 31 was designed both to capitalize on labour in such demands as a six-and-a-half-day work week, and to minimize political insurgency. One of the key features of indenture history, therefore, is the heroic effort of labourers like Dhiren to rouse collective action against the injustices of an inherently exploitative system, typified in the apartheid-like measures of Ordinance 31.

Beeharry's timeline is carefully constructed around the period in which the otherwise unregulated use of labour underwent an initial

phase of reform which would later evolve into the mutually binding contractual obligation of indenture.[66] But Beeharry rewrites (as much as he
faithfully documents) history, exposing colonial records as self-congratu-
latory narratives of legislative achievement. Specifically, he frees indentured peoples from the footnotes of colonial history, giving voice to their
contributions as active agents of legislative and social change. He accom-
plishes this by illustrating the subtle and overt levels in which subaltern
agency might have been enacted.

A generation of elders such as the introspective Ghosh Babu and the
tragic Ramprasad are shown to be eyewitnesses to the undue severity of
indentured existence at its earliest and most abusive stages. Beeharry accordingly demonstrates that the transmission of oral history, filtered
through personal testimonies and communal folklore, is a legitimate
and effective vehicle of political agency. In this sense, it is Ramprasad's
testimony of past events, together with the dire circumstances of his premature death, that fuels Dhiren's own conviction to denounce the various injustices of the plantation colony:

> What had happened to Ramprasad would go on happening to all immi-
> grants, loyal or not, because nobody, neither the Protector of immigrants
> checked whether medical facilities and medicine were available to the sick
> labourers nor did the planters grant them time off as sick leave but squeezed
> the maximum out of them till they could no more and gave up the ghost ...
> he felt a wave of indignation surge inside his breast at the injustices that
> man could inflict on his own kind.[67]

Social realism and epic intent often jostle for narrative supremacy in
That Others Might Live, the former usually prevails in matters of historical
accuracy while the latter tends to dominate character and political/social
commentary. Thus, despite the fact that Dhiren assumes a mythic stature
by the end of the novel, he is never shown to operate far from the real
historical forces and influences of those around him. His involvement in
grass roots activism – particularly his efforts to circulate a petition against
Ordinance 31 – is directly influenced by the actions of Adolphe de Plevitz,[68]
a planter of German descent who championed the labourers' struggle
against the various levels of plantocratic bureaucracy.[69]

Beeharry pays homage to this historical figure for having championed
the labourers' revolt against Ordinance 31, actions which initiated its
repeal, the appointment of the British Royal Commission of 1872–4 to
investigate allegations of exploitation, and the subsequent passing of

new labour laws in 1878, upon which the indenture system was eventually modelled. For this reason, perhaps, de Plevitz is primarily presented in the text as an orator whose greatest influence is found in his vociferous denouncement of the abuses of the Pass System: 'The law of 1867 is not a piece of legislation; it is a sword hanging over the heads of the immigrants. It has given rise to so many abuses that, unless the Secretary of State revokes it, soon there will be more slaves in this country than free men.'[70]

But Beeharry's depiction of de Plevitz as a figure who remains behind the political scene also functions as a subversive narrative ploy, for the prime movers in the struggle for emancipation are shown to be the labourers themselves. Indeed, while de Plevitz actually appears in Mauritian annals because he earned the governor's appellation as 'the unofficial protector of the immigrants,'[71] the same acknowledgment has eluded the labourers themselves. Such historical gaps, particularly in the context of Mauritian history as the stage on which indentured labour came to be a systemized and regulated infrastructure, makes Beeharry's revisionist reading of subaltern agency particularly powerful. It is also significant that Beeharry describes political agency not solely as a product of individual heroism, but also as a quiet cultural revolution in which all members of the community are involved. For example, the conscientious ensurance of cultural survival – be it in the form of private daily acts, such as the upkeep of eating habits and social customs, or in more public collective efforts, such as the construction of baitkas[72] where people gather to faithfully reenact ceremonial rites and practices – is as integral a part of revolutionary struggle as public acts of political insurgency.

Even though Beeharry's text often suffers from 'an overly didactic explanation of the working of historical forces,'[73] he rarely idealizes the labourers' plight. Instead, he critically addresses the extent to which internal dissension hinders the efforts of reformers like Dhiren. This phenomenon is deftly captured in the figure of the sirdar (the plantation foreman or supervisor, often of the labourers' own ethnic origin). In fact, it is Dhiren's former supervisor, Sirdar Santoshi, whose own petty rivalries (and fears of reprisal from colonial authorities) result in Dhiren's tragic death on his wedding day. Thus, even Dhiren's opening of a school to instruct local children in matters of 'the Indian dialects and hygiene,' seals his reputation as 'an agitator' intent on jeopardizing his kinsmen's livelihoods.[74] However severe such opponents are shown to be, Beeharry is equally insistent that Dhiren's greatest opposition is found in the plantation system itself, which denies the labourers even the most basic freedom of mobility in the deliberate effort to prevent collective action.

Beeharry further widens the site of collective struggle in his thematization of the even greater restrictions imposed on the female subaltern as a sexual object and in her subordinate social status in the plantation economy. In the case of the early stages of indenture that the novel depicts, women were historically subjected to the additional peril of finding themselves among a conspicuous minority, which made them vulnerable to various forms of exploitation.[75] A Carter states:

> After 1842, the majority of women migrating to Mauritius were not indentured as labourers and consequently their position on estates was even more insecure and their earnings and allowances more negligible than those of men ... Women who migrated singly were offered employment as domestic servants, or were married from the depot to Indian immigrants in the colony.[76]

The plight of the indentured woman is movingly portrayed in the tragic figure of Anjani. Not only is Anjani the victim of sexual exploitation (she is 'rescued' from orphanhood by a French planter only to become his concubine), but she is also ostracized by her own community. In fact, it is difficult not to recall the tragedy of Thomas Hardy's Tess in Anjani's character.[77] Like Tess, Anjani is condemned by the systems of class and patriarchy which brandish her a fallen woman. Though Manish is relatively impervious to local scandals, he resists Anjani's overtures in the knowledge of her tainted status as a planter's mistress. Unlike Hardy's tragic heroine, however, Anjani suffers the additional stigma of her Indianness in a racially hierarchized system. As Tinker asserts, even those women who were seen as legitimate members of their own community (in their status as wives) were denied similar validation by the colonial infrastructure: 'Indian wives did not find a recognized place in the law of Mauritius (and later of the West Indies) based upon European, Christian rules of marriage.'[78]

In the same manner in which Beeharry critiques European and South Asian forms of cultural chauvinism, he is equally careful not to ascribe racial prejudice to any particular ethnic group. To this end, the narrative includes a subtext which implicitly critiques the pervading interracial tensions between the South Asian and his/her Creole or Malagash counterpart.[79] In Anjani and Mlle Jeanne's fate, therefore, it is clear that sexual transactions are the primary arena in which racial prejudice is most openly pronounced. Even the heroic Dhiren warrants critical scrutiny, therefore, when he instinctively attributes Jeanne's sullied sexual reputation to her 'impure' Creole ancestry. However, what begins as Dhiren's racial prejudice ends as a newly acquired awareness of and sensitivity to the systemic exploitation of female sexuality across the racial divide: 'what he had seen with his own eyes on the river bank was only the toll paid by servants to the lust of their masters. After all that was quite a common thing in India. Did not the Zamindars have their own goondas who went about in the countryside picking up women for their masters?'[80]

Anjani's eventual suicide in the wake of her grief over Dhiren's death seems unnecessarily tragic, but her symbolic plunge into the dreaded *kala pani* on the return journey exposes the extent to which both old and new worlds are equally implicated in the continued oppression of women. On the one hand, the future seems as perilous a space as the foreboding waters that transport these women as metaphoric vessels of the very customs that will ensure their continued subordination overseas. On the other hand, Anjani's inability to imagine life beyond Mauritian shores crystallizes her integral place in the new world, if only as a testament to the inescapable need for gender reform alongside other reformatory measures.

While the name of the incoming ship, the *Ganges*, underscores the sacred ties that bind, the departing ship, the *Maha Ranee* (Queen), pays tribute to the power of the female spirit, alluding perhaps to the capacity for heroism that Anjani's narrative discloses as forcefully as Dhiren's. To this end, both Anjani's and Dhiren's narratives underscore the epic reach of a text which 'becomes instrumental in shaping the world-view of succeeding ages, so that, in the words of the tale, past *exempla* and present needs find a continuous and unbroken meeting ground.'[81] As such, they symbolize the newly emergent image of the tribe as a group united across religious, caste, race, and gender differences.

The narrative circularity of *That Others Might Live* appears to project a distinctly Hindu ethos in its spiritual reconnection with the sacred homeland: 'Far away the signal mountain and summits of the Moka Range, towering high over the town, stood serene and peaceful under a canopy of gloss white clouds and of blue heavens.'[82] Despite its circularity, however, the narrative bears the lessons of history while affirming that even the most seemingly helpless figures carry the potential for transformative action, and by propelling its characters forward into an uncertain future that is nonetheless theirs to define. Beeharry's characters thus set the stage for an epic imaginary that deconstructs the imperialist projection of the indentured labourer as a passive receptacle of history, or its reading of Mauritian society as a derelict 'barracoon,' indelibly overshadowed by the 'lifeless system' of the imperial machine. This is because the diasporic subject's seemingly commonplace struggle for survival is an intrinsically heroic act which writes into being the tale of a new tribe.

4 'Passenger Indians' and Dispossessed Citizens in Uganda and South Africa: Peter Nazareth's *In a Brown Mantle* and Farida Karodia's *Daughters of the Twilight*

Middlemen and 'Mister Browns'

The South Asian presence in Africa predates the colonial era. Under the jurisdiction of the Arab sultanate of Zanzibar, South Asians enjoyed a favourable reputation as coastal settlers and savvy traders.[1] Social historians such as Dent Ocaya-Lakidi agree,[2] however, that once South Asian peoples arrived in the thousands as British colonial subjects, anti-South Asian feeling surfaced in images of Punjabis policing the East Africa Protectorate; of Gujarati merchants amassing commercial strongholds; of the particularly alien practices and customs of Hindu migrants; of the ubiquitous indentured labourers' seeming usurpation of 'the indigenous workers' rightful, negotiated place in the socio-economic hierarchy';[3] and, eventually, of nationalistic zeal directed outward to the Indian subcontinent rather than synchronized with the African call to independence.[4]

In Kenyan author Ngũgĩ wa Thiong'o's first novel, *Weep Not, Child*, a Bildungsroman set during the height of the Mau Mau armed resistance to British colonial rule, an omniscient narrator speaking from the perspective of the indigenous African states:

> The Indian traders were said to be very rich. They too employed some black boys whom they treated as nothing. You could never like the Indians because their customs were strange and funny in a bad way ... The Indians feared Europeans and if you went to buy in a shop and a white man found you, the Indian would stop selling to you and, trembling all over, would begin to serve him ... You did not know what to call the Indian. Was he also a white man? Did he too come from England?[5]

Here, Ngũgĩ captures the image of duplicity which has plagued South Asian diasporic peoples since their settlement on the African continent in the nineteenth century, namely, the stereotype of Indians as a colonized people who appear to act as 'colonizing immigrants' in their socio-economic role as 'middlemen.'[6] Ngũgĩ must have recognized the need to challenge such forms of ethnic essentialism when he suggested to Nazareth that he write a novel about Indians in East Africa,[7] responding specifically, it would seem, to the image of the South Asian as the proverbial 'middleman' or 'Mr Brown.'[8]

Caught uneasily between a racially divisive European ideology and an emergent pan-African consciousness, each of which has used the label 'Asian/Indian' in essentialist terms,[9] South Asian diasporic authors have since sought not only to self-critically redress the 'middleman' stereotype but also to affirm the South Asian diaspora's by now multigenerational history of settlement in the continent. In his own scholarship on East African literature, Peter Nazareth echoes historian Ocaya-Lakidi's assertion that racial prejudices in East Africa were first entrenched in black consciousness as the instrument of imperialism to put its 'exploitative policies into effect,'[10] only to be further deployed in the neoimperial interests of a post-independence elite.

Continental African writing by the diasporic community is thus hardly reminiscent of Deepchand Beeharry's epic tale of the indentured labourers' odyssey as a spiritually allied group of pioneering settlers. In fact, the differences between South Asian migration history to Mauritius and continental Africa are numerous enough to warrant comment. Even when factoring in the older presence of South Asian peoples along the East African coast, it is safe to say that the diaspora of the mainland has never come close to forming the majority populace it has in the island of Mauritius. Migratory patterns in East Africa quickly reveal the tale of a doubly displaced diaspora whose subsequent emigrations[11] to the United States, Canada, and England, and return journeys to the Indian subcontinent since the 1960s has left what Michael Twaddle refers to as 'residual communities' or 'roughly one half of 1 per cent of the current estimated total populations.'[12] In stark contrast stands the diaspora in South Africa, which effectively forms the largest hub of the old South Asian diaspora. The population of 'ethnic Indians' in South Africa (the 2001 census puts them at 1,115,467)[13] rivals that of Trinidad and Guyana combined. Unlike the East African context, this is a steadily growing population (seeing a growth of a little under 100,000 since the 1996 census), the vast majority of whom are South Africans by birth. However, there are many significant points of confluence between the East and South African context. First, each of these diasporas constitutes a racially marginalized minority. Second, each diaspora has been (or, in the case of South Africa, continues to be) determined by its place within the triadic axis, where it has vied for political or cultural representation and territory within indigenous African and European settler societies. Third, this has produced the distinctive 'middleman' condition, particularly as it applies to the free passengers who, in their position as merchants, traders, clerics, and administrators of Empire, fell somewhere between the racial and structural hierarchies of the colony. And finally, under native majorities in Uganda or white supremacy in South Africa, each diaspora has found itself dispossessed by programmatic forms of relocation and exile.

Continental Africa invited the highest proportion of free passengers (more commonly referred to as passenger Indians in this region) during the colonial era. These migrants travelled of their own volition to continental Africa alongside the steadily growing community of indentured labourers. Indeed, South African writing by this diaspora is filled with individualized portraits of the kinds of personal ambitions that might have motivated emigration during this period. Imraan Coovadia's 2001 debut novel *The Wedding* constructs the movement of the passenger Indian as an imperial quest narrative that begins with the conception of a grand dream of epic proportions. In his dissatisfaction with colonial India, the protagonist Ismet sets his sights on a new land, in the ironic terms of imperial adventure, conquest, and self-aggrandizement reminiscent of the colonial boy's adventure tale embodied by H. Rider Haggard's *King Solomon's Mines* or Rudyard Kipling's 'The Man Who Would Be King': 'With Khateja by his side, he saw himself forging a commercial empire, founding a dynasty, patronizing a culture. A sea change. Riches, dragons, treasure, barrels, roaring crowds, strange territory, trading delegations.'[14] The reversal of the imperial adventure narrative in the hopes and dreams of the colonized subject seeking self-betterment in the colonial outpost provides a comic example of the various motivations and experiences that might have served as a catalyst for migration to the continent, and one which deviates considerably from the narratives of trauma associated with bonded labour.

The passenger Indian thus tells a story of a differently constructed subdiaspora that adds to the diversity of the cultural, religious, linguistic, and socio-economic make-up of the larger diaspora of which it is a part. This included an unprecedented level of occupational diversity as well, where the migrants' livelihoods were earned as agricultural labourers on sugar plantations and manual labourers on the East Africa Railway; as petty traders and merchants; as professionals schooled in medicine, law, accountancy, and teaching; and, last but not least, as clerics and lower-end administrators for the ever-expansive colonial bureaucracy. The greater affluence and mobility of these settlers also facilitated the ensurance of closer ties, if not frequent returns, to the motherland. Marriages, for instance, continued to be arranged with the help of relatives back home. Together, these factors underscore the extent to which the diasporic communities of East and South Africa came to form a more diversified and mobile body of migrants and settlers. This is a far cry from the caricatural 'Indian shopkeeper' who earns the disdain of Ngũgĩ's Kikuyu characters, [15] or of the obsequious servant and docile labourer created in the European writer's imagination. [16]

A Voice Apart, A Literature in Exile

Even though a great number of South Asian peoples continue to make their home in Africa, their literature often describes communities wedged between contending powers, internally split by a host of inter- and intracommunal differences and dislocated, either by voluntary or forced exile, from their African homelands. Exile has undoubtedly been a recurring motif in the lives of South Asians whose ancestors' place in the African continent was inextricably tied to the infrastructures of the colony, the dismantling of which necessarily destabilized their sense of security and belonging therein. Uganda and South Africa offer an important basis for comparison, considering the forms of extreme dispossession, physical and socio-political, experienced by the diaspora in both locations. The early body of writing represented here by the novels of South African Farida Karodia and Ugandan Peter Nazareth have looked less toward their own historic beginnings in the African continent than to the more immediately felt effects of decolonization and apartheid – socio-political movements which have radically disrupted the lives and livelihoods of South Asian diasporic peoples themselves.

To some, then, it might come as little surprise that diasporic peoples have rarely been factored into the articulation of an African socio-political identity and, by extension, its national literatures. In Robert Gregory's 1981 survey of the Asian contribution to East African literature, this body of writing is said to have begun and ended in the 'period of transition, the decade before independence and the decade after.' [17]

Several decades later, it is easy to contest this conclusion. For one, the dispersal of post-colonial writers across the globe has often facilitated greater publishing opportunities, to which the post-millennium spate of Africa-based novels by older and younger generations of diasporic South Asians alike attests. Moreover, the unfolding historical forces – such as a post-Amin Uganda or a post-apartheid South Africa – which often reverse patterns of migration, remind us that diasporic experience is never irreversibly fixed to the various posts of history, but is continually repositioned by changing material and other conditions.[18] For example, the eventual collapse of the national economy would compel subsequent Ugandan leaders to reopen the doors to Asian immigration and facilitate the repossession of their assets.[19]

Similarly, since authors such as Farida Karodia have chosen to return to a post-apartheid South Africa, one might optimistically speculate that South African literature might also look forward to the broadening of its literary frontiers. In fact, this seems to have begun with the publication of Imraan Coovadia's *The Wedding* (2001) and Neela Govender's *Acacia Thorn in My Heart* (2001), two examples of post-millennium fiction from the perspective of the Indo-African community. Though the latter is a francophone novel (Govender was born in the Natal colony in the 1940s, but has spent most of her life in France), it has much in common with Karodia's first novel. This includes its rural South African setting and the entrepreneurial spirit of the family patriarch as a tenant farmer, its semiautobiographical narrative, and its generic echoes as a female Bildungsroman filtered through the perspective of a young Indian girl's daily travails, including the sacrifices and indignities suffered for the sake of a colonial education. In fact, the emergence of another generation of writers suggests that South Africa might gradually become another major hub of South Asian diasporic fiction, second only to the Caribbean. With these demographic patterns in mind, it appears that one might already speak of two waves as well as two generations of diasporic writing in South Africa: the period of writing initiated during and in response to the apartheid years and the post-1990s period which signalled the regime's demise.

The apartheid years saw the publication of shorter works, the most renowned of which is Ahmed Essop's short story collection *Haji Musa and the Hindu Fire Walker* (1988), a cross-section of Essop's literary career which began as early as 1969. Another example is Agnes Sam's *Jesus is Indian* (1989), a collection culled from the author's exilic perspective in the United Kingdom. A fourth-generation descendant of indentured labourers, Sam brings the indenture narrative to the short story genre. In the aptly titled story 'And They Christened It Indenture,' Sam's characters evoke a historical genealogy and collective consciousness within the vocabulary and poetics of indentureship. Interestingly, in the South African context, indenture history is often approached through the genre of autobiography rather than fiction; some better known examples include Dr K. Goonam's *Coolie Doctor – An Autobiography* (1991) and Jay Naidoo's *Coolie Location* (1990).

The novelists of note during this period are Farida Karodia and Achmat Dangor, both of whom launched their literary careers in North America, and both of whom give voice to 'coloured' characters with cultural and ancestral roots in the Indian communities. While a younger generation of novelists has since emerged in the post-apartheid period, this older generation of writers is still very much a part of the cultural and literary conversation; three have published novels since 2000 (Essop wrote his novel *The Third Prophecy* in 2004). Though this is necessarily a body of writing in gestation, it is not premature to observe a few interesting differences between the earlier and later fiction. In those works written in the most repressive climate of anti-apartheid activism and reprisal – Farida Karodia's *Daughters of the Twilight* (1986) and Achmat Dangor's *Waiting for Leila* (1978) are the most striking examples – ethnic particularity is often subsumed in the interest of cross-racial alliances. When speaking of Indo-South African fiction written in the 1980s, Pallavi Rastoji notes that this is the 'decade that saw the urgent need to unite the nonwhite population in order to dismantle apartheid. In this body of writing, Indians often defy the divisive categories of apartheid by absorbing themselves into alternative identities.' [20]

Cross-racial alliances are characterized as a necessary weapon and effective symbol against the entrenched political and other divisions created by the apartheid state. It is in the later fiction, then, that ethnic self-assertion is approached more forcefully. As Rastoji suggests, however, this is still a fledgling body of writing within what is also a fledgling post-apartheid state:

Indian fiction following the dissolution of apartheid in 1990 takes on a different hue, although its transformation is not as radical as one might imagine it to be. Even though Mandela promised a 'rainbow nation' that would evolve along nonracial lines, many South Africans of Indian extract felt excluded from the promise of the postcolonial nation that seemed to be still predicated along the black and white binary. In this fiction, Indians

tend to assert their Indianness in more explicit ways and without necessarily taking on larger communal identities to locate political authority,
even as they remain acutely aware of the racial interconnectedness of all
South Africans.[21]

Though circumstances and context necessarily differ, a similar pattern
of strategic representation can be found among the first generation of
Indo-Caribbean writers who also find themselves overshadowed by black/
white polarity in the decades leading up to independence and the con-
solidation of the West Indies Federation, specifically. As will be seen in
chapter 5, the Caribbean also gave rise to the kind of triadic axis that
was particular to South and East Africa, in the dynamic created by the
European settler, the African indigene, and the Asian minority. Of
course, no group could claim indigeneity, nor was the 'middleman status'
the prevailing sentiment against which Indo-Caribbean writers asserted
their own identity; Indo-Caribbeans were nonetheless faced with a similar sense of political invisibility in relation to the white colonizer and the
dominant African diaspora. Thus, where Afro-Caribbean characters took
centre stage over and above the 'ethnic Indian,' it was not in the spirit of
self-erasure so much as in the ensurance, both as a politically strategic
measure and as a genuine display of interracial solidarity, of collective
participation in the anti-imperial struggle. Here, too, the impulse was
promulgated by the desire to advocate non-white solidarity, which was
encapsulated by the political and ideological platform of black alterity,
the ripples of which were felt across the globe via pan-Africanism, the
civil rights movement, and revolutionary figures such as Steven Biko in
South Africa and Marcus Garvey in the West Indies.

In the case of East Africa, it would seem that the era of decolonization
shifted rather than terminated the base of literary production by South
Asians in the wake of their exodus from their African homelands. To this
end, Nazareth more accurately contends that, given the exilic perspective of many of its writers, Ugandan literature often needs to be 'tracked
down' before it can be considered part of the canon of African literature.[22] Renewed scholarly engagement with this more recent corpus of
writing invites our rereading of the first generation of writers such as
Karodia and Nazareth within an equally current critical and theoretical
framework. For instance, early critical reception of Nazareth's two novels,
In a Brown Mantle and *The General Is Up*, championed his caricature of Idi
Amin, but glossed over his critique of the ethnic rivalries besieging
African nations. In a more recent assessment, African scholars such as

Tirop Peter Simatei have turned their focus to the other, more self-critical dimensions of diasporic writing.[23] Commenting on Indo-African writers Peter Nazareth, M.G. Vassanji, and Jameela Siddiqi Simatei states: '[ils] ont tenté d'évaluer les rapports de forces qui ont présidé à la création de nations homogènes au détriment de minorités d'origine exogène et ont, surtout, essayé d'évaluer la responsabilité de chacune des parties en présence.'[24]

Apart from Malawian author David Rubadiri's *No Bride Price* (1967), which Nazareth refers to as one of his primary influences, and Behadur Tejani's *Day After Tomorrow* (1971), Nazareth's *In a Brown Mantle* is the first and earliest textual representation of the Asian community in East Africa, and certainly one of the least idyllic visions of African multiculturalism. David Rubadiri's novel appears to be one of the first to advocate, with cautious optimism, not only the possibility of interracial union in a post-independence era but the acceptance of its preexistence, particularly in the relationships between Indian men and African women, in African history. As the Indian female character tells her father,

'Look at it this way Daddy ... the Indian has penetrated more into the African life than even the best missionaries and the best administrators. He has rubbed shoulders with the most traditional and primitive in the remotest corners of this country and yet has remained a world utterly and irrevocably apart.

'IndoAfrican children are entirely from Indian fathers and African mothers.'[25]

Echoing the ill-fated but inexorable romantic union between Njoroje and Deepa in M.G. Vassanji's *The In-Between World of Vikram Lall* (2003), Rubadiri anticipates that it will be subsequent generations who will most radically challenge cultural norms in their attempt to bring the pattern of interracial union out of the realm of social taboo. In *No Bride Price*, Rubadiri shows that the African male attempts to challenge prevailing racial prejudices, be it by means of attempted courtship or in the harbouring of desire for an Indian girl. The second generation bears the banner of optimism heralded by national independence, a trope that is echoed but quickly derailed in Nazareth's more cynical version of both interracial relations and the nation-state in his own first novel *In a Brown Mantle*.

Writing by and about the South Asian diaspora in East Africa still constitutes a very small forum of representation compared to the situation in South Africa, where the population continues to increase. In this regard, it is also notable that writers from this region who now live abroad seem to prefer the label of 'East African' rather than the national appellation particular to their place of birth. For Uganda-born writers, this is perhaps an understandable response to the denial of national citizenship at the inception of statehood. But I believe it is also indicative of other kinds of patterns specific to the region as a whole. For one, it speaks to the pattern of migration outward, delineated by Robert Gregory, in the volatile decades before and after decolonization. Diasporic South Asians who are twice removed from the ancestral land, as colonized subjects at home and abroad, come to identify their African homes as intimately connected with the broader cartographies of empire over and above the delineated geography of statehood.

The East Africa Protectorate remains the primary label of identification for those migrants who came and left under its jurisdiction. It also speaks to the pattern of mobility within the protectorate that is particular to the 'passenger Indian.' Not bound to the colonial project or plantation with the kind of regulated authority imposed upon the bonded labourer, the passenger Indian was freer to chart his/her own destiny across the imperial map. This is poignantly underscored by Vassanji's personal history as the son of migrants born in Kenya and brought up in Tanzania. The kind of interconnected social, commercial, and personal networks that South Asian diasporic peoples developed across the colonial outposts of the East Africa Protectorate are captured in Nazareth's work, where ideas, goods, and people are shown to move fluidly across the colony. *In a Brown Mantle* captures this phenomenon in the figure of Pius Cota, a Goan revoluntionary whose martyrdom in a neighbouring colony (a thinly disguised Kenya), becomes the object of reverence and political controversy in the neighbouring Indo-African community. Similarly, Vassanji's *The In-Between World of Vikram Lall* captures the intersecting movements and migrations of free passengers, indentured labourers, and their descendants. In the repeated displacements endured by the protagonist's family, from the relative comfort of a small Asian enclave in Nakuru to their acute sense of vulnerability in a colonial outpost targeted by the Mau Mau freedom fighters, and then again from their numerous commercial successes and failures in the bustling city centres of Mombasa and Nairobi, the Lall family respond to and are irrevocably shaped by the various forces of colonial life.

Women writers have, since the publication of Nazareth's work, come to play an important role in the reshaping of the aesthetic features and modes of representation found in Indo-African fiction. Here, Ugandan-born Jameela Siddiqi stands out. Echoing Nazareth's satirical indictment against black and Indian political opportunism and ethnocentrism alike, Siddiqi picks up where Nazareth signs off, bringing the tale of the exiled tribe out of Africa, and into the double diaspora of the present. Setting her comic first novel, *The Feast of the Nine Virgins* (2001), in the migrant dens of 'Wembley and Tooting,' the African-born South Asian, like Rushdie's India-born Gibreel Farishta in *Satanic Verses*, falls once again into the cold, unwelcoming lap of Mother Empire, only to be reborn as a migrant mutant of sorts, an oddity to both the former colonizer and to his/her ancestral kith and kin. Like the Caribbean double diaspora, the figurative process of mutation is compounded by an added layer of cultural schizophrenia for those who have not one but two ancestral homelands to preserve and reproduce in the new 'new land.' Siddiqi self-consciously comments on this phenomenon in her own reflections on the ironies of diasporic subjectivity which inform her writing:

> So, whatever happened to 'When in Rome?' Because when in East Africa they tried to recreate India, and then, on being expelled to Britain, they transported that same second hand slice of India, but this time with the added delicious effort to try and recreate colonial Africa in Wembley and Tooting. Africa's yesteryear trader is now the British Asian restaurateur introducing his largely well-to-do English clientele to a unique Indian-African food experience. Strangely enough, it is a food experience that is new even for 'real' Indians and Pakistanis, many of whom would be hard pressed to mark a cross on a blank map of Africa to show the exact location of Uganda.
>
> But that is today's story, and it is a story that has now taken on global proportions with the East African Asian Diaspora representing an even larger cultural monolith through being equally well established further afield in the USA, Canada and Australia. But that perhaps is a subject for one of my future books.[26]

Similarly, women writers such as Agnes Sam rewrite, from the female perspective, the trope of the seemingly impossible African-Asian romance. Though Vassanji also challenges convention in the Njoroje-Deepa affair, the romantic subtext is nonetheless filtered through the split cultural consciousness of the male protagonist. Similarly, while Karodia's *Daughters of the Twilight* also thematizes the Indian female body as the site upon which racial taboos are figuratively and literally 'violated,' the novel limits

its discussion to the imperial racial binary of Oriental female / White male interrelation. Her character's brief sexual encounter and infatuation with her white neighbour essentially robs Yasmin of her innocence and childhood. In Agnes Sam's 'The Well-Loved Woman,' the narrator inverts racial and gender norms entirely. Here, the protagonist Chantal becomes infatuated with an African male, who by virtue of his race and her own community's prejudices, remains an intangible enigma that prompts more questions than it does answers: 'How had she never seen him before? When had he come? Or had he always stood there without her noticing him? Where did he disappear to at night? Why did no one ever speak to him? And why did he stand there like that? As if he were waiting – without hope.'[27] The narrative thus reorients the standard foci through which interracial unions, as an already taboo subject matter, have been traditionally filtered: the African male becomes the object of Indian female desire while the imperial and gender hierarchies represented by the white male are conspicuously absent. Instead, Indian prejudices and mores prevent the union from progressing from private imagined fantasy to openly lived experience. Chantal's greater rebellion against gender norms is projected through the lens of interracial desire, but her independent spirit is publicly censured at the slightest indication of transgression: '"An Indian girl speaking with an African man!" sent shockwaves through the community. "No one in this city will marry you now! We'll have to send for a husband from India for you!"' they cried.'[28]

The 'Twilight' Narratives of Apartheid and Neocolonialism

Nazareth's *In a Brown Mantle* (1972) and Farida Karodia's *Daughters of the Twilight* (1986) are first novels that reclaim, if not help set, the stage of self-representation for the Asian minority of Africa. Not only do these novels provide insight into interracial politics at the particularly volatile periods of decolonization and the creation of the apartheid state respectively, they also offer a highly particularized glimpse of the South Asian diaspora itself. While Nazareth satirizes the absurdly complex network of interethnic rivalry and tension besieging Uganda, Karodia focuses on an interracial family as a reflection rather than an anomaly of the multiracial South African populace.[29] Nazareth's *In a Brown Mantle* is a fictional account of Uganda's rise to independence and its subsequent drive to wrestle commercial strongholds from the 'Asians' or 'Mr Browns' of East Africa. Farida Karodia's *Daughters of the Twilight* recalls the similar fate awaiting South Asian migrants in South Africa, not from the African indigene but from the apartheid regime, as she depicts their eviction from their properties, businesses, and homes under the Group Areas Act of 1950, one of apartheid's principal laws of relocation and racial segregation.[30] In fact, the novel thematizes the various social, material, and psychological effects of racial segregration on the ethnic minority, including the process of relocation, the phenomenon of 'reclassification' (ethnic self-identification for bureaucratic purposes), and the varying degrees of exclusion, belonging, and cross-racial alliance predicated on the differences between rural and urban existence. The phenomenon of 'relocation' or internal dispossession within the adoptive homeland is repeated across the diaspora where ethnic alliances produce other forms of apartheid. Thus, under the racialized policies of President Forbes Burnham at the birth of Guyanese independence, Indo-Guyanese peoples are shown to experience similar forms of dispossession, though at the hands of the African diaspora rather than of the white settler. Such forms of coerced relocation are featured in Jan Shinebourne's *Timepiece*, a novel which documents the increasing entrenchment of Afro-Indian racial tension during the early years of Burnham's dictatorship: 'She had come to live with them to escape the racial disturbances which began in Georgetown in 1961, spread to many other parts of the country and did not end until 1964, by which time fifteen thousand people, mostly Indo-Guyanese, had been forced to move from their homes and settle elsewhere.'[31]

Born in Uganda in 1940, author/scholar Peter Nazareth is a second-generation Goan whose father migrated to what was then the British East Africa Protectorate at the turn of the twentieth century. Indeed, Nazareth might be called the quintessential diasporic subject, given a family history which includes Malaysia (his mother's birthplace), his Goan father, and his own subsequent move to the United States in the 1970s. Similarly, Farida Karodia is a second-generation South African, for whom the process of migration signals her own circuitous journey between the Eastern Cape and Canada, where she lived between 1968 and 1994, and her Gujarati father's migration to colonial South Africa, a generation earlier.

Unlike Nazareth, Karodia did not initiate her literary career while living in her country of birth, but rather joins her exiled peers who were unable to write freely in a repressive atmosphere. Not surprisingly, apartheid's strict censorship laws stifled any literary activity of protest. Karodia is thus a part of 'a floating exile community' of South African writers who 'continued to write about South African matters even after decades of living elsewhere.'[32] In a rare profile of the author's literary career, Anver

Versi states that Karodia's exile came about when she discovered that she had been blacklisted as 'an enemy of the state.'[33] Facing a forced internment in her own country after a short period of residence in Zambia, Karodia opted instead to seek refuge in Canada where she would pen two novels, *Daughters of the Twilight* (1986) and *A Shattering of Silence* (1993), and a short story collection, *Against an African Sky and Other Stories* (1997). Though Karodia's first novel did not receive the critical attention or acclaim it deserves in Canada, where it was published, it was nominated for the Fawcett Literature Prize in Great Britain. Its subsequent reworking as the first part of a three-part multigenerational saga entitled *Other Secrets*, published by Penguin in 2000, also received a prestigious nomination, the International IMPAC Dublin Literary Award, though it too did not enjoy a long shelf-life in print. Like many of her literary peers, Karodia has since made the journey back to a 'New South Africa'[34] and most recently published another novel entitled *Boundaries* (2003), which is set entirely in her native South Africa. One might hope if not predict that Karodia's return home and continued creative output might rekindle scholarly and commercial interest in her oeuvre, resurrecting those of her earlier works which have fallen out of print.

Nazareth's *In a Brown Mantle* is unique in that it was written and published in the author's native Uganda,[35] a few days before President Idi Amin Dada ordered the expulsion of the country's 'Asian' population. The novel sold out in its first printing by the East African Literature Bureau and its enormous success led to a Yale fellowship that would help launch Nazareth's prestigious academic career.[36] In fact, the novel itself eerily prophesies both Amin's overthrow of Uganda's first President Milton Obote and what would be Nazareth's own exile as a result of the expulsion edict of 5 November 1972.[37] What is interesting here though is that Nazareth's first novel addresses this community not from a retrospective distance but from the author's insider perspective as one of many citizens in a plural Ugandan society. Though written from his vantage point in the United States, Nazareth's subsequent novel, *The General Is Up* (1991), also deals exclusively with the African context. Echoing the trope of the 'mad king' prefigured in Caribbean and Latin American literature, this novel is a scathing satire of the infamous general-turned-president,[38] and can be seen as a sequel to the first, describing as it does the arduous and chaotic moment of departure for the South Asian diasporic community. Though it is a little-known work, *In a Brown Mantle* stands as a significant landmark in Indo-African writing, one which deserves critical attention.

Nazareth and Karodia are unique voices in African literature. They do not fully belong to the small minority of writers of European origin who speak from the historical centre of institutionalized power nor do they belong to the vast majority of indigenous African writers who speak from the cultural and political centre of the post-colonial condition. This liminal condition should not, however, be misconstrued as a site of privileged mobility. In Salman Rushdie's transnational worldview, an immigrant or exile's displacement from the homeland results in a split or 'double perspective'[39] which forces the individual to acknowledge the shifting and relative nature of identity. Though the diasporic writer's simultaneously 'plural and partial'[40] imagination mirrors Rushdie's deployment of the double perspective as a narrative device which reveals a decentred or multiply positioned consciousness, Karodia and Nazareth insist that for the second-generation South Asian in Africa, 'in-betweenness' is usually an imposed condition of marginalization within the natal land itself – or, as Rushdie poetically states, 'that form of internal exile which in South Africa is called the "homeland."'[41]

In the extreme cases of Uganda and South Africa, therefore, this interstitial condition is brought about by exclusivist doctrines and often draconian measures. What the in-between, or to use Karodia's titular phrase, 'twilight' atmosphere of these texts underlines is the diasporic community's sense of volatility in Africa as a twice-displaced people, that is, both in their historical displacement from the Indian subcontinent and in their status as a political and racial minority in the new land. Hence, the twilight state condemns the sons and daughters of the diaspora to an uncertain personal and collective destiny. This condition acts as a central metaphor for a state of belonging that is perpetually put into question, sometimes violently so. In this light, Arlene A. Elder justly concludes that to the writer of South Asian origin in Africa, 'the African world ... is one in which race and culture, rather than place of birth, are crucial.'[42] From albeit contrasting perspectives, therefore, Nazareth and Karodia emphasize the imperative of racial and cultural collaboration, not only in the sense of equality and belonging, but also in the interest of opening up inherently segregationist societies to the possibility of pluricultural statehood.

Although both texts are explicit in their identification with a pan-African consciousness that denounces white supremacy, they also turn a self-critical gaze to their own communities' narratives of exclusion. Diasporic writers are keenly aware that theirs is a twofold task: they must not only subvert dominant discourses but also, as Arun Mukherjee more accurately suggests, highlight the historical realities that have been buried or forgotten by the grand narratives of history.[43] These writers deconstruct the grand narrative of imperialism and at the same time engage in the discourse of self-representation. When filtered through the workings of a formal narrative strategy, the emphasis on subjective experience in each of these novels is played out as a tension between individualism and an 'agential politics of identity'[44] that is simultaneously self-interrogative.

Karodia not only indicts the institutionalization of apartheid, but also subtly balances her judgment of racist colonial practices in her characters' intermittent reflections on Indian history: 'India! India! You're always comparing this country to India. The British had their faults, I'd be the last one to deny that, but ... Who can forget the atrocities committed by Indian upon Indian?'[45] Similarly, the sectarian and other rivalries within the South Asian community described in Nazareth's novels undermine the diasporic subject's tendency to imagine the 'Asian' community in idealistic or nostalgic terms, a fact that makes ironic the ethnocultural unity implied by the conferred label. This foregrounding of cultural and historical relativity in the interest of demythologizing India as an unblemished if not utopic ethnocultural space, or of debunking false dichotomies that only reinforce the rhetoric of bias and prejudice within the adopted land persists in the writing of a younger generation. In Coovadia's *The Wedding*, a novel set in India and Africa – 'worlds apart' that are bridged in the heroic leaps of faith taken by the immigrant – India is similarly demythologized as a land that is far from the cohesive whole projected in the homeward gaze of the diasporic subject: 'Now, in a happier time, my grandfather would have refuted these words. What India did this Vikram imagine was there? Throwing around all this talk was irresponsible. The only India he had seen was a million squabbling fiefdoms and hostile tribes quarreling over the land. Where were these "united as one man" Indians going to come from?'[46]

Sons and Daughters of the Dispossessed

Daughters of the Twilight is not the first South African novel by a writer of Indian origin, but it is one of the earliest representations of the Indian perspective. Bernth Lindfors suggests that 'South Africa's first Indian novel' is Ansuyah R. Singh's *Behold the Earth Mourns*, published circa 1960 and long out of circulation. Lindfors describes the novel as 'a forgotten piece of South African fiction ... unnoticed by literary commentators for more than thirty years.'[47] Lindfors's reading of the distinctly Hindu ethos that informs Indian resistance in South Africa is definitively absent in Karodia's novel. As a call to mobilization across the racial chasm that divides South Africa's disenfranchised groups, Karodia's novel seemingly transcends the Gandhian-inspired battle cry of *satyagraha* (nonviolent resistance), if only by virtue of the latter's deference to a caste and race consciousness.[48]

Though the novel has since been reworked as the first part of a larger multigenerational saga, Karodia herself admits to initially having wanted to maintain the integrity of each piece, having written the project as a trilogy. In this regard, she notes that *Daughters of the Twilight* has generally remained intact since its republication in *Other Secrets*. As Rajendra Chetty notes, in her summary of the latter work's publication history, 'Basically, *Daughters* has remained the same; just some of the details like names have changed – the writer fictionalized the name of the town from Sterkstroom to Soetstroom. But, in fact, all three parts can be considered as distinct books within the one new book.'[49] Given the integrity of *Daughters in the Twilight*, even in its reworking, I have opted to limit my discussion to the work as the author's debut novel, given its conceptualization and publication in the apartheid era, which, as I have noted, has had a considerable impact on the style, tone, and content of this earlier period of fiction.

Karodia's first novel is a semiautobiographical reflection of her own hybrid South African identity as the daughter of a Gujarati-Muslim father and a 'coloured' mother who 'were the only Indians in the town.'[50] Set entirely in the author's place of birth – a rural township in the Eastern Cape that is far from the hubbub of an increasingly urbanized diasporic population – Karodia's novel also breaks the stereotype of ethnic and religious ghettoization that is commonly associated with South Asian peoples. The rural setting, however, should not be read as an anomaly either. In her discussion of Karodia's work since her return to South Africa, Rajendra Chetty states, 'Karodia notes in her text that it was relatively common in the days before mass relocation (the Group Areas Act decreed that the different races shall live apart) to find solitary Asian traders living and conducting business in the heart of the white rural communities.'[51] Though the family patriarch Abdul is insistent that his eldest daughter marry a Muslim South Asian, his sense of religious piety is commensurate with a pluricultural ethos of communal belonging, one that is textually represented by his 'coloured' wife, Mevrou; the family's sympathetic white neighbour, Dora Oliphant; and an indigenous African 'squatter,' Daniel. The family is a racial conglomeration of outcasts who, albeit to varying degrees, share a history of economic and social disenfranchisement.

Like Achmat Dangor, Karodia provides an alternate version of the characteristically Hindu-Indian portrait of the old South Asian diaspora. In Dangor's 1997 novel *Kafka's Curse*, religion complicates post-apartheid subjecthood further still. Describing the marginal position of Islam within a predominantly Judaeo-Christian society, Dangor's novel echoes the anxieties felt by the Muslim and Hindu communities of the Indo-Caribbean. As will be seen in chapter 6 on Trinidad, however, in Indo-Caribbean literature representations of Islam are fleeting if not reductive, relative to the dominant position of Hinduism in the diaspora itself. In the African context, the minority position of Muslim South Asians must be qualified where Islam itself has a long-standing tradition which predates colonial history. For this reason, perhaps, in Dangor's novel Islamic identity becomes an explicit layer of diasporic subjectivity, often over and above ethnic allegiance and identification.

Although Nazareth's novel is critical of patriarchal attitudes, his female characters function primarily as symbols of the prostitution and corruption of African culture rather than as active agents of change. Subsequently, the gradual disintegration of nationalist ideals within a post-independence society is typified in the protagonist's objectification of women in his frequent 'wenching.'[52] In contrast, Karodia's text deconstructs a male-centred narrative in which women are shown to be side-lined in the struggle for independence. In her early novels, for instance, female characters are preparing to situate themselves or are already immersed within liberation struggles which also include an engagement with feminist politics. In Karodia's *A Shattering of Silence*, a political novel depicting Mozambique's violent uprising against Portuguese rule, a woman of Goan origins is a key player in the underground resistance (an interesting counterpoint to the figure of Pius Cota depicted in Nazareth's first novel). Similarly, in *Daughters of the Twilight*, Meena evolves into a highly politicized being in her discovery that self-actualization often necessitates a militant assertion of selfhood.

Daughters of the Twilight assumes the form of a Bildungsroman which traces the social and psychological development of the protagonist, Meena, alongside the official gestation of the apartheid state. As such, it charts the impact of the dehumanizing apartheid law, the Group Areas Act, a policy which forcibly seized the properties, businesses, and homes of non-white peoples, subsequently designating the least inhabitable stretches of land for occupation by the people it categorically

dispossessed. The highest percentage of those to have felt the consequences of the Group Areas Act of 1950 were Indian or 'coloured.'[53]
The 'coloured' and 'Indian' communities 'have long and consistently
called for the abolition of the Act,'[54] a fact that is alluded to in the increasing politicization of Meena.

Interestingly, Karodia situates the beginning of the family's displacement and marginalization in the colonial South Africa that ushered in
indentured labourers, thus establishing the family's genealogy within its
nomenclature and mythology. Meena says of her father:

> He had come from India in search of adventure. At the age of fifteen he
> arrived in Durban with other Indian immigrants who had come to South
> Africa as indentured labourers to work the sugar plantations in Natal. He
> had arrived in the period following the turmoil created by Mahatma
> Gandhi's call for civil disobedience, a time when the provinces of Natal and
> Transvaal had passed laws restricting the movement of Indians from one
> area to another ... But Papa, like thousands of other Indians, had managed
> to slip through the borders and had escaped to Dordrecht ... and then
> settled in Sterkstroom.[55]

Reflecting a common trend in the history of indenture, a great many labourers in South Africa remained behind after the termination of their
contracts, and came to be known as 'freed labourers.'[56] The glossing over
of Abdul's migration history makes the delineation between his status as
a freed labourer or passenger Indian rather ambiguous. Though he is
clearly shown to have worked alongside other labourers prior to his entrepreneurial debut as a small goods merchant, the ambiguity surrounding Abdul's migration history is a strategic narrative ploy insofar as it
demonstrates the homogenization of the Indian as a subordinate labour
force in the eyes of the apartheid regime.

Nor is this view diminished for subsequent generations born in the
adoptive land. For South Africa's 'daughters' such as Meena and Yasmin,
racial injustice is initiated in a colonial school curriculum embedded in
European ideals which clash with the 'South African Indian's' daily lives.
The curriculum functions as a denigration of the contributions of the
indentured labourer to the colonial economy: 'There, to my horror, be-
neath the oval stamp on the inside cover were the carefully printed words
of a jingle: "Coolie, coolie, ring the bell; coolie, coolie, go to hell."'[57]
Karodia seems particularly critical of the deployment of such stereotypes
within an education system that 'standardizes' the 'nineteenth-century

official stereotype which had posited the dualistic coolie character –
yielding and bowed before the plantation manager,'[58] and is offensive
to European sensibility as a subaltern of the lowest degree. Indeed, the
coolie stereotype is not a simple marker of difference but a far more
insidious linkage between race and class, which, when perpetuated in
the school curriculum, ensures the continued racial and social subordination of the descendants of indentured labourers and ethnic Indians
generally. Interestingly, Abdul's double association with two contradictory images – the mercantile settler as a duplicitous economic pariah
and the bonded labourer as a racial and economic subordinate – effectively cancels each stereotype out. This in turn subtly reveals the narrative of upward mobility achieved through individual industry and
self-empowerment implied by Abdul's transformation from labourer to
self-made entrepreneur.

When the Mohammed family is evicted from their property and business, the experience of displacement is accordingly described as a multigenerational legacy grounded in colonial history: '"When will it end,
Delia? When? All my life I've been kicked around."'[59] For the dispossessed, then, 'home' functions as a more fluid, transmutable metaphor
for the unity found in kinship rather than as a fixed symbol of physical
or material stability. Thus, with a family genealogy that is defined both by
voluntary and involuntary forms of displacement, home most viscerally
signifies as a sense of connectedness to others over and above a romantic
attachment to place:

> We were leaving behind us not only our home but also a big chunk of our
> lives. Tears slid down Ma's cheeks as she watched Gladys's forlorn figure in
> the rear-view mirror.
> I turned around for a last look. Both she and Daniel had been such
> an integral part of our lives, the many threads woven into the fabric of
> our existence.[60]

In the absence of a terra firma, or a land to claim as home, filial and
non-filial relationships become the stabilizing tools for selfhood and belonging. However, in a racially divisive context, these stabilizing threads
of human connection are also pitted against a Hegelian dialectic of suspicion and mistrust. Perhaps in response to the often contradictory
nature of human relations, Meena's first-person narrative is delivered as
a productive rather than self-effacing dialectic between constrasting perspectives. Adopting what Miki Flockemann calls the narrative's 'dual

focus,' a pattern of inter-subjectivity embedded in black women's writing, the protagonist's development is played out as a critical dialogue with her older sister, Yasmin (a role model and foil). In her comparative analysis of the use of the Bildungsroman in Caribbean and African women's writing, Flockemann suggests that the dual focus creates an interlacing of perspective in light of other women's experiences which in turn subverts the traditional construction of the Bildungsroman as a male-centred, linear progression toward dominant national ideals. For the subaltern female, such a progression merely culminates in the stark options available for women of colour in a colonial or post-colonial context. In contrast, the dialogic interplay between two closely related characters engenders a critical negotiation between self/other so as to ensure that 'selfhood is not defined by the ruling hegemonies, but in opposition to them through an identification with the local community, [such that] the construction of an alternative selfhood seems possible.'[61] Meena's story pivots around a similar axis of inter-subjectivity, which primarily includes her older sister whose subordinate position is a shared condition that each figure nonetheless processes in highly individual ways.

In her claim 'to be just what I am,'[62] Meena begins to resist the colonial and patriarchal practices within which the subaltern female is doubly circumscribed. The father's pragmatic understanding of his daughters' education as ensurance of her marriageability – '"Perhaps an education will help to make the package more attractive"'[63] – betrays a myopic view that is little better than the assimilative educational practices of the state which delimit the social and professional 'possibilities available for non-white girls.'[64] By observing the kind of restrictive social mobility afforded her sister by means of a private education for 'coloured girls,' Meena astutely perceives the intersecting hegemonies of imperialism and Western capitalism with its racialized class structures. Moreover, Meena sees in her own and her sister's destiny within the tightly controlled social parameters of the apartheid system the Indo-African's often dichotomized position between an active identification with African liberation struggles and a conciliatory approach to the dominant system in the ensurance of greater social mobility.[65]

Yasmin's gradual 'Westernization' also makes evident Ngũgĩ's concept of 'colonial alienation' in his assessment of the impact of the colonial education system on the child's psyche, in its gradual distancing of the child from the familiar markers of an indigenous culture by means of a deracinated curriculum which encourages colonial mimicry while denying entry into the racial hierarchy.[66] Consequently, Meena's older sister

Yasmin is shown to have internalized an Orientalist tradition which arrests her sexual development behind the objectifying gaze of the colonizer. In this regard, she also brings to view Gayatri Spivak's paradigm of the subaltern female who, caught between the imperatives of patriarchy and imperialism, inevitably carries over the traces of the essentialist discourses she attempts to resist.[67] In this regard, Yasmin's one and only act of rebellion is still contingent upon her self-image as a sexualized object, for her albeit transgressive infatuation with a white South African male, rather than bridging the racial divide, only serves to perpetuate her status as the gendered 'other.' Yasmin's rape by this neighbourhood bully is thus an ironic critique of her naive hope that racist doctrines will be subverted by individual acts of interracial union – a romantic idealism that seems unattainable without a concomitant dismantling of the ideological infrastructures that facilitate her oppression as a woman of colour.

Neither Nazareth nor Karodia evoke the paradigm of hybridity as a utopic solution to racist ideology. In fact, Nazareth rejects the contention of his diasporic counterpart Behadur Tejani[68] that racial harmony can be actualized by means of interracial marriages, or by bringing together the best of Indian and African cultures. In the case of the apartheid regime where 'coloured' peoples are denied equality on the very basis of their miscegenation,[69] a utopic view of interracial mixing is rendered particularly inoperative. Homi Bhabha's paradigm of hybridity as 'the strategic reversal of the process of domination,'[70] insofar as it subverts the essentialist binary of self/other, seems inapplicable in a system that consciously marks the hybrid individual as a site of shame.[71]

In Karodia's novel, hybridity as a site of shame is explicitly embodied in Yasmin's rape and subsequent rejection of her 'half-breed' child. Yasmin's rejection of her child implicitly echoes her own sense of shame as the product of interracial marriage. Similarly, racial miscegenation as an officially encoded strategy of cultural and political marginalization is brought to bear on Meena's developing awareness as a racially marked entity. Having to choose between her status as coloured or Indian, Meena must ironically affirm her hybridity at the expense of her Indianness so as to facilitate her entry into an urban school for coloureds. In other words, Meena's reclassification is hardly a self-empowering celebration of her mixed ancestry; rather, it is a capitulation to a government-enforced policy in which both coloured and Indian function as fixed and mutually exclusive racial categories. The Mohammed family's hybrid identity can therefore only become a subversive site of resistance as a critical pronouncement of selfhood over the discursive deracinating practices that contain it.

Meena's first-hand experience of the apartheid bureaucracy in 'Pretoria, the administrative capital'[72] is thus a jarring awakening to race-as-construct. Meena's awakening is poetically symbolized in the striking contrast between a monochromatic world of bureaucratized racial binaries and the uncontainable variety of the natural world:

> The heaviness which had threatened to stifle me was lifting. Images collided ... the purple masses of jacaranda blossoms, the patterns of light and shadow on the street as the sun broke through the intertwining branches, the blue of the sky reflected in the windows. What a fool I had been to let myself be upset by that Afrikaaner. My eyes and mind were once again in harmony.[73]

In her renewed sense of self-possession, Meena's political awakening is subsequently aroused in her discovery of the South African left as a multiracial body: 'Again, to my surprise, despite the strict segregation of races, I found whites and blacks surreptitiously squeezed into the small room ... We were soon joined by four other people, three of them Indian.'[74] Karodia deftly challenges the Empire's antimiscegenation laws by subtly aligning the multiracial body with the variegated colours of the South African landscape, and suggesting that racial hybridity is a 'natural' outcome of colonial migration.

Elleke Boehmer contends that quite often the denouements found in South African fiction written in the 1980s, the last decade of apartheid, are punctuated by death, near-death, departure, or escape. Boehmer attributes this pattern to a narrative uncertainty that involved 'an unwillingness or an inability to comment on what might follow ... a refusal even to go as far as anticipating any ultimate end and therefore any possibility of a new beginning.'[75] To a certain extent, this is true for both Nazareth's and Karodia's novels, each of which is set in a period of political transition that seems to foreclose the possibility of acceptance, integration, and equal citizenship for its diasporic subjects. Narrated from the perspective of the exile in London, *In a Brown Mantle* paradoxically begins where its narrator's history as a 'Damibian' (the fictional naming of Uganda) citizen has been abruptly foreclosed. *Daughters of the Twilight* ends with Yasmin's desertion of her child and family, an act of embittered escape from the only meaningful markers of belonging. The narrative is thereby punctuated with a sense of foreboding, such that the concluding image is as barren and hopeless as Yasmin's new predicament of loss and dispossession: '"This place is like a desert ... It won't be long before they'll be back again with their dogs and their guns."'[76]

Stylistically, however, Nazareth's and Karodia's novels could not convey their messages more differently. Karodia's drier, understated prose reflects the narrator's quiet sense of despair in the early stages of what would continue to be the regime's stranglehold on its population, and also reflects an earlier stage of South African writing as a form of 'bear[ing] witness' to the atrocities of the present.[77] As her narrative moves toward the possibility of racial and cultural collaboration without giving in to utopic visions of interracial harmony, her tentative gesture is mirrored in a sparingly descriptive prose, and punctuated by celebrations of the subtly interwoven patterns of colour that grace the South African landscape:

> The orange orb suspended above the distant horizon had turned the bleached grass into a field of fire. As it dipped below the mountains it splattered the sky with pinks, softening the colours on the ground until the thorn scrub spread out lilac shadows. Then, as it dipped even lower, those lilac shadows ran together in dusky hues. [78]

In contrast, Nazareth's humourously irreverent text, set in the purportedly liberating post-colonial moment, comes across not only as a wry comment on the stillborn aspirations of nascent post-colonial states, but also as an ironic 'unmasking' of the narrator's own 'authorship' – that is, as a narrative strategy of resistance against one kind of 'authoritarian' control for another. Upon first read, Nazareth's satire resembles other African 'post-colonial dystopias,'[79] most notably Ngũgĩ's *Devil on the Cross*. Reading much like a socialist manifesto steeped in the references, personages (most notably Nkrumah and Lumumba), and rhetoric of African liberation struggles, *In a Brown Mantle* sits comfortably within the canon of post-colonial African literature. However, the author's nuancing not only of diasporic South Asians as a variously allied political and ethnocultural body, but also of post-colonial societies as highly individual entities – a fact that is exemplified in the novel's repeated references to the stark difference between Kenya's and Uganda's respective levels of 'struggle' for independence – suggests that the novel resonates beyond the central thrust of its anticolonial themes.

As it was completed in the year preceding Amin's overthrow of Milton Obote, and published only days before Amin's Asian Expulsion Edict, several critics have also recognized the prophetic quality of this novel. *In a Brown Mantle* subscribes to what its author/scholar has identified as a common trend in Ugandan literature, that is, its thematization of post-coloniality as a symbolic anticipation of 'an Amin.'[80] Critic Abasi Kiyimba states that the only two African novels to have 'most directly' depicted Amin's notorious leadership are Nazareth's second novel *The General Is Up* and Alumidi Osinya's *The Amazing Saga of Field Marshal Abdullah Salim Fisi (Or How the Hyena Got His)*.[81] I would suggest that both *In a Brown Mantle* and *The General Is Up* can be read as two important chapters in the saga of Indian-African relations under the dictatorship of Idi Amin. The novel poignantly opens to newspaper headlines announcing an assassination attempt on the nation's first president. Nationhood is poetically referred to as 'a machine of perpetual immobility'[82] in which it is not only the 'Mr Browns' of Africa who are the figurative stillborns of the nascent post-colonial state, but also indigenous Africans who find themselves disenfranchised by its political elite.

Nazareth can be said to have acknowledged his friend Ngũgĩ's suggestion by writing a novel about the seemingly underrepresented if not misrepresented 'Mr Browns,' while also following his own desire to write 'a novel about Goans which was simultaneously a political novel about Africa.'[83] In turning his attention to the Goan community, Nazareth vehemently reaffirms his contention that 'there never was an "Asian community" in East Africa. There were several different "tribes," all mutually exclusive: Patels, Ismailis, Sikhs, Bohras, Goans, etc.'[84] As the subjects of centuries of Portuguese rule and, in its aftermath, what would be perceived by many Goans as an Indian occupation, Nazareth's Goan characters certainly challenge any homogenizing view of South Asian history and identity. Primarily employed as British civil servants in East Africa, Goans constituted what might loosely be referred to as the lower middle class within a racialized colonial hierarchy. The Goan self-image as a religiously, ethnically, politically, and socio-economically distinct minority lays bare the misconception of the 'Asian community' as an ideologically cohesive monolith.

Recounting the story of his personal rise and fall from the ranks of the new African government, the protagonist-narrator Joseph D'Souza writes from the perspective of an exile in a frigid London rooming house. As such, the narrative is structured as a flashback which occasionally returns to D'Souza's present condition as a man without land or currency, a predicament that is tragi-comically prefigured in his failed attempt to dupe a British-made electric heater into accepting 'third world' money. Indeed, the opening scene is reminiscent of Sam Selvon's *The Lonely Londoners*, in which another substandard heating device gives little comfort or warmth to a displaced coterie of West Indian émigrés. Like Moses and his disheartened fellow denizens, D'Souza echoes the portrait of the doubly disenfranchised citizen characteristic of early immigrant writing in a post-war era. Finding himself similarly displaced, in England and Africa, by the 'brown mantle of his skin,' D'Souza's transhistorical perspective as a thrice-removed minority – that is, a Goan within a dominant Indian diaspora; an Asian minority in Africa; and a visible minority among the European population – also marks a new perspective in the body of post-colonial literature.

D'Souza's own increasing opportunism is a cynical reflection of the newly formed bourgeoisie. Consequently, his disillusionment is not with 'the African people,' nor is it levelled against the elite of which he is a part, but rather it is with the rabid individualism ushered in by late capitalism. As D'Souza remarks, 'the common people ... did not seem to particularly think in racialistic terms except insofar as they felt they had suffered at the hands of businessmen who where Indian.'[85] In spite of his own class privileges, however, D'Souza's corruptibility is also prefigured as a compensatory drive to cash in on what he perceives to be his decreasing net worth as a disposable symbol of ethnic diversity. D'Souza's insecurity is compounded when he witnesses the rhetoric of multicultural fraternity dovetail into a nativist discourse that is, itself, an inchoate mixture of Negritude and the European call to 'native paramountcy.' As Arlene Elder explains, native paramountcy signalled the weakening Empire's strategic shift in supporting indigenous African rights so as to '[undermine] the collective strength of the non-European populations.'[86] Nazareth captures the call to native paramountcy in the following passage:

> The colonial government had already seen the writing on the wall, it had felt the wind of change, and it had now changed its tactics. Instead of denouncing Africans as savages incapable of ruling themselves, thus providing a moral basis for continued rule, the colonial Government had now turned round and begun claiming that her rule had been one long training session so that the Africans could eventually rule themselves. [87]

In this regard, Nazareth's text is situated within the dyadic axis of indigenous/diasporic interrelation. As subtext, the narrative of native paramountcy that shapes and consumes Nazareth's characters is echoed in Indo-Fijian author Satendra Nandan's *The Wounded Sea*, where diasporic South Asians are also pitted directly against the indigenous population and its claims to political ascendancy and land rights.

As the emerging President Robert Kyeyune's speech writer, D'Souza is quick to identify the ideological dissonance between the president's view of the African 'people' in racially homogenous terms and his own reading of the same in the idealistic coda of historical affinity among a group whose experiences coalesce as racialized colonial subjects. The novel pivots around the mounting conflict between Kyeyune and D'Souza, a symbol of the disintegration of black-brown relations at the level of the body politic, which D'Souza refers to as the 'two pieces of the wing of an aeroplane separated by a hairline crack.'[88] But the crack only becomes a full-scale rupture in the hands of GombeKukwaya, the novel's thinly veiled caricature of Idi Amin. In his portrait of Idi Amin as an ogreish thug with 'fishbowl eyes' and the animalistic nickname of The Cow, Nazareth eerily anticipates Ngũgĩ's *Devil on the Cross* (1982), an account of the brutalizing effects of neoimperial hegemony on the material and spiritual well-being of the African people. D'Souza's dream of a multiracial Africa is dealt its final blow when The Cow's discriminatory politics are couched in a Negritudinist elevation of Africa's 'grand and glorious'[89] past which is put to the service of a nativist argument aimed specifically at the Indian mercantile class whose assets and properties represent the obstacle to indigenous African prosperity.

Simatei's comparative analysis of Nazareth's and Vassanji's East African novels (mentioned earlier) has perhaps afforded a reassessment and softening of his earlier critique that Nazareth's focus on the rising bourgeoisie's collusion with neoimperial interests overshadows a concomitant assessment of his 'Asian' characters' implication in 'their own hegemonic behaviour and ambitions.'[90] The novel itself provides numerous examples to repudiate this charge. Functioning outside the purview of colonial ideology and Western influence, The Abala Goan Institute is caricatured as the nerve centre of the diaspora's 'club mentality,' an ethnocentric attitude which ironically begins in the Goans' voluntary segregation from the greater Indian population. In her study of the Goan community in the Ugandan capital, Jane Kuper can be seen to confirm Nazareth's view of the proliferating divisions within the South Asian diasporic community: 'For the Goans, the "others" were "Indians", while the "Indians" in turn joked about the Goans as "Brown Europeans."'[91]

Not only are the Goans of Uganda shown to bear the label of 'Indian' in the most ambiguous sense, they are also shown to be further split over the question of allegiance to the British Empire. Nazareth reminds his reader that South Asians have borne a much older history of conquest, and accordingly attempts to explain Goan attitudes within the wider framework of subcontinental history:

> My father came to Damibia in the early nineteen-twenties from Goa, a small country within the continent of India ... Hardly anybody paid any attention to Goa until India decided a few years ago to re-conquer it from the Portuguese, who had ruled it for four hundred and fifty years ... The history of Goa is full of conquests and reconquests – rule by Hindu empire-builders, Moslem imperialists, and finally the Portuguese ... One strand of the Goans always resisted, and the period of foreign rule is often interrupted for a few short years by independence, rule by the Goans themselves.[92]

Though Nazareth's version of subcontinental history is grossly oversimplified, what is significant here is his rendering of diasporic individuals as historical beings whose multiple positionings lay bare the intersecting trajectories of intercultural contact and conflict. As Nazareth himself comments, 'Goan history could be part of his [narrator's] consciousness and part of his excuse.'[93]

In fact, Nazareth's portrait of a fractured diasporic community illustrates the extent to which ethnocentrism impedes national unity at the intra- and intercommunal level. However, Nazareth never restricts his satirical gaze to a particular group. The 'club mentality' which comes to exemplify the Goan population is in fact shown to be equally true of African traditionalists for whom tribal loyalties trump both intertribal and interethnic unions. This is brought to light in the trope of the impossible Afro-Asian romance. During his carefree university days, D'Souza's relationship with Grace, an 'African beauty queen,' is matter-of-factly described as little more than a fleeting affair given the protectionist tribal custom of endogamy practised by Grace's family. While the novel does not proffer a complex portrait of interethnic relations beyond their representational value as the normative patterns of racial division, the satirical thrust of the novel is directed as much outward, to the fractured body politic, as it is inward, to the diasporic body and its own 'racist fictions of purity.'[94]

In one of his earlier surveys of Asian-African literature, Nazareth coins the term 'Brownitude,' referring to a mode of cultural discourse which combined the spirit of Negritude as a form of racial self-empowerment with the imperialist construction of Africa as 'the dark continent,' a colour-coded recipe which the South Asian writer then deploys in the interest of writing against the middleman stereotype. Nazareth cites Ahmed

Virjee's poem 'Black on Brown' as the exemplary expression of this thankfully short-lived genre. Drawing directly on the imagery associated with the indentured labourers who were such a predominant feature across the East Africa Railway, Virjee extols the Asian work ethic, his industry, and his fellowship. Using the symbol of the 'tortuous railways' and 'endless roads'[95] upon which the labourer toiled, Virjee concludes that hardship was not in vain, for it underscores the extent to which the Asian played his part in the 'civilizing mission.' In his own novel, Nazareth alludes to Brownitude discourse in the persona of Bernie Rodrigues, a high-ranking Goan official who champions the civilizing influence of the British in Africa for having turned a primitive backwater into 'the Apple of the Lord's eye.'[96]

While racially motivated differences are mostly shown to work to the detriment of the community, sowing the seeds of political immobilization and civil unrest, other patterns of difference are articulated as productive or at least realistic expressions of heterogeneity. Hence, the narrative is dotted with characters whose status as first-generation immigrants reveals a varied range of orientations to African politics. For instance, D'Souza's father's policy of non-interference in what he refers to as 'someone else's fight' is characteristically motivated by the first generation's atavistic longing to return, in life or death, to the ancestral homeland. To illustrate that a diversity of opinion exists even among the first generation, the narrator recalls the heated debate which once ensued between his father and Pius Cota, a committed Goan revolutionary from the neighbouring Azingwe (a fictionalized Kenya). Cota deftly sidesteps his peers' political apathy by shifting the question of political involvement from the older to the younger generation. In so doing, he enables the young D'Souza to reconceptualize his African identity as 'part of the new generation, with roots here and with new ideas.' Cota's deeply felt identification with 'the colonized' helps crystallize D'Souza's political awakening: 'I couldn't quite accept that all the "white" people were superior to all of us "coloured" people.'[97] In the father's ethnocentrism and Rodrigues's colonial mimicry, Nazareth appears to acknowledge what Kiyimba calls the 'Asian share of blame in the racial intolerance that contributed to the tension that Idi Amin caused to explode';[98] on the other hand, Nazareth also rewrites the master narrative of African nationalism in the figure of Cota as revolutionary and martyr to the anti-imperial struggle, while at least gesturing toward a theorization of diasporic subjectivity as a transformative response to changing material conditions.

D'Souza's final expression of national belonging is an ironic declaration of love for his African homeland as its 'bastard son': "'Goodbye, Mother Africa," I said, as the plane lifted off. "Your bastard son loved you.'"[99] D'Souza's diasporic subjectivity as the illegitimate offspring of a pluricultural state paradoxically affirms as it releases any authoritative claims to African citizenship. The use of the confessional mode to convey D'Souza's own downwardly spiralling tale of political and moral bankruptcy results in a level of narrative ambiguity that metonymically echoes the protagonist's ambiguous citizenry. D'Souza's narrative discloses an epistemic disparity between utterance and meaning in the Bakhtinian sense of an 'authorial unmasking through a language that is double-accented.'[100] Though his story is presented as a clear indictment of a fraudulent body politic, D'Souza's dubious narrative authority muddies the line between victim and victimizer, patriot and opportunist, citizen and denizen.

The delegitimization of the protagonist-narrator in his multifold subject-position as witness, perpetrator, lackey, and victim does not collapse under the post-modern semantics of subjective indeterminacy. Though D'Souza's perspective is often filtered through the loosely veiled guise of what Simatei amusingly refers to as a 'sloganeering socialist,'[101] the protagonist's multiply positioned identity between variously conflicting allegiances invests his dogmatism with irony. In fact, meaning and, with it, judgment and accusation, is deferred, exposing the constructed and mutable concept of race, since it is racial discourse that continues to hold entire communities hostage to a ghettoizing politics of blame. In D'Souza's narrative, the politics of blame is at least momentarily recast at the discursive intersection between race and class interests, so that no member of African society is entirely culpable nor entirely free of the sadly ongoing 'business' of racial profiling and ethnic essentialism.

On 12 April 2007, an anti-Asian demonstration erupted in the Ugandan capital of Kampala against the 'Government plan to give away part of Mabira Forest to the Sugar Corporation of Uganda (SCOUL), which is part of the Indian-owned Mehta Group.'[102] The recent targeting of the entire ethnic community over the actions of the government and the Mehta group might explain, at least in part, why so few Ugandan-Asians have accepted these new gestures of inclusion and made the voyage back to their African homes. The recent backlash against the Asian community underscores the fact that Peter Nazareth's little-known novel, *In a Brown Mantle*, has as much resonance today as it did in 1972. Linking the two – the current event with the fictionalization of its historical antecedent – effectively relocates a forty-year-old text in the present once again. Hence, Nazareth's text is a cautionary reminder that the narratives of our times often betray a continuum of interethnic violence initiated or exacerbated in the colonial era. But the text also dares us to surmount the posts that pin us down to the impasses of history insofar as it rescues the African-Asian character from the figurative and literal ghetto of ethnic typecasting and racial scapegoating, thereby critically relocating the South Asian diaspora within larger patterns of historical injustice.

In a Brown Mantle and Daughters of the Twilight seek to participate in the ongoing debate of African liberation struggles and thus form part of the canon of post-colonial African literature. Wedged precariously between often complicit and competing master narratives, these texts deploy the diasporic subject's 'twilight' or 'in-between' perspective to open up the discourse of national identity and belonging in (self-) interrogative terms. When set against the backdrop of a changing political landscape to which the diasporic subject cannot make indigenous claims but nevertheless identifies as the adopted 'homeland,' particularly as a second- or subsequent- generation citizen, the 'Asian/Indian' character manifests a self-conscious awareness of the relative nature of belonging, while asserting a distinctive coda of 'ethnic' affiliations.

These novels, each of which depicts the historical moment that would invariably turn diasporic subjects into dispossessed citizens in their natal lands, paradoxically serve as a testament to the diaspora's identification with greater African society. Highlighting the disjunctive nature of the community as a heterogeneous and, by extension, variously allied body, these texts espouse an alternate politics of inclusion in the evocation of difference, not as a basis for discrimination but as a shared feature of community. Poised as their protagonists are on the brink of major political upheaval, neither Karodia nor Nazareth offer idealistic solutions to state oppression; rather, each of their narratives moves toward a way out of racial division and mistrust by reframing the politics of blame in the poetics of a shared history of discrimination and suffering.

PART THREE

The Caribbean

5 New Configurations of Identity for the Indo-Guyanese 'This Time Generation': Rooplall Monar's *Janjhat* and Narmala Shewcharan's *Tomorrow Is Another Day*

Not Columbus's 'Indies'

In his discussion of the African diaspora, Stuart Hall jokes that the Asian presence in the Caribbean reveals the paradoxical truth of Columbus's mistaken impression that he had, in fact, arrived in the 'Indies' in 1492. As Hall ironically comments, 'You *can* find "Asia" by sailing west.'[1] Caribbean writers most certainly cannot escape the irony of the epic blunder in the eventual encounter of the misnamed American 'Indians' with the Indian indentured labourer, and the subsequent patterns of misrepresentation that would be the hallmark of official colonial records. As Sam Selvon writes, 'Christopher Columbus must be killing himself with laugh, but he should wait until he hear the whole story. We find Columbus had a brother who was a tally clerk counting the first East Indians who ever came to Trinidad as they land off the ship. He can't understand them when they talk, so he spelling and writing down the names what he think he hear, and allocated groups to the sugarcane plantations regardless of skill or craft, caste or religion'[2]

Between 1838 (a few short years after the abolition of slavery) and 1917 (the official end of indenture), over half a million indentured labourers arrived in the British Empire's Caribbean colonies. These included the smaller islands of Jamaica, Grenada, St Vincent, and Walcott's native St Lucia, but by far the most visible presence was to be found in Guyana, South America, and its closest island-neighbour, Trinidad.[3] Mirroring the other island colonies of the Empire, the South Asian diasporic communities of the Caribbean were primarily composed of indentured labourers brought in by the European plantocracy to replace freed African slaves. At the end of their contracts, a staggering 75 per cent of these immigrants chose to remain in the Caribbean, some because of the expense of the return passage 'home' or because of the numerous other financial and technical obstacles with which they were so often confronted, some because of the agonizing prospect of the interminable sea voyage back to the Indian subcontinent, and some because of the earnest desire to settle in the new land.

When indentured peoples became the primary labour force on the plantation, they remained a relatively segregated community under the auspices of the colonial system, first by means of the Pass System (established in Mauritius)[4] and later by means of colonial institutions such as missionary schools.[5] Also, many indentured peoples forfeited a return passage home for the opportunity to purchase Crown land in the island interiors which, in turn, resulted in their isolation well into the earlier part of the twentieth century. Together, these factors have helped preserve the religious and social structures of South Asian peoples in the Caribbean. However, as illustrated in Deepchand Beeharry's *That Others Might Live*, the sense of 'commonality' uniting South Asian diasporic peoples came about as early as the arduous sea voyage from the Indian subcontinent to the colonies, and is thereby predicated on their historical and spiritual bond as *jahaji-bhai* (ship brothers)[6] or fellow-travellers and émigrés. For those making the journey to the Caribbean, the waters were already cast with the ghostly shadow of the Atlantic slave trade, and the distance between the motherland and the 'new world' was the greatest that South Asian émigrés had ever known.

Neither Indo-Guyanese nor Indo-Trinidadian writers speak of a minority experience. The former can boast of their earlier arrival in the region and of their status as an ethnic majority which lasted for almost a century. In fact, by the turn of the twentieth century, Guyana's census revealed that the South Asian diasporic community constituted the largest ethnic group therein (42 per cent of the total population); by the 1960s they constituted a slim majority of the country's population (50.2 per cent of the total population).[7] The unusual concentration of South Asian diasporic peoples within an equally anomalous English-speaking South American country makes Guyana's position in Latin America unique. As one of Britain's major plantation colonies in the Americas – one which relied on a labour force of African slaves, South Asian indentured labourers, and, to a lesser extent, Chinese immigrants – Guyana continues to identify itself as an extension of the Caribbean region, particularly to the nations of the former West Indies. Though the Dutch were the first to establish a colony along the Guyana coast (which also includes present-day Surinam and French Guiana), the British occupation since 1831 has left by far the greater impression on Guyanese society.[8]

Guyana is also linked to the Caribbean archipelago in terms of its Amerindian populations. In fact, in spite of the genocide carried out against Amerindian peoples since Columbus's arrival and the subsequent tendency to exclude indigenous cultures in discussions of contemporary Caribbean society, Amerindians such as the Arawaks still maintain a modest minority status in present-day Guyana.[9] While writers such as Wilson Harris cast indigenous peoples at the centre of the Guyanese cross-cultural imagination, Indo-Guyanese writers rarely evoke the voices, characters, and histories of indigenous peoples. Cyril Dabydeen is one of the few such writers to illustrate the imprint of indigenous civilizations on the Indo-Guyanese consciousness.[10]

Guyana, itself an Amerindian word for 'land of water,' came to be known as the Land of Six Peoples, which includes African, South Asian, indigenous, European, Chinese, and Portuguese peoples,[11] though the first three groups are the most visible members of contemporary Guyanese society. 'East Indian' has been the term deployed throughout the British Caribbean to describe peoples of South Asian origin. It is a peculiar legacy of Caribbean history, which once again recalls Columbus's epic blunder. As Selvon's comment reveals, the labelling of indigenous peoples as 'Indians' is a misnomer which has caused some consternation among the peoples of the South Asian diaspora. The term 'East Indian' was thus coined to distinguish between the immigrants from the 'East' and the misnamed Amerindians. To complicate matters, the term 'West Indian' came to refer to the British colonies of the Caribbean, thereby resulting in a further distinction between 'East' and 'West' Indians (the former associated with the South Asian diaspora and the latter with the African diaspora). Usage of the term 'East Indian' persists across the Caribbean region, particularly at the level of local parlance. Selvon, for one, rejects such labels as absurd constructs which only reinforce ethnic rivalries and racial segregation: 'This starts to be bewildering, and gets even more so, for when we have East Indians born in Trinidad, we should have to call them East Indian Trinidadians. And the people living in these islands are called Westindians. So by definition, what we have here is really an *East Indian Trinidadian West Indian*.'[12]

Nevertheless, Selvon has argued for ethnic self-assertion as a 'proclamation of what East Indians in the Caribbean have accomplished.'[13] Similarly, Cyril Dabydeen remarks, 'Ethnicity is a key marker; it's what sometimes feeds our work, where we find the particularities, even the resonance, for what we create.'[14] Both Dabydeen and Selvon would agree, however, that ethnic self-assertion does not preclude national participation. Similarly, Frank Birbalsingh suggests that the South Asian diaspora in the Caribbean is no different from other immigrant groups, whose literatures have been influenced by historical circumstances and their bearing on ethnic configurations. For this reason, perhaps, the label 'East Indian' is perceived to be a colonial relic that is not reflective of the complex, multiply positioned identity of the diasporic subject whose hybrid identity has been rooted in the Caribbean for almost two centuries. Birbalsingh suggests that the term 'Indo-Caribbean' presents a more accurate reflection of the process of indigenization of South Asian culture in the Caribbean region, while also signifying the diaspora's distinctiveness from a dominant Creole culture grounded in Christianity and largely 'Western' cultural norms influenced as much by Europe as by North America.[15]

British imperial history has played no small part in forging ethnic delineations in the Caribbean region. As Brian Moore suggests, up to the nineteenth century Guyana was an 'ethnically compartmentalized society' constructed around the division of labour under a colonial plantation system.[16] Within such a structure, the newly arrived indentured labourers were seen as expedient replacements for an earlier diaspora who had fought long and hard for their freedom. For the African diaspora, the promise of emancipation might well have appeared to be grossly mocked in the indentured labourers' seeming acceptance of the very same plantation existence, and in the Empire's almost seamless substitution of one kind of exploitable human labour force for another. As David Dabydeen notes, this initial disruption of the narrative of emancipation was further complicated over time, and on a number of other political, social and economic levels:

> Afro-Guyanese argued that the Indian presence depressed wages, and the Indian habit of frugality and asceticism gave them an advantage since they were willing to survive on very little … Moreover, Indians had been given land in lieu of a return passage home upon the expiration of their indentureship contract, to encourage the retention of seasoned labour. The freed Africans however had to purchase Crown lands, the cost of which was prohibitively high … In short the Indians were seen as stealing their rightful inheritance, newcomers and interlopers accorded legal protections and material privileges denied to slave and ex-slave populations.[17]

Like their Trinidadian counterparts, many Indo-Guyanese writers address not only the metanarrative of imperialism, but also the African diaspora's perceptions of social and economic betrayal in the appearance of the new labour diaspora. They do so by providing a materialist reading of racial segregation as it was instituted under a colonial plantation system and carried over to the post-colonial era in the division of labour between the largely urbanized Afro-Caribbean and the rural Indo-Caribbean. They also give voice to the diasporic subject's religious beliefs and cultural values as they are internally and externally perceived to be at odds with Christian, black, and Creole identity. Having said this, it should be noted that ethnic configurations are necessarily changing among increasingly urbanized younger generations who are influenced not only by the changes taking place in their society at the local level but also by larger globalizing forces and a new cyber culture. Narmala Shewcharan's and Rooplall Monar's novels capture this transition at its earliest stages.

Historically, however, it is clear that the indentured community in the Caribbean found themselves in an uncomfortable position between the recently freed African slaves and the European plantocracy. This position should not be confused with the duplicitous 'middleman' label that stigmatized the South Asian trader/merchant in East or South Africa,[18] but it was nonetheless rife with similar consequences of social and cultural ostracism that would have been felt well after decolonization. As Birbalsingh explains, there are several factors which account for the South Asian immigrant's strained position among African, European, and Creole peoples. South Asians brought with them altogether alien 'languages, customs, religions, dress and culture in an English-speaking, Christian society'[19] and in a creolized culture bearing African roots. And, as in the other colonies of the Empire, the indentured labourers were perpetually haunted by the 'coolie' stereotype, given the identification of 'coolie-work' with the drudgery of manual labour and the stigma of social inferiority. In Mahadai Das's anthologized poem, 'They Came in Ships,' the speaker begs the question of her 'coolie' ancestors: 'Was your blood spilled so I might reject my history – forget tears among the paddy leaves.'[20] Similarly, in David Dabydeen's signature poem 'Coolie Odyssey,' the speaker, from his vantage point in the double diaspora, describes his migrant sensibility in the mythopoetics of indenture, which first exposes the imperial myth (if not the imperial lie) that migration would benefit the colonized subject:

Still we persist before the grave
Seeking fables.
We plunder for the maps of El Dorado
To make beautiful our minds in an England
Starved of Gold.'[21]

Indo-Caribbean Literature: A New Creolité

Guyana is the birthplace of the English-language indenture narrative. Written at the height of the indenture system by a young India-born British barrister, Edward Jenkins's *Lutchmee and Dilloo: A Study of West Indian Life* (1877) is the first novel to describe indentured existence. Commissioned by the Aborigines Protection Society and Anti-Slavery Society, Jenkins reported on the conditions meted out to the labourer under the indenture system in British colonial Guyana in an earlier documentary piece entitled *The Coolie: His Rights and Wrongs* (1871). Jenkins's dedication to the cause soon developed into a fictional venture which offered a more descriptive portrait of the people who suffered daily under the dehumanizing system. In his introduction to the newly reprinted edition of the novel, David Dabydeen suggests that Jenkins's advocacy for the underdog was, much like the earlier abolitionist movement itself, rooted as much in the ideals of the civilizing mission as in purely humanitarian impulses. In *Lutchmee and Dilloo*, it is the self-ennobling discourse of Empire that drives character and plot. Though the novel aims for historical accuracy in depicting the injustices of indenture for the 'Guianese coolie,' Dabydeen rightly suggests that the Indo-Guyanese characters themselves remain 'indentured to his [Jenkins'] authorial voice.'[22]

But Jenkins's work accrues considerable value as a literary artefact: first, it sought to champion the cause of the 'lowly coolie' in the increasingly militarized and jingoistic pro-imperial climate of the late nineteenth century. Second, Jenkins's keen sense of the impact of indentureship not only on body and mind but also on the spiritual and cultural identity of the diasporic individual was quite without precedent. Indeed, this would have been the very first English-language fiction on the Indian diaspora. Jenkins even anticipates the central import of the sacred epic the *Ramayana* in the diaspora, drawing on the storytelling devices of the Indian epic and its beloved personas of Rama, Sita, and the monkey-god Hanuman in the shaping of his own tale: 'Of the Bengal village in Behar, where the hero and heroine of our story were born and had lived, the only other character yet presented to the reader, Hunoomaun, was the "chokedar," or watchman; a character, at the time we are writing of, found all over Bengal.'[23] The kind of empathy for the Indo-Guyanese plight found in Jenkins's early abolitionist-inspired fiction is loosely echoed in Trinidad's A.R.F. Webber's *Those That Be in Bondage: A Tale of Indian Indentures and Sunlit Western Waters* (1917), but more notably in the work of Guyana's Edgar Mittelholzer.

Completed in 1938, published in 1941, and republished in 1970, Mittelholzer's little-known novel is a slightly different fare to that of Jenkins's *Lutchmee and Dilloo*. Situating his Indo-Guyanese characters in the post-indenture period, Mittelholzer's novel incorporates many of the themes raised by the Indo-Caribbean writer him/herself, including the younger generation's willing conversion to Christianity as the only available means of self-advancement in a system designed to muzzle religious tolerance and cultural diversity, or the treatment of the female subaltern as the Oriental object of imperial male fantasy. Arnold Itwaru's novel *Shanti* reveals the buried history of sexual abuse across racial lines in his depiction of the rape of an Indo-Guyanese girl by a white overseer, or again in the blunt editorial comments made about the colonizer's view of Indian women, such as the following: 'vigorous, fuckable female animals at his disposal and pleasure.'[24] Similarly, Mahadai Das reminds her readers that, as a gendered minority, *jahaji-bhain* have suffered as 'one third-quota, coolie woman.'[25]

In one of the few extant reviews of Mittelholzer's *Corentyne Thunder* (1941; 1970), Wyck Williams argues that this little-circulated text signals the birth of the Guyanese novel, thereby challenging Wilson Harris's *Palace of the Peacock* (1970) and its heretofore unrivalled place in the canon. Williams's reasoning is as follows:

> Its depiction of landscape (internal and external) offers insights into the Guyanese psyche: the colonial crucible in which our identities took form, the rippling effects down through generations … That bond between land and people was never stronger than in Berbice county, never more boldly depicted than in *Corentyne Thunder*. For those born after Independence Mittelholzer's novel has the verve to forge emotional links with the past, to broaden our understanding of a region traditionally identified with one ethnic group.[26]

Corentyne Thunder dares enter the inner sanctum of the 'East Indian,' breathing life into a subject matter that would hardly have been deemed worthy of public attention, much less aesthetic expression, at its time of publication. Guyanese novelists tend to agree with Williams's assessment of the importance of Mittleholzer's novel in the development of the local canon, but they do so with a more critical eye to the author's representation of the Indo-Guyanese plantation community. As Jan Shinebourne remarks, in an interview with Frank Birbalsingh, 'Mittelholzer's *Corentyne Thunder* hit me for six. I felt so thrilled when I opened it and found that somebody had described the same landscape, climate, rivers, trees, people, speech – everything that I wanted to do.'[27] However, Shinebourne tempers her praise in a later comment about the novel's 'glamorized picture of rural Berbice.'[28]

The Indo-Guyanese novel, from its earliest example in the form of Peter Kempadoo's *Guiana Boy* (self-published in 1960, and republished as *Guyana Boy* in 2002), has been largely concerned with the coastal community of Berbice county, initially immortalized in *Corentyne Thunder*. As Jeremy Poynting notes, Guyanese literature is marked by the particularities of the Guyanese landscape: the three major rivers of Essequibo, Demerera, and Berbice and the villages that border them; and the five distinct spaces of coastland, inhabited hinterland, city, sugar estate community, and the foreboding uninhabited wilderness.[29] In spite of its aesthetic and other limitations, from its very first pages *Corentyne Thunder* captures the metaphysical intensity of diasporic experience for the labourer who remains spiritually and mentally tethered to the new land well after the legal contract that ensured his social and physical bondage has expired:

> A tale we are about to tell of Ramgollal, the cow-minder, who lived on the Corentyne coast of British Guiana, the only British colony on the mainland of South America. Ramgollal was small in body and rather short and very thin. He was an East Indian who had arrived in British Guiana in 1898 as an immigrant indentured to a sugar estate. He had worked very hard. He had faithfully served out the period of his indenture, and now at sixty-three years of age he minded cows on the savannah of the Corentyne coast, his own lord and guide.[30]

The Indo-Guyanese, as the subject of English-language fiction, has thus predated the birth of the Indo-Guyanese novel itself, which is said to have begun with Kempadoo's aforementioned first novel, *Guiana Boy*. Like most of the early novels of the period, Kempadoo's was also written from the perspective of the twice-removed diaspora, as an immigrant abroad. Indeed, Rooplall Monar, the entirely self-published Sheik M. Sadeek, and the newly emergent Moses Nagamootoo are the only three novelists to have stayed in Guyana, though there are some examples of reverse journeys home, such as that of Peter Kempadoo in the 1970s. The early generation of Indo-Guyanese novelists who came to form the double diaspora in England or Canada include David Dabydeen, Cyril Dabydeen, Arnold Itwaru, and Sasenarine Persaud. Not surprisingly, these writers look to their early fictional endeavours as a means of coming to terms with the culture shock of the immigrant experience itself. One such example is David Dabydeen's *The Intended* (1991), which is a semiautobiographical portrait of the author's struggles as a young immigrant who, following the colonial model of self-actualization in the Western metropolis, finds that he, too, is another 'lonely Londoner.' In a very different turn from Selvon's West Indian or black coterie of characters in *Lonely Londoners*, however, the protagonist first befriends Shaz, a British-born Pakistani, though he is nonetheless self-consciously aware that 'I was an Indian West Indian Guyanese, the most mixed up of the lot ... the only real hint of our shared Asian-ness was the brownness of our skins.'[31]

The Indo-Caribbean novel has emerged as a male-dominated genre. Like other regions boasting larger diasporic populations, however, it has since come to include women writers. Here, Narmala Shewcharan stands out as the first Indo-Guyanese female novelist. However, Jan Shinebourne, of mixed ancestry (a Chinese father and a Chinese/Indian mother), penned two earlier novels, *Timepiece* (1986) and *Last English Plantation* (1988), the latter of which has been hailed as the 'first attempt in the contemporary novel of the Anglophone Caribbean to reconstruct Indian female experience from an Indian female perspective. It is also the first novel to give the Indian female character a central place in the scheme of things.'[32] Shewcharan and Shinebourne have been joined by Ryhaan Shah, whose debut novel *A Silent Life* (2004) provides an unusual insider glimpse into a Muslim Indo-Guyanese family.

As will be seen in chapter 6 on Trinidad, where Muslim characters do appear in the greater body of Indo-Caribbean literature, they are minor characters who are somewhat reductively imagined. The absence of complex Muslim characters in Indo-Caribbean writing might simply reflect the distribution of religious groups in the region. For instance, an overwhelming 85 per cent of the indentured labourers who immigrated to Trinidad were Hindus.[33] Historian Brinsley Samaroo confirms that religious adherence in Indo-Caribbean society had a two-pronged effect on its respective communities: on the one hand, it broke, in the form of transnational religious organizations as well as in the process of religious syncretism, patterns of 'incipient communalism'; on the other hand, Indian-trained or imported religious leaders 'brought with them many of the prejudices ... which had divided India over the centuries.'[34] Others suggest that it was the Muslim Shia community who 'retreated from public view' in the aftermath of the Muharram Massacre of 1884, when colonial authorities opened fire on a crowd of men, women, and children in what had come to be the dominant multiracial festival on the island, the Hosay Festival (the Shia-Muslim Festival of Muharram). Seeing in the festival's ability to mobilize people of various creeds and races a threat to the 'colonial state' at a time of heightened unrest on the island, the colonial authorities saw fit to destroy and ban the procession using the harshest means.[35] Trinidadian Ismith Khan's novel is particularly striking for its descriptions of the Hosay Festival and its vibrant street procession. In this sense, *The Jumbie Bird* (1961) is a significant work for bringing Muslim identities to view not in the myopic framework of minor characters but in the arena of cultural history and national lore.[36]

In the Guyanese context, Ryhaan Shah's is an interesting new perspective which adds to the spectrum of Indo-Caribbean diversity, thereby shifting the standard foci away from the themes, norms, and references associated with the dominant Hindu diaspora. Cyril Dabydeen also pushes the creative envelope in his distinctly post-modern novel *Drums of My Flesh* (2005), where a young protagonist named Boyo befriends an eccentric mendicant, Jaffe, who helps him make sense of his increasingly chaotic world. Jaffe, who looks to his own Islamic faith for spiritual guidance, becomes the narrative's shaping mytho-cultural consciousness and repository of racial memory. This is an interesting narrative ploy, for it brings the Guyana of the protagonist-narrator's past into the projected fold of his daughter's increasingly uncertain future as a global citizen poised on the threshold of radical environmental and political change in a post-9/11 era.

Indo-Guyanese writing has been and continues to be enriched by the Creole identities of the Caribbean. Drawing on her own mixed race background, Jan Shinebourne brings the experiences of the ethnic Indian and Chinese-Guyanese communities to life in her two novels *Timepiece* and *The Last English Plantation*. More recently, Oonya Kempadoo (Peter Kempadoo's daughter of mixed Indian, Scottish, and Amerindian origins, born in London but raised in Guyana) has followed in her father's footsteps, though she belongs squarely to the post-independence generation of writers insofar as she unflinchingly confronts the racial prejudices besieging contemporary Guyana. In her use of the mango tree as a central symbol in her first novel *Buxton Spice* (1998), she creates a metaphorical landscape that is consistent with Caribbean women's writing more generally. Indeed, I am reminded of Jamaican Michelle Cliff's fictional autobiography, *Abeng*, where the mango, both as a transplanted fruit and highly adaptive, indigenized resource, is a productive, fecund countersymbol of hybridity and variegation in an otherwise racially segregated society. Though Oonya Kempadoo's first novel is set in 1970s Guyana, the frank descriptions of the protagonist-narrator Lula's sexual awakening fuse an otherwise disjointed narrative. (This structural characteristic is typical of the female Bildungsroman penned by other Caribbean women writers including Lakshmi Persaud, Michelle Cliff, Cristina Garcia, and Jamaica Kincaid.) However, the country's growing racial divide is never far from the young girl's daily musings. Referring to the destruction of a local village mosque by a rioting mob, Lula comments, 'The only warring I could remember was what Mums said was a rally. I remember PNC people running down the street with flames in bottles.'[37]

For the Indo-Guyanese writer the principal catalyst for creative expression has been the relatively untold history of indenture and the unique sense of cultural displacement felt by this plantation community. As a handful of the first generation of Indo-Guyanese writers illustrates, plantation estate or village life are central concerns for the descendants of indentured labourers. Indeed, the editors of the first major anthology of Indo-Guyanese literature suggest that the largely rural setting of the community might account for the late emergence of the Indo-Guyanese novel itself, particularly in comparison to the development of Indo-Trinidadian literature. Joel Benjamin, editor of *They Came in Ships: An Anthology of Indo-Guyanese Writing* (1998), provides an important correlation between the Indo-Guyanese community's socio-economic conditions and scant literary production: 'A sociological explanation might point to the later access of the Indo-Guyanese community to education, the narrower base of professional elite and the fact that a far higher production of the community remained in the sugar industry or in the rural villages.'[38]

Indo-Guyanese writers nonetheless echo the motifs and thematics of wider Caribbean literature in many ways: in their emphasis on the recent memory of colonization and anticolonial struggle; in their indictment of neoimperial practices, particularly as they are channelled through the tourist industry, the degradation of local agriculture, and

urban development; in their oft-echoed articulation of the exilic or
immigrant experience in the Western metropolis; in their narrativization of a fragmented memory as a symptom of dislocation; in their per-
sonification of a lush tropical landscape; and in their use of Creole as
the language of speech and/or narration. One might say that these are
the generally overlapping concerns of the diasporic Caribbean writer.
However, Indo-Caribbean writers tend to part company with their diasporic counterparts not only in their narrativization of indenture history
but also of the post-colonial moment as an uneasy response to the now
dominant Afro-Caribbean or Creole culture. As the older generation
of Rooplall Monar's Indo-Guyanese community lament, 'the world of
sacred ceremonies [is] threatened by creole ways.'[39]

This is not to suggest that the Indo-Caribbean community categorically resists a Creole aesthetic. On the contrary, the processes of transculturation are as much a part of Indo-Caribbean experience as are the
atavistic resonances of a distant cultural past; for instance, religious syncretism is evident in the Indo-Caribbean's identification with certain
aspects of Obeah or, again, in the 'carnivalization' of the Muslim Hosay
Festival (the traditionally somber Islamic observance of Muharram).
Linguistic hybridization is most strongly evident in the mixing of various
forms of Creole with Hindi/Bhojpuri vocabulary. Items of consumption
such as food (roti, curry, chutney) are rife with examples of hybridization; and, of course, interracial mixing is the most outward expression of
a 'shared' Creole identity. In the spirit of cultural hybridization, the
Indo-Guyanese residents depicted throughout Rooplall Monar's work
are shown to break into 'a mixture of Hindi melodies and creole
rhymes';[40] similarly, many contemporary Indo-Caribbean writers, including Rooplall Monar, David Dabydeen, Cyril Dabydeen, Harishchandra
Khemraj, Jan Shinebourne, and Narmala Shewcharan, underline the
unity of peoples 'who have passed through the estate experience of slavery and indenture.'[41] David Dabydeen and Sharlow Mohammed thematize this historical bridge most explicitly in their historical novels *The
Counting House* (1996) and *When Gods Were Slaves* (1993), respectively.

What is unique to South Asian diasporic peoples in the Caribbean
context, therefore, is the extent to which a distinct cultural identity has
been maintained in the process of transplantation, over several generations, and in spite of the processes of colonization, assimilation,
and creolization. During his own sojourn in Trinidad, Derek Walcott
marvelled over not merely the ubiquitous presence of South Asian
peoples in the Caribbean, but also the poetics of triumphant survival

embodied in their cultural life. Musing over an Indo-Trinidadian performance of the *Ramleela,* a dramatization of the Hindu epic, the *Ramayana,* Walcott writes:

> I misread the event through a visual echo of History – the cane fields, indenture, the evocation of vanished armies, temples, and trumpeting elephants – when all around me there was quite the opposite: elation, delight in the boys' screams, in the sweet stall, in more and more costumed characters appearing; a delight of conviction, not loss.[42]

The parallels with Trinidad are most readily apparent in the Indo-Guyanese writer's emphasis on a group whose core sociocultural values, together with a common history of indenture, have helped transcend intracommunal differences, at least in relation to the wider Caribbean society. Indo-Guyanese writers such as Rooplall Monar, Sheikh M. Sadeek, David Dabydeen, Cyril Dabydeen, and Jan Shinebourne provide, from an insider's perspective, the particular vicissitudes and connections formed among the descendants of indentured peoples within the spiritual and social parameters of a largely community-oriented existence.

However, a younger generation of authors such as Narmala Shewcharan and Harishchandra Khemraj, Churaumanie Bissundyal, and Ryhaan Shah signal a new stage in Indo-Guyanese fiction in their portraits of a progressive shift away from the rural, communal existence of the older generation. This mirrors the changes that have taken place in Caribbean nations themselves. First, the industrialization of the plantation economy and its subsequent disruption of the estate community is evidenced in the younger generation's exodus to urban centres. Second, greater access to colonial education further distanced the younger generation from the beliefs, languages, and values of their more tradition-bound elders. And, third, the increased level of emigration to Europe and North America for higher education and employment has unalterably widened the gulf between young and old. The differences between a rural and progressively urbanized diasporic community, together with the growing gulf between older and younger generations, are brought to light in Monar's *Janjhat* (1989) and Shewcharan's *Tomorrow Is Another Day* (1994). These novels are strikingly different in setting, tone, and style but they point to a development in the Indo-Guyanese novel from an earlier generation's focus on the secluded estate community to a younger generation's more politicized interest in urban Guyanese society.

Monar and Shewcharan also present different linguistic innovations in Indo-Guyanese and Caribbean fiction. For example, Monar uses a version of creolized English that is steeped in the syntax, vocabulary, and rhythm of Hindi/Bhojpuri.[43] *Janjhat* is perhaps the first novel to employ Indo-Guyanese Creole as the language of dialogue and narration. Monar's use of this particular version of Creole as both the language of character and consciousness, together with his explicit use of Hindi/ Urdu terminology (such as the titular *Janjhat*, a Hindi/Urdu term for 'an unnecessary problem') without an accompanying glossary, also suggests that South Asian languages have come to constitute an indelible part of the vocabulary and flavour of the Caribbean subject's polyglot identity.

Sasenarine Persaud, best known as a short story writer, rails against the occlusion of Indo-Guyanese 'Hindi-English' in discussions of Caribbean Creole. In his 2000 reflection piece on the art of the short story, the author laments:

> And then there was this big noise in 'Caribbean Literature,' intensifying with Kamau Brathwaite's Nation Language making the rounds and being recognized – totally forgetting about all those Indians in Trinidad and Guyana, zapping them ... To me this was the Guyana I had left behind come back to haunt me, only now in literature – black racism in literature ... Yes, perhaps Naipaul had watered his Hindi down and Selvon was too removed from his. They wrote in a different time with a different compunction: 'to make it' in a Euro-world. I didn't care if I 'made it' in any world. I had a vision I would pursue. So I had to do something – better than Naipaul, better than Selvon – to demonstrate that living Hindi-English would not be made invisible by anybody else's nation language. I would use my knowledge of spoken and written Hindi to take this notion apart. A political act.[44]

What Persaud alludes to here as a living 'Hindi-English' that is distinct from other kinds of Creoles, specifically the Afro-centric basis of Edward Kamau Braithwaite's 'nation language,' is the broadening of the meaning of 'Creole' itself.[45] Creolization reflects the 'cross-cultural' spectrum of Caribbean society, particularized and refashioned through the ethnic and linguistic plurality of its diasporic communities. In the Indo-Guyanese context, creolization occurs in the mixing of Hindi, Urdu, and Bhojpuri lexical elements, in the anglicization of Hindi, Urdu, or Bhojpuri expressions and in the hybridization of South Asian lexical and syntactical elements with English vocabulary, such as the pattern of emphatic word-doubling found in 'tru-tru.'[46]

Shewcharan has also stretched the contours of English-language fiction to include Indo-Guyanese Creole as the language of speech and narration in her short story 'Janjhat: Bhola Ram and the "Going Away Plan."'[47] In her novel, however, Creole functions as a diglossic language that is employed as a mark of class distinction. In keeping with the use of English as the language of officialdom and, by extension, the formal basis of narration, Creole is associated with informal, colloquial speech. Moreover, in a multiracial urban context, Shewcharan's characters utilize a form of Creole, akin to Braithwaite's concept of the creolized English that is common to West Indian peoples, as the lingua franca of her Guyanese characters, rather than the highly localized brand of Creole spoken by the Indo-Guyanese community.

Published only a few years apart and set in the period of Guyana's first independent government, led by Forbes Burnham,[48] both novels explore the gender, generational, and class differences that make up the Indo-Guyanese response to a rapidly changing society and its newly forming relationship to the outside world. In turn, they consider the inextricable interrelationship between the individual, the diasporic community, and the state. In this complex equation, the subaltern female assumes a doubly symbolic role as cultural preserver and the often unwitting symbol of assimilation. Monar and Shewcharan present a challenging voice in Indo-Caribbean fiction in their respective investigations of gender inequality as it is further determined by class or race politics. In fact, Monar proves to be a laudable exception within a male-dominated literary tradition that has generally stereotyped South Asian diasporic female characters in its 'typical passive-victim focus.'[49] Similarly, in her cross-sectional portrait of Indo-Guyanese women, each of whom confronts the political and economic hardships of post-independence Guyana from conflicting class-based and generational perspectives, Shewcharan seems wary of Western feminism insofar as it oversimplifies the 'postcolonial Woman' as 'a metaphor for "the good"' or as a dehistoricized symbol of victimhood.[50] In this vein, Shewcharan's novel breaks with the common expression of Caribbean women's lives through the genres of fictional autobiography or the Bildungsroman.[51] Instead, the journalistic flavour of Shewcharan's political novel is reminiscent of the 'political post-colonial dystopia' typified in earlier novels written in the decades following independence.[52]

Monar and Shewcharan's works seem to suggest that feminist readings of Caribbean women's narratives that do not consider the specificities of caste, ethnicity, and religion in relation to the socio-economic lives of women only partly account for Indo-Caribbean female subjectivity.

Ameena Gafoor echoes this position, suggesting, in her own reading of Shinebourne's *The Last English Plantation*, that 'the challenge for Caribbean feminist scholarship is no longer to deconstruct male cultural paradigms ... in an effort to change the tradition that has silenced and marginalized us, but ... by analyzing the centrality of female experience that has so far remained unexplored.'[53] A first step in this process is, of course, to shift the narrative focus to the inner workings of Indo-Caribbean female consciousness, in contrast to her earlier representation in fixed wooden roles as a dutiful wife, mother, daughter; as an object of imperial male fantasy; or as an ethno-cultural commodity enshrouded by the veil of custom and propriety.

Monar and Shewcharan accordingly write with an awareness of gender construction as it has evolved in plantation societies, challenging official colonial discourse which contends that indenture served as an unqualified form of female emancipation from a repressive Hindu patriarchy and its caste system.[54] In *Janjhat*, for instance, the older generation recall the common patterns of violence against women to which colonial authorities turned a blind eye, thereby challenging continued assertions that 'the early period of indenture resulted in an improved status and mobility for the majority of South Asian women, relative to that in India.'[55] Historian Patricia Mohammed suggests that the indentureship and post-indentureship period put gender relations and norms, as well as the constructs of masculinity and femininity that underpinned them, in flux.[56] The sexual, material, and social liberties that women might have exerted or enjoyed at the early stages of indenture, when the vast majority of women emigrated as autonomous agents (that is, as independent wage-earners) rather than as male appendages in a family unit, necessarily affected male behaviour as well. This is manifested in the male population's sense of emasculation, loss of control, and loss of face or *izzat* (the Hindu/Urdu word for pride) not only under the watchful gaze of their own community but also that of the European, African, and Chinese male. Progressively, women came to be looked upon as necessary ingredients in the restructuring of the worker's existence instead of as temporary units of labour; this greatly altered a woman's place in the plantation structure, and it is a pattern that is repeated across other plantation societies. As Shireen Latif attests, in her study of Indo-Fijian women's lives in a plantation economy, in the 'newly settled peasant household, the tendency was to withdraw women from agricultural work and confine them to the domestic sphere.'[57] In other words, the creation of a new group of freed settlers resulted in the reconstitution of the patriarchal family unit, one which first and foremost necessitated stringent control over female sexuality so as to curb the threat of female desertion, self-empowerment, or other forms of disruption to the restitution of male authority.

Monar and Shewcharan also challenge existing arguments that the Indo-Guyanese peoples' low participation in education by the turn of the century was due to communal insularity or gender-biased attitudes to education.[58] Rather, in the recurring motif of regret over the inaccessibility of education, or, indeed, the futility of education in light of the limited chances of occupational mobility, these texts illustrate the more realistic perception among Indo-Guyanese peoples that education and its rewards are usually reserved for the privileged few, or for those willing to eschew their religious beliefs in exchange for a missionary education. In fact, the rural community is shown to revere its educated members; conversely, for those whose material survival outweighs larger ambitions, education is a painful source of inner conflict and regret: '"Estate work ain't get a future," he told himself, cursing his fate, wondering why he couldn't take education.'[59] In Shewcharan's more cynical urban community, education crumbles into an empty symbol of elitism governed by a system in which socio-economic advancement is mainly fuelled by political patronage. In a corrupt and racially exclusive infrastructure, education offers little more than a means of escape to 'the richman's country.'[60] The recurring motif of the 'brain drain' and the general exodus of Guyana's younger citizens thus functions as a disruptive subtext throughout *Tomorrow Is Another Day*, wherein the queues for immigration visas are as long as the 'food lines.'

Leaving Behind the Plantation Estate 'Logie'

Rooplall Monar is a twice-honoured recipient of the Guyana Prize for his short story collection, *Backdam People*, and his poetry collection, *Koker*.[61] Like most of his Indo-Guyanese contemporaries, Monar is the descendant of indentured labourers whose fiction turns to plantation estate life for its realistic texture and setting. Though this rural backdrop is a common feature among the fictions of the first wave of Indo-Guyanese writers, Monar's compassionate and detailed portraits of plantation estate life in the post-indenture period are a significant contribution to Guyanese literature. Throughout his work, Monar pays homage to his community's cultural resilience in spite of the demoralizing history of indentureship, offering a uniquely sympathetic, feminist, and tragic-comic approach to the estate or village settlement. Monar's own history on the Lusignan and Annandale sugar estates together with his varied background as an estate bookkeeper, journalist, and practitioner of folk medicine are reflected in his judicious collation of the diverse voices of his community, his trained attention to the physical and psychological repercussions of plantation work, and his detailed account of the central role of socioreligious practices in the spiritual and emotional well-being of a community that has historically faced both economic privations and the psychosocial effects of cultural displacement.

At first glimpse, Monar's novel is so vivid a portrait of the rural community that the politics of contemporary Guyanese society seem far removed from the daily concerns of people whose lives still revolve around 'backdam wuk' – the same labour-intensive livelihood of their ancestors. Jeremy Poynting defines 'backdam wuk' as follows:

> The backdam was the distant part of the estate to which the workers had to walk up to five miles in the darkness of the early morning before they started work. But the backdam was also the place where the cultivation of the estate merged into the wilderness of the savannah and where the estate workers had the freedom to gather fruits and firewood and sometimes cultivate their own plots.[62]

Though Monar goes to great lengths to realistically portray the plantation estate community, his thematic concerns transcend the legacies of indenture existence. In *Janjhat*, for instance, Monar subtly weaves the goings-on of the wider political fabric in and out of his narrative in such a way that his novel is as much a realistic slice of village life as it is a loosely veiled political allegory of those who articulate their 'independence' as a critical negotiation between the individual's loyalty to the diasporic community and participation in wider Guyanese society. Moreover, Monar's critical awareness of gender and generational differences, which are often grounds for intracommunal conflict and repression, simultaneously challenges nostalgic and prejudicial oversimplifications of this otherwise complex, heterogeneous, and ever-changing community.

In *Janjhat*, the changes taking place within the Lusignan and neighbouring plantation communities are subtly tied to wider Guyanese society. Indeed, through the older generation's perspective, Monar captures the structural changes that have occurred over the course of Guyana's recent history, particularly the major structural shift from plantation estate communities to new village settlements. For the older generation who has straddled both the close quarters of estate 'logies' and the more private, independent 'Housing Scheme'[63] of the village settlement, the changes in lifestyle are a continual source of internalized and externalized tension. In addition to their restructured accommodations, the older generation is shown to straddle a colonial and post-colonial era which, among other things, has rendered obsolete the plantation estate system and the patterns of coexistence and camaraderie shared among its inhabitants. Thus, when Big-Bye mooma, the principle spokesperson of the older generation declares, "'Eh, eh, since this country get freedom is everything changing overnight,'"[64] her observation is less a hopeful celebration of independence than it is an ironic lament for the gradual disintegration of a heretofore insular and self-protective community. A similar lament is echoed in Shinebourne's novel Timepiece, where the city-dwelling protagonist Sandra returns to the old village estate only to find that it has become a virtual ghost town. When she asks one of the few remaining inhabitants, a young boy nonchalantly smoking a cigarette by the roadside – an image that strikes the protagonist as dissonant with the ghostlike state of a once vibrant neighbourhood – he matter-of-factly replies: 'Estate work dead. Estate don' pay no kinda money. Estate only employing a few people nowadays. Pure machinery doing everything. Me old lady tell me long ago was pure estate work round he'. But not now.'[65]

Monar's use of a traditional marriage plot as a central narrative device accrues greater significance in the diaspora. By the mid-to late nineteenth century, marriage was a vehicle for the restoration of the patriarchal family unit, which was shattered by the wholly disproportionate gender ratio (women being the conspicuous minority) in the early period of indenture. Moreover, the common practice of endogamy among Hindus and Muslims of the diaspora ensures the survival of religious belief and custom. However, while the marriage plot in Janjhat playfully plunges the reader into a seemingly idyllic communal setting, it fast becomes apparent that the community is propelled by a false sense of security in its judicious upkeep of the status quo. This is because the community's expectations of how the newly wedded couple will live up to their 'traditional' conjugal roles are quickly disrupted by Data, the rebellious young bride around whom the narrative revolves. The marriage plot thus plays itself out as two principle dialectics of struggle: first, as a woman's resistance to a traditional patriarchal Hindu structure, and second, as the broader debate over cultural assimilation that is echoed across Indo-Caribbean and, indeed, other diasporic societies.[66] The disruption of the traditional marriage plot offers alternate possibilities in the subaltern female's struggle for self-determination; in turn, the subverted marriage plot bears new symbolic resonance in the diaspora where the subaltern female's attempt to redefine gender norms is further complicated by the community's perception that any such acts of rebellion are evidence of the corrupting influences of external forces rather than expressions of female agency.

It is significant that Data's struggle is waged on the 'home' front, therefore, the principle site in which the marriage contract ensures the uninterrupted transfer of heteronormative and patriarchal codes.[67] The home is a matriarchal domain insofar as it facilitates the dictates of tradition. For South Asian diasporic communities, female-inscribed domestic space functions as both the guardian and preserver of cultural continuity; ironically, then, it is in the private, interior spaces of female domestic life that external forces, including the compromising effects of physical displacement, cultural marginalization, and the prospect of assimilation, are most actively gauged. As a pun on the Indo-Guyanese-accented 'daughter,' Data's unwanted nickname comically symbolizes the imposition of assigned gender roles at the expense of more complex expressions of female subjectivity. In this sense, Data's battle is directed against her tyranically orthodox mother-in-law, Big-Bye mooma, for it is upon the matriarch's shoulders that the upkeep of tradition most heavily falls. In contrast, Data's young husband Big-Bye and his peers seem more preoccupied by sexual fantasies and chauvinistic posturing than by religious or cultural observances. However, even though males have a distinct advantage in their less *duty*-bound role and as the more socially mobile members of their community, neither gender is free from the watchful eye of the community. Data's increasing sense of self-determination is given an ironic boost when she becomes the source of courage for her husband Big-Bye in his own private struggle against the shackles of conformity. Indeed, Big-Bye is shown to be as beleaguered as his young bride by the constructs of propriety and the chauvinistic trappings of tradition: '"A proper Hindu boy don't do that wickedness," his mooma would say, as if she knew what was in his mind.'[68]

Monar makes it clear that Data does not reject her identity as 'a good Hindu girl' as much as she wishes to break out of a system that renders women continually dependent on others in their roles as 'datas' (daughters) and 'doolahins' (brides): 'She didn't want to be addressed as doolahin any longer. She didn't want to be treated as a protected bride, fed, pampered and chided.'[69] In her resistance to the perception of women as passive, dependent members of their society, Data does not reject the role she has to play in ensuring her community and family's welfare. Rather, her assertion of independence is a 'gradual and disciplined'[70] assertion of selfhood in the concomitant observance of custom, the daily concerns of material survival, and the possibility of participation outside the socially restrictive parameters of village life.

Data's struggle for independence acts as an allegory for the community's fate in a post-independence era. In Data's negotiation between selfhood and competing cultural codes, Monar seems to capture the community's struggle for cultural autonomy beyond the paralyzing fear of assimilation. In turn, Data's emphasis on a form of material self-sufficiency that is not so individualistic as to compromise the foundation of *jahaji*-hood and its systems of collective action serves as an alternate model for independence at the national level. To this end, Monar's novel addresses the interrelated issues of nationhood and ethnocultural belonging that Guyanese author Janice Shinebourne stresses as the necessary concerns of writers who emerged in the context of 'an extremely rapid transition between revolutionary times and conservative, racial, chauvanistic nationalism.'[71] For the diasporic community, therefore, the upkeep of tradition is not a private matter but a collective concern, nor merely a cultural preoccupation but a political statement.

The marks of urbanization, industrialization, materialism, and 'Americanization' in a post-independence Guyana, together with a dominant Afro-Guyanese body politic, are viewed as the sources of corrosion of a core set of values and beliefs as they are encoded in everything from a woman's dress to her concept of family life and her individual ambitions: "'You hardly find a good Hindu woman today. Nice house full they eye. Is everybody come selfish after independence. No closeness anymore. Young gal want to live town life.'"[72] As the primary bearer of tradition, then, the South Asian diasporic woman becomes the central symbol of change: she is an active agent of change in her conscious disruption of cultural expectations. She is also a passive symbol of change, for her body is under constant surveillance for the external markers of sexual and social compromise. In this sense, the female diasporic body is encoded with the diaspora's migration history, the body becoming a human billboard for changes that are interpreted as assaults to cultural identity and ancestral memory. For the older generation, the changes brought about by the country's independence are principally assessed in its growing influence over the visual signs of transgression found among a younger generation of women: "'But these present-day young girls: too much lip-stick, high-heel shoe, short dress ... eh-eh, going cinema, not doing regular puja ...; *This time generation quick to give you bad name.* Them young gal fuget they culture and self-respect."'[73]

Monar's realistic account of a multigenerational Indo-Guyanese community closely reflects the processes of acculturation found in the diasporic context, for change operates at the generational level as well as in terms of contact with other groups.[74] In Monar's text, interethnic contact is no less potent because it transpires at a more discrete level in the form of media access, an 'English' education, and pop culture – the shared language of the imagined (national) community: "'This radio and newspaper and commercial eddication destroying young people."'[75] Cross-cultural contact also occurs in the form of a growing trend of consumerism of both American and Indian imported products. The younger generation's less restrictive working conditions in a post-plantation economy, as well as a modest diversification of labour, facilitates patterns of consumerism that the older generation could ill afford. In other words, the very terms and basis of contact are themselves changing according to the community's material and historical circumstances.

For Big-Bye mooma and her peers, therefore, individual endurance is inextricably tied to a sense of collective and spiritual solidarity most often achieved in the observance of religious and cultural ceremonies that not only help preserve custom and tradition but act as a viable counter-culture to an oppressive plantation system. Thus, as Big-Bye mooma looks back on the ravages of estate life – particularly for women who were subject not only to the drudgery of plantation labour but also to the threat of sexual exploitation[76] – she finds that a spiritually united front is its only redemptive feature. Instead of bemoaning 'backdam wuk,' Big-Bye mooma waxes nostalgic over the 'estate days': 'Such days gave her life a meaning. They spiced its blandness; though they sharpened the nostalgia for living on the estate where every part of life revolved around the gods and their observance ... To deviate from that part was to find only emptiness, haunting memories, bereft of any glory or pride.'[77] Similarly, for the older men of the community, drunken camaraderie and religious observances serve as the only antidote to the spiritual emptiness of plantation life: 'Felt moments of happiness only when he was involved in the religious festivals or lost in sessions of rum-fired reminiscence.'[78] The older generation thus evokes an ironic nostalgia, not for the distant India of the past but for the close quarters and shared experience of estate life. Indeed, the older generation does not look back to the motherland for a model of cultural preservation since India's entry into a globalized economy is itself a potential source of cultural corrosion: "'Is the Bombay film, and juke box responsible for that.'"[79] Consequently, the community is shown to stand anachronistically against both the motherland and the host society, for each now bears the signs of change that the older generation regards as the disintegration of the unique spiritual strength and communal bond of the *jahaji-bhai(n)*.

As a member of the new generation of Indo-Guyanese women, Data's struggle for her independence does not operate in the simplistic confrontation between tradition and modernity, or between the older generation and the cinema-going, radio-tuned youth. Such simplistic binaries are shown to melt into empty cultural codes, as is evidenced in her peers' donning of the outward signs of change without a concomitant awareness of the imbalances of power inherent within and without the community. ·
In fact, Data is shown to dissociate herself from the majority of her female peers who lend credence to the older generation's fear that modernity is synonymous with Western consumerism and an empty pop culture at the expense of a deeply rooted spiritual and cultural heritage:

> It had become clearer to her that she wanted to be more than Chan, though she admired Chan's bold and independent spirit. No. Chan was just an ordinary housewife. She depending on she husband. In one way Chan still tie-down ... Not me. Oh no! Data wanted to be herself ... where she could do her own thinking, aspire to live her own dreams, start building a future for her unborn children ... Yes! become herself. Her own person.[80]

Data rests on the critical precipice between her elders' nostalgic reveries and her peers' seemingly misguided attempts at challenging the status quo, wishing to expand the possibilities of what 'a good Hindu girl' might imply for a nation that is itself breaking free from the shackles of its colonial past and entering a world of uncertain tomorrows.

As a fourth-generation descendant of indentured labourers, Shewcharan shares Monar's background. As the first Indo-Guyanese female novelist, Shewcharan also has a status in the canon of Guyanese literature that is similar to the one held by Lakshmi Persaud in the canon of Trinidadian literature; she is also one of the few Indo-Caribbean women writers (including Shani Mootoo and Niala Maharaj) to enter the consciousness of a male protagonist. Describing post-independence Guyana through a brand of documentary realism that immediately resonates with her journalistic background, Shewcharan's *Tomorrow Is Another Day* primarily aims to expose the active participation and subsequent disenfranchisement (and resultant sense of betrayal) of the Indo-Guyanese populace from the political machinery in the transition to statehood. Shewcharan sets her novel against the political backdrop of 1980s Guyana, the country's most tumultuous period since its inception in 1970 as a Co-operative Socialist Republic under PNC (People's National Congress) leader Forbes Burnham. Forbes Burnham came to power in a coalition government in 1964. Eventually Burnham distanced himself from (Indo-Guyanese) Dr Cheddi Jagan's PPP (People's Progressive Party), the first party to win general elections in 1953 under universal adult suffrage. Burnham was Chairman of PPP until 1955 when he split to form his own party, the PNC, and his defection is said to have created the racial split in contemporary Guyanese politics since he primarily relied on the urban Afro-Guyanese population for political support. Burnham is also accused of political betrayal both for his widely disputed electoral victories and for a fraudulent socialist policy that was, behind the scenes, a CIA-backed government.

Whereas Monar's characters are made to realistically confront the encroachment of a progressively materialist and consumer-driven society, Shewcharan's characters confirm the political and social morass into which post-independence Guyana has plunged. In an uncanny inversion of Monar's depiction of generational conflict, Shewcharan differentiates between an older generation's continued sense of interconnectedness and a younger generation's adaptation to a new dog-eat-dog ethics of survival. Moreover, the post-independence context has ironically brought about a total collapse in gender communication in a newly emancipated society. This is highly reminiscent of Shinebourne's *Timepiece* where male chauvinism becomes a metonym for national chauvinism in its erection of barriers that inhibit social advancement, intellectual honesty, and personal growth. In Shewcharan's novel, however, it is the disintegrating family unit that mirrors the state of the nation. The elements of social fragmentation and cultural assimilation that are beginning to touch the rural community are shown to have besieged urban society. Shewcharan's urban portrait is constructed as a fragmented assortment of competing private interests, in such a way that the ideological and interracial reconstitution of 'community' itself becomes an indispensable ingredient in the reconstruction of Guyanese society as a whole.

From the outset, Shewcharan's novel is a direct indictment of Burnham's policy of racial polarization. As such, the narrative commences with the last attempt of an Indo-Guyanese politician, Jagru, a leading member of the opposition, to join forces with the 'Official Party.' Jagru's defection mirrors that of the real-life figure of Forbes Burnham, though here the

terms of defection are reversed, an 'East Indian' joining the predominantly Afro-centric party in what he believes to be a conciliative gesture
that will eventually bridge the racial divide. Though Jagru's motivations
are shown to be well-intentioned, his political naivety is quickly exposed
by his family and friends who can see that the 'East Indian' figurehead
helps the official party deflect charges of racial bias. Jagru's precarious
position immediately recalls the dyadic axis of the Ugandan context as it
was tragic-comically configured in the character of Joseph D'Souza (in
Nazareth's *In a Brown Mantle*), the disillusioned right-hand man of an
ascendant African president in search of a political and a racial scape-
goat. Indeed, the thematic echo is doubly reinforced in Shewcharan's
portrait of an ailing political regime that uses racial division as a conven-
ient smokescreen to camouflage neocolonial policy and internal corruption, and the country's gradual economic collapse brought about by
increasing IMF debt and the subsequent crippling of local industry.

In addition, Shewcharan provides a brief caricature of Forbes Burnham
in the shadowy figure of the out-going Prime Minister Rouche. Rouche
stands at the epicentre of a fractured and dispirited national consciousness whose 'Official Party's' platform is addressed to a primarily middle
class, urban, black and Creole electorate: 'Rouche had won the support
of *his own* people, as he liked to call them. His appeals had been directed
at them in exclusive denial of the many other races which inhabited the
land, including those whose forebears had come as indentured immigrants.'[81] Much like Nazareth, Shewcharan is also quick to point out
that the East Indian is not the only casualty of Rouche's bankrupt government. In turn, the novel shares a thematic echo with her short story
'Janjhat,' in her documentary depiction of the daily inequities of the
Burnham dictatorship, its defunct bureaucratic structure, its rampant
black market trade, and its widespread shortages of goods which culminated in seemingly endless 'queues for basic food items that were a
familiar feature of city life after 1981.'[82] Indeed, the author's description of the various means by which the ordinary citizen strives to eke
out a living in the face of impoverishment is as much an indictment of
a morally bankrupt government as it is a testament to human ingenuity
and spiritual resilience. For instance, the only way that the ordinary
citizen can survive on the system of food rations is through individual
resourcefulness. Aunt Adee, a market vendor, suggests to a desperate
Chandi, a young mother left to fend for her family's survival, that she
put her children to work at the food lines by standing in for the elderly
at a nominal fee.

Since no member of society is entirely free of the indignity of the food line, it also becomes the central metaphor for the coming together of otherwise socially and racially stratified groups. The stark juxtaposition of Chandi's impoverishment with the urban middle class is brought to light in this context:

> She had met them in town today: Radika and her mother-in-law, Kunti. She had helped them out by queuing for them in one of the food lines. She had told them her story ... She hungered for listeners and for their easy words of sympathy, but she stilled an impulse to go and knock at their door. She could not afford the luxury.[83]

Echoing Monar's multigenerational portrait, Shewcharan exposes the mis-representation of subaltern women 'as harmonious symbols of historical continuity.'[84] Shewcharan's narrative offers more varied articulations of female subjectivity than does Monar's, however, in light of contemporary urban life and its wider spectrum of social and class differences. In this sense, Chandi, Asha, and Radika are representative figures of a younger generation of Indo-Guyanese women whose cultural outlooks are shown to be filtered through competing class interests.

For Chandi, who has followed the traditional pattern of an early marriage and motherhood, the principal site of struggle is economic rather than cultural. In her impoverished state, she is saddled with the seemingly impossible task of ensuring her family's survival. In contrast, as a single woman without the burdens of familial responsibility, Asha's unorthodox involvement in her brothers' smuggling ring is less a symbol of her 'emancipation' than a symptom of her country's stunted economic and social growth. Finally, as a member of the country's elite, Jagru's unsympathetic wife Radika is desperate to free herself from an empty bourgeois existence, though she continues to remain immune, if not callously indifferent, to the plight of her less fortunate female peers. In the variously positioned identities of her diasporic characters, Shewcharan also establishes a basis of comparison between the male and female Indo-Guyanese response to post-colonial society. The breakdown in gender communication in the urban context reveals the extent to which political activism and agency are themselves delimited by patriarchal codes which harness both men and women within predictable social expectations and behavioural patterns. Thus, on the one hand, Asha begins to share Jagru's political convictions: 'She'd managed to keep apart, to remain as a distant observer, looking on at this panorama of bad times. But

Jagru's energy made her wonder if she shouldn't abandon that role, become more active. Perhaps change was possible, if people joined together in hope and determination.'[85] On the other hand, Jagru's idealism is compromised by his latent sexism: 'Jagru at last became aware that she was struggling, trying to get him off her. He sat up in concern. Had he hurt her?'[86]

In the recurring motif of possible new beginnings, Shewcharan's narrative celebrates the strength of the human spirit not as it is embodied in individuals but as it is fostered in the lap of kinship and collective action. The Indo-Guyanese community's deeply rooted tradition of familial piety, communal solidarity, and cultural resilience serves as a spiritual suture that has the potential to mend the rift in human interrelations further compounded, after centuries of racial division under colonial rule, by the individualism of late capitalism. This is not to suggest that Shewcharan idealizes the Indo-Guyanese community. Rather, in the polarized racial and cultural climate of post-independence Guyana, she singles out the older generation as a symbol of cross-cultural unity in their ability to remember a shared history of oppression. In this sense, it is the collective action taken by Jagru's mother, Kunti, and her Afro-Guyanese friend, Aunt Adee, that saves Chandi and her family from starvation and social collapse. In the contemporary moment, this interracial act of compassion envelops wider Guyanese society in the paradigm of the moral basis of community: 'He'd grown to appreciate the warmth which lay under Aunt Adee's appearance. It was people like her who gave the lie to stories of racial unrest, which were always being promoted by unscrupulous politicians looking after their own interests.'[87]

As a representative of an older generation of women, Kunti echoes Big-Bye mooma's despair over the disintegration of core cultural values, and shares her memories of communal kinship in the experience of 'backdam wuk.' However, Kunti's identification with other women of colour and her exposure to the multiracial texture of urban life extends her conception of communality to include 'others' like Aunt Adee. This is not to suggest that cross-racial alliance is absent in the plantation estate. For instance, in Shinebourne's second novel *The Last English Plantation*, an older generation of women of South Asian and African origin are shown to collaborate in their role as local healers, and the confluence of their knowledge systems serves as a remedial countersite to the suffering of two oppressed groups. Similarly, as public activists and agitators, Kunti and Aunt Adee's alliance echoes the parallel struggles of colonized subjects against the plantation system, which resulted in the first abolition to end slavery and the 'second abolition' to end indenture.[88] Ironically, then, while the ethnocentric basis of Big-Bye mooma's sense of community is shown to hinder the younger generation's development, the older generation of Shewcharan's community acts as the collective conscience of a newly 'independent' society that has spiralled into social collapse: 'What kind of generation was it that knew nothing of right and wrong.'[89]

Monar and Shewcharan's novels provide a cross-sectional portrait of Indo-Guyanese society, through a self-critical lens that questions the role that Indo-Guyanese subjects might play in the shaping of a new national consciousness. As such, these are honest attempts at reassessing the relationship between the individual and the imagined community. Though inescapably conscious of their recent colonial past, these authors look inward to the issues of racial and cultural rivalry, gender and generational differences, and the shared struggle for survival underlying their country's collective plight. The focus of resistance is no longer simply the colonial or neocolonial apparatus but the complex internal fabric of Guyanese society. In both novels, diasporic experience affects the question of 'independence' at the individual and the collective level. On the one hand, diasporic experience is shown to produce a reactionary and essentialist politics of identity which resists change in the often illusive veil of nostalgia or in the interest of self-preservation. The rural diasporic community's instinct for cultural survival at the expense of wider Guyanese society mirrors the individual's instinct for self-preservation at all costs, including the welfare of others – a reaction that is reinforced in an urban landscape overrun by the effects of social dysfunction, political cynicism, economic hardship, and human detachment. Conversely, diasporic experience acts as a symbol of cross-cultural commonality/communality, at least in the Guyanese citizens' shared histories of oppression. Monar and Shewcharan's novels thus envision the quest for 'independence' as a conscientious negotiation between private, communal, and national interests, thereby realigning the Indo-Guyanese struggle for political and social representation within the nation's search for a better tomorrow.

6 Indo-Trinidadian Fictions of Community within the Metanarratives of 'Faith': Lakshmi Persaud's *Butterfly in the Wind* and Sharlow Mohammed's *The Elect*

Not '*East Indian Trinidadian West Indians*'!

Trinidad is home to the largest South Asian diasporic community in the Caribbean archipelago. Indentured peoples began to disembark from the first ship the *Fatel Rozack* (itself a mispronunciation of *Fath al Razack*), to arrive on its shores on 30 May 1845, which has since become the nationally celebrated Indian Arrival Day.[1] Historically, the South Asian population of Trinidad and Tobago has shared a near-majority status with people of African origins: since a 1987 census, ethnic ratios have remained relatively stable at 42 per cent black, 40 per cent East Indian, 16 percent other/mixed, and 2 per cent white.[2] However, recent statistical data reveals a slight shift in ethnic ratios, the Indo-Caribbean population assuming the dominant position by 0.7 per cent.[3]

Even as one of the largest and oldest ethnic collectives in the Caribbean region, however, there is a certain veil of mystery surrounding Indo-Caribbean peoples, one that is poignantly captured in the Afro-Caribbean writer's perspective. For example, St Lucian poet Derek Walcott admits to a tourist-like fascination with the Indo-Trinidadian peoples' 'delight of conviction on the edge of the Caroni Plain.'[4] Similarly, Barbadian novelist George Lamming confesses that he, like most Afro-Caribbean peoples, 'lived in an involuntary, almost unconscious segregation from the world of Indians'[5] in spite of the fact that the 'Indian presence is no less Caribbean in its formation than that of their African comrades.'[6] Indeed, this level of segregation, though gradually being dismantled by Trinidad's youngest generation, is nonetheless still a visible aspect of Trinbagonian life.

In his 1992 study of Caribbean literature, Michael Dash draws on Edouard Glissant's theorization of Caribbean peoples as a creolized collective.[7] Because of their transcultural aesthetic, Dash argues that Caribbean literature is best approached in regional terms over and above its particular articulations of nationhood or ethnicity. In fact, Dash's view corresponds with the fluid metaphor of the sea (found in numerous examples of Afro-Caribbean writing)[8] as a unifying principle between the island societies of the archipelago, the fluid undercurrent metonymically bridging a shared history as plantation colonies and diasporic bodies. Focusing almost exclusively on Afro-Caribbean history and literatures, however, Dash overlooks a fundamental distinction between the 'kinds' of diasporic peoples that make up this Caribbean collective; that is to say, Glissant's own differentiation between the 'transplanted' diaspora (indentured labourers) and the 'transferred' diaspora (African slaves). As Glissant states:

> I feel that what makes this difference between a people that survives elsewhere, *that maintains its original nature*, and a population that is transformed elsewhere *into another people* (without, however, succumbing to the reductive pressures of the Other) and that thus enters the constantly shifting and variable processes of creolization (of relationship, of relativity), is that the latter has not brought with it, not collectively continued, the methods of existence and survival, both material and spiritual, which it practised before being uprooted.[9]

Glissant's concept of a collective of creolized subjects denies neither the Indo-Caribbean the possibility of a hybrid identity nor the Afro-Caribbean the possibility of cultural continuity. Rather, his typology points to the important historical distinction between the respective narratives of slavery and indenture, a distinction that must be taken into consideration in any study seeking to theorize and historicize the Caribbean. The indentured labour diaspora closely corresponds to Glissant's model of peoples whose largely voluntary en masse migration facilitated the physical transplantation of the tools (foods, clothing, and artefacts) and knowledge systems (sacred religious texts) which helped ensure cultural survival in the new land. Glissant's distinction is made evident in the common image of Indo-Caribbean enclaves – Vijay Mishra's 'little Indias'[10] – which partly reveal the structure of plantation society as a racially divided system of labour and partly disclose the tendency for cultural preservation of the transplanted South Asian diasporic community itself.

Though a widely applicable hermeneutics, Dash's regionalization of Caribbean identity precludes a specialized view of the particular developments, features, and concerns of Indo-Caribbean writing. Indo-Caribbean peoples' unique configuration as a labour diaspora affiliated through shared ethnic, religious, and linguistic ties has necessarily produced a differently constituted migrant group in the Caribbean. For Indo-Caribbeans, the Middle Passage becomes the culturally specific *kala pani*, a symbol of rupture steeped not in the trauma of enslavement but in the implicit invocation of the Hindu caste system; and the labourers' experience of plantation life, though filled with hardship and struggle, must be qualified in the context of a post-emancipation economy, and in light of migration and settlement as a largely voluntary process. For the Indo-Caribbean, settlement in the New World speaks as much to a history of segregation from other diasporic groups as it does of integration and creolization. Dash's theorization of Caribbean literature within the larger post-modern paradigms of hybridization discounts the historical conditions and cultural characteristics of indentured peoples, whose transplanted traditions, religious rites, languages, customs, and, perhaps most importantly, unique sense of place in the Americas attest to the distinct perspective from which Indo-Caribbean writers participate in the cross-cultural dialogues of the Caribbean imagination.

One of the most striking differences between Afro-Caribbean and Indo-Caribbean literature is the depiction of community not as a syncretic and transcultural entity,[11] but rather as a fraternity of ethnic, cultural, and historical ties whose principal impulse is its resistance to the accelerated processes of fragmentation and flux brought about by cultural displacement. Indeed, the central metaphor of the sea is absent in novels that are so often set in the island interior's sugar belt, the traditional setting of the indentured labourer's plantation estate dwellings and rural village centres. This is poetically underscored in the opening paragraph of Sharlow's *The Elect* (1992), where the protagonist feels unable to challenge the grand narratives of European imperial history because of his own decidedly limited perspective within a seemingly land-locked horizon[12]:

> Tom didn't know if he believed teacher MacDonald when he told the class the earth was round. He told them how they could prove it by standing on a beach and watching the ships come in; they would see the mast first, long before the hull; this showed the earth was like a ball. Trouble was Tom had never been to the sea, never seen a real ship, and as for knowing what a hull was ...[13]

A Literature 'at Home'

When Indo-Caribbean literature has been compared to the greater body of Caribbean literature in the past, it has primarily been discussed in terms of the common tropes of rootlessness and homelessness established in V.S. Naipaul's Trinidad-based novels, such as *A House for Mr Biswas* or *The Mimic Men*. To this end, Victor Ramraj concludes that Naipaul's metaphor of the 'enigma of arrival' or the exilic condition (be it in the Caribbean island of birth, the Indian motherland, or the seat of Empire) is also the prevailing Indo-Caribbean condition.[14] This reading of the diaspora is poetically mirrored in the adoption of the *Ramayana*, the Hindu epic whose central themes of exile, suffering, struggle, and eventual return resonates with a Hindu community now separated from its sacred homeland.[15]

In fact, Naipaul's recurring theme of the permanently displaced cosmopolitan and colonial subject is also echoed across the body of Caribbean literature and its reiteration of 'qualities of exile and dislocation.'[16] However, as Frank Birbalsingh more accurately points out, it is important to contextualize Naipaul's paradigmatic sense of 'homelessness' as the result of the 'doubly marginalized' condition of the Indo-Caribbean, that is, the legacy of a colonial condition that situates Caribbean peoples 'on the fringes of the European-American metropolis' and the status of Indo-Caribbean peoples as cultural outsiders 'within this already dependent and devalued creole culture.'[17] Naipaul's metaphor of the diasporic subject's prevailing desire to flee the colonial periphery for the imperial centre, evoked as the proverbial 'escape to an autumn pavement,'[18] is sadly confirmed in the fact that Sharlow Mohammed is one of the only novelists to date who has never left his native Trinidad.

Naipaul's metaphor of rootlessness bears particular resonance among the first generation of Indo-Caribbean writers and, more generally, the post-war generation of Caribbean writers who saw the colonial metropolis as a vehicle for personal self-advancement, particularly for those hoping to find publishers at a time when Britain was receptive to the colonial 'historical connection.'[19] This is echoed in the personal testimonies of several writers of the period, including Sam Selvon, V.S. Naipaul, and his own brother, Shiva Naipaul. This generation was necessarily disheartened by both the climate of interracial mistrust and betrayal that seems to pervade the post-war era, and the turbulent and more often than not interethnically divisive politics of decolonization which put into question the individual and collective fate of diasporic

South Asians, even where their grass roots activism and political leadership were visible and effective features of anticolonial struggle. For many, this emigration did help launch what would become prestigious literary careers, but for others it proved to be an exercise in futility. For example, Ismith Khan, who emigrated in the 1950s where he proceeded to write three novels, *Jumbie Bird* (1961), *The Obeah Man* (1964, 1994), and *The Crucifixion* (1987), laments that the United States was not quite as ready for Creole English writing and ethnocultural themes specific to the Caribbean as Britain might have been.[20]

The regional and largely Afro-centric approach of the West Indies Federation may also account for the tendency of ethnic self-erasure in favour of a greater expression of regional unity. For instance, in many of Sam Selvon's novels, the brutally honest portrait of a motley *crüe* of West Indian émigrés appears to project an Afro-centric portrait of Caribbean society, locating anti-imperial struggle in the creolized 'nation-language' championed by Edward Kamau Braithwaite and its implicit call to black consciousness and black power. Interestingly, it is the title character of Moses and his fellow pan-African denizens for which Selvon is best known, rather than for his earlier depictions of the Indo-Caribbean peasantry, such as the kind found in his first novel, *A Brighter Sun* (1952). In a slightly different vein, Ismith Khan attempts to account for his own relative obscurity in the international marketplace because he projected ethnic 'Indian' identity at a time when it was de rigeur to speak of the Caribbean as a distinctly Afro-centric space:

> *Jumbie Bird* is a novel about identity, which was a fashionable literary theme in the 1950s when Sam Selvon, Lamming and others were writing novels ... But there is something special about the novel which I don't see, for instance, in Selvon's work or V.S. Naipaul's: the strong feeling for India. The characters of Selvon and Naipaul talk about identity too, but Kale Khan asserts the power of his Indianness and the value of connectedness with India in a way that is unique to Caribbean literature.[21]

Even those works which do include ethnic Indian characters and are entirely set within the ethnic enclave – for example, Naipaul's Fuente Grove in *The Mystic Masseur* (1957), or Harold Sonny Ladoo's Tola District in *No Pain Like This Body* (1972) – do not directly historicize the legacies of, or address the inequities meted out by, the indenture system. Rather, they describe the daily vicissitudes and degradations of the Indo-Trinidadian peasantry, whose lives seem out of step with modernity since they are still synchronized with the violence and unpredictability of the seasons and the elements, and with the rituals, rites, and social mores of ancient custom. In either case, these are characters who are often terrifyingly out of sync with their environment, if not wholly incapacitated in the radical restructuring of that environment. This is hauntingly depicted in Ladoo's novel about the unrelenting patterns of domestic violence, ritualized behaviour, and daily hardship suffered by his rural-bound characters. For many of these older writers, then, the 'Indian world and Indian ways'[22] impede the process of acculturation in the new world, or, in the case of Naipaul, they impede the possibility of racial belonging for the colonized subject in the imperial centre or global stage.

Sharlow, born in 1949 in Longdenville, a rural township in central Trinidad, breaks with the themes and tropes established by his male predecessors. Unlike those of the pre- and post-independence generation, Sharlow remained on the island of his birth, and his works tend not to reflect the anxiety over ethnic difference that is evident among the earlier generation. Sharlow's prolific oeuvre (his output is comparable to that of Selvon) also deserves praise for its scope and thematic innovation, particularly for his pioneering works *When Gods Were Slaves* (1993) and *The Promise* (1995). The former is one of the first Indo-Caribbean novels (along with that of Indo-Guyanese novelist and scholar David Dabydeen) and certainly the first major Indo-Trinidadian work to enter the consciousness of the African slave, in its narrativization of the crossing of the Middle Passage to the injustices suffered at the hands of the plantation owner. As Birbalsingh points out, 'We may consider this a unique achievement since it is not matched by any of the three major Indo-Trinidadian novelists – V.S. Naipaul, Samuel Selvon or Ismith Khan, and it holds out hope that for all the cultural differences that separate the two ethnic groups, Indo-Trinidadians and Afro-Trinidadians are fundamentally united by a common nationality.' [23]

More notable perhaps is *The Promise*, the novel for which Sharlow draws his creative inspiration from the colonial archives of the indenture period, commemorating, in the form of the indenture narrative, the parallel journey across the Atlantic of indentured Indians. Again, I must cite Birbalsingh's 1995 lone review of the novel: ' *The Promise* can be said to do for Indian indentureship what novels by Phillips and D'Aguiar do for African slavery: present basic facts of Caribbean history in all their human complexity.'[24] *The Promise* fictionalizes the historic moment of arrival of indentured labourers in 'Chinitat.'[25] Recalling Beeharry's *That Others Might Live*, the novel also humanizes the various catalysts for migration and the injustices meted out by the colonial overseer or plantation owner in the early years following abolition. In a novel that gives as much narrative voice to the European character as to the Indian character, the reader is also able to see the evolution, or devolution as the case may be, of John Paul, from a well-intentioned abolitionist to a Christian zealot who sees in the 'coolies' a people with 'no language, no manners, no religion' and subsequently deserving of the master's scorn and the master's whip, even in the aftermath of emancipation.[26]

These indenture narratives present a new frontier in Indo-Trinidadian writing, since they seem to have arisen, along with the growing body of scholarship, through the restoration of and access to archival data on the early stages of indentureship, from recruitment in India to arrival in the plantation colony. Indeed, there are only two other full-length novels currently in print that draw directly on historical records which make evident the kinds of social patterns and conditions of recruitment, the fatalities and dehumanizing experience on board the human cargo ships, and the deracinating bureaucratic processes of arrival and dispersal in the plantation: they are Ron Ramdin's *Rama's Voyage* (2004), and the even lesser-known *Chalo Chinidad: 'Let's Go Trinidad,'* by Jang B. Bhagirathee (2003).[27] As I have suggested, Deepchand Beeharry's *That Others Might Live* is a foundational text for its depiction, several decades earlier, of the traumatic journey across the *kala pani* and for its judicious re-creation of the indenture system on the plantation itself. In the aforementioned Trinidadian novels, the greater emphasis placed on the journey itself, as well as the recruitment practices in the subcontinent, is driven by a historiographic impulse to excavate the forgotten 'other Middle Passage' (Ramdin's term),[28] from the annals of colonial history and national lore. This shift in emphasis (on departure and journey) marks an important development in Indo-Trinidadian fiction, namely, the birth of the *kala pani* narrative which strives to recuperate the untold histories, not only of the process of settlement in the plantation colony, but also of what the impetus and process of migration might have involved for the colonial subject living in the shadow of the British Raj.

The turn away from social realism and satire as genres which aided in the assertion and interrogation of the limits of ethnic affiliation suggests that a younger generation of writers is also increasingly comfortable in its self-identification as a distinct ethnic community. Perhaps the most interesting example of this shift manifests itself in the 2001 publication of Kirk Budhooram's *The Festival*, which has been termed the 'first mystery/suspense novel by an IndoTrinidadian.'[29] As a detective genre,

Budhooram's *The Festival* presents the community as a colourful back-drop for other kinds of social and psychological 'interrogations' that are themselves framed within the intrigues of wider Trinidadian society. And as the *kala pani* narratives of Sharlow and others seem to suggest, the process of indigenization includes a historiographic reclamation, restoration, and revaluation of the indenture period and experience. Once overshadowed by the master narratives of Europe, Africa, and India alike, now these recent novels by the younger generation of writers facilitate the recovery of diasporic memory while redressing an obvious gap in the wider historical consciousness of the Caribbean population.

As Birbalsingh affirms, in his anthology of Indo-Caribbean writing,[30] Naipaul's answer to the question of belonging (that rootlessness is not simply the symptom of colonial alienation but also a governing feature of modernity) seems unsatisfactory to a younger generation of Indo-Caribbean writers. Indeed, the question itself can be said to have been reformulated in texts which not only depict an almost bicentennial community but also the indigenization of its culture in the Caribbean landscape. In fact, the neurosis of displacement and colonial mimicry that pervaded Naipaul's reading of the Caribbean – a reading which incited a great deal of criticism[31] – has been at least partially allayed in more recently published Indo-Caribbean fiction.

Moreover, Naipaul's paradigmatic 'enigma of arrival,' which speaks to the anxieties of diasporic subjectivity, has been considerably nuanced, if not overturned, by writers such as Sharlow and Persaud whose writing has emerged some three decades after the decolonization of the British Caribbean. In novels which focus almost exclusively on the Indo-Trinidadian community, Sharlow and Persaud portray the diaspora as a long-established, multigenerational institution which is now as surely embedded in the Caribbean landscape as it is spiritually sustained by its South Asian cultural heritage. In fact, the naturalistic flavour of each of these novels is made tangible in detailed descriptions of the daily patterns of communal life as the unifying feature of Indo-Trinidadian experience. Indeed, if the paradigm of exile found in Caribbean literature appears in these novels, it does not function as an overriding symbol of rootlessness, at least not within the protective enclave of community in which the majority of its members are shown to be quite 'at home.' Indeed, for those writers, who are now several generations removed from the time of their ancestors' enigmatic arrival in the Caribbean, the common tropes of cultural alienation and 'familiar temporariness' are considerably tempered.[32] This is because these writers' major preoccupation is with the internal factors which threaten to undermine the integrity of the diasporic community, on the one hand, and continue to compromise interethnic relations, on the other.

In Lakshmi Persaud's first novel *Butterfly in the Wind* (1990),[33] the various autobiographical details of her protagonist's life create the distinctly 'South Asian' flavour found in other Indo-Trinidadian novels, such as Niala Maharaj's *Like Heaven* (2006) or even V.S. Naipaul's Trinidad novels, such as *The Mystic Masseur* and *The Suffrage of Elvira*. These details include her family's Hindu-Brahmin background; the centrality of the *Ramayana* in daily prayers and religious ceremonies; the daily use of religious lingo (such as *kathas*, *pujas*, and *siwala*), traditional foods (such as *roti*, *gulabjamans*, and *chatni*) and cultural objects (such as *lota*, *chulha*, and *orhni*); and the prevalence of Urdu/Hindi modes of address (like *didi* and *pundit*). In her intimate familiarity with these cultural markers, Persaud's protagonist, Kamla Maharaj, greatly resembles Naipaul's Indo-Trinidadian protagonists; she is a descendant of indentured labourers whose life is circumscribed by the tightly woven cultural and spiritual fabric of her local community. However, the female novelist rarely betrays the feeling that her transplanted community is a mere replica of the originary homeland, or, as Naipaul recently put it, 'a kind of India ... which we could, as it were, unroll like a carpet on the flat land.'[34] On the contrary, Persaud's detailed descriptions of home, family, community and culture animate, in the context of the everyday, what Walcott refers to in his observation of an Indo-Trinidadian performance of the *Ramleela*,[35] thousands of miles and several generations removed from the motherland, that is, not 'loss' but a 'delight of conviction.'[36]

Be it the anxiety of exile or the delight of conviction, Indo-Caribbean writers not only give voice to the specificities of South Asian diasporic experience, but they also make evident the process of indigenization of South Asian culture in the diasporic location. Persaud's description of her community as a foundational history rather than as an elusive sign of displacement clearly resonates with this 'delight of conviction.' Indeed, the community is itself a formative text in her protagonist Kamla's development, in such a way that her seemingly innocent childhood observations are windows to an ancient wisdom; through these observations she taps into living systems of knowledge found in such acts as her grandmother's mustard oil massages, her mother's elaborate *pujas*, and her own generally infectious participation in the 'simple joys' of life, such as buying her favourite South Asian sweetmeats from the local market or picking just the right kind of flowers for temple offerings. In fact, the poetics of the tropical landscape, which is 'central to the process of self-possession,'[37] for Caribbean diasporic peoples, assumes a double resonance in Persaud's *Butterfly in the Wind*. Here, nature is not only invested with the character and history of the island tropics but also with the rich sensory details and vocabulary of South Asian culture. In her loving catalogue of the foods, names, rituals, flora, and fauna that have been introduced to and indigenized in the Caribbean by indentured peoples and their descendants Persaud widens the paradigm of creolité to include other cultural traditions.[38]

Fictions of 'Faith' in the Diasporic Community

Although Persaud has lived in Britain for the latter half of her life, her ties to family, her frequent returns to her native Trinidad, and her former teaching career in Trinidad and Jamaica are apparent in an oeuvre that is imaginatively situated exclusively in the Caribbean. Persaud is also the first Indo-Trinidadian female writer to have written a 'full-length work.'[39] Other female Indo-Trinidadian writers have since contributed to the growing stream of novel production, including the Vancouver-based Shani Mootoo (*Cereus Blooms at Night* [1996] and *He Drown She in the Sea* [2005]); the Toronto-based Ramabai Espinet (her first novel is *The Swinging Bridge* [2003]); the New York-based Joy Mahabir (her first novel is *Jouvert* [2006]); Niala Maharaj whose first novel *Like Heaven* (2006) was written during her residency in the Netherlands; and, most recently, the India-based Peggy Mohan's *Jahajin* (2007). These writers are also widening the geopolitical frame of reference and readership for those who form part of the double diaspora, which has traditionally been mapped within the anglophone metropolises of North America and Europe.

Persaud remains the most prolific among her female peers, having written four novels to date, two of which are set entirely in the village of Pasea, in the Tunapuna district, where the author spent her childhood. Her first novel, *Butterfly in the Wind*, is a fictional autobiography that is strung together as a series of interwoven sketches which describe, from the first-person perspective, a young girl's development within a close-knit Hindu community. Persaud's second novel, *Sastra* (1993), is also set in her childhood community of Tunapuna. *Sastra* is, in many ways, a sequel to *Butterfly in the Wind*, insofar as the female protagonist becomes a fully formed character in the negotiation between personal, familial, religio-cultural, class/caste, and colonial expectations. Persaud's third novel is a significant departure from her previous works. *For the Love of My*

Name (2000) is a fictional account of the Burnham years of Guyana's tumultuous political history. Here, we see her creative vision spanning outward, beyond community and nation, and assuming a regional Caribbean
consciousness and sensibility. Not only does her Guyana-based novel set
up an interesting point of comparison with Narmala Shewcharan's
Tomorrow Is Another Day, but it also reinforces the concept of an island
subjectivity which is, in turn, enlivened by a pan-archipelagic, if not pan-
American, network of interrelation. In her most recent novel to date,
Raise the Lanterns High (2004), Persaud bridges the mythic distances between ancient India and contemporary Trinidad, bringing her oeuvre full
circle, from ancestral land to natal island home.

In terms of the body of Indo-Caribbean literature, *Butterfly in the Wind*
marks a significant turning point. It offers, in the form of a fictional autobiography, an unprecedented portrait of 1940s Trinidad, filtered through
the consciousness of a Hindu girl who is nurtured and protected by
her relatively well-to-do family. Persaud's novel offers a unique 'female
perspective of the more often than not antagonistic interplay between
her orthodox Hindu upbringing and a European colonial education.
However, her retrospective is often impeded by a degree of narrative
dissonance wherever the author seems to struggle to bring together a
fragmented memoir of events.[40] Subsequently, this novel often strikes an
uneasy balance between genres, as it is devoid of the post-modern strat-
egies of irony and metafiction which evoke the fallibility of memory or
the distorting effects of nostalgia.

Unlike Persaud, Sharlow has been referred to as a minor figure in
Indo-Trinidadian literature,[41] even though his is one of the only bodies
of fiction to rival, in scope and number, the prolific output of novels by
his literary predecessors Naipaul and Selvon. His first works, the companion novellas *Requiem for a Village* and *Apartheid Love* (1982), trace the
impact of fundamentalist American evangelical missions in the rural
Trinidad interior, and thus set the stage for his first full-length novel, *The
Elect* (1992). Sharlow's visibility and marketability have been considerably obscured by his permanent residence in his native island, his seemingly reclusive nature, his largely self-published body of works, and what
can best be described as his acute sense of marginalization and critical
neglect in comparison to his émigré peers.

Sharlow's *The Elect* is also notable as an early example of a growing
body of writing to focus on post-independence Trinidad. Persaud's somewhat idyllic view, at least of her own familial and cultural milieu in colonial Trinidad, is greatly problematized by Sharlow's satirical indictment

of the far less 'wholesome' diasporic community of Palmist, at least as it has come to be overrun by external and internal forms of corruption. Though Sharlow seems more critical than Persaud of the inherent tensions within the diasporic community itself, he nonetheless confirms the latter's projection that the underpinning structure of the community is its collective ethos or sense of fraternity, particularly when 'constituted negatively' against discriminatory or alienating practices.[42]

Sharlow's examination of the extent to which religious conversion acts as an assult on the individual psyche is reminiscent of Shani Mootoo's *Cereus Blooms at Night* – a novel which indicts the Canadian Presbyterian Mission's deracinatory policy of making education accessible to the indentured labourer's children on the condition of religious conversion. Sharlow's protagonist, Tom, is a casualty of this religious indoctrination and its complicity in colonial policy. Indeed, like Mootoo's haunting figure of Ramchandin in *Cereus Blooms at Night*,[43] Tom is stigmatized as a cultural outsider whose own parents' Hindu practices and beliefs appear foreign and incomprehensible.[44] But unlike Mootoo's unequivocal attack on the Canadian Presbyterian Mission's racist practices, Tom's Presbyterian background is used as an ironic counterpoint to the economically exploitative agenda of the American Evangelical missions, which were to emerge in full and unrelenting force by the 1970s and 1980s – the period in which *The Elect* is primarily set. These competing religious missions underscore the author's critical commentary on the imperceptible transition from a colonial to a neocolonial era, and the altogether bitter irony that religion/religious doctrine can rend asunder the diasporic community as readily as it has held it together.

Birbalsingh has accurately noted that in Sharlow's short fiction the author 'fuses Naipaulian techniques such as caricature, farce, irony and repartee, with comic resources of Trinidad creole speech to produce a keen satirical edge.'[45] A further comparison could be made between Naipaul's first novel, *The Mystic Masseur*, and Sharlow's *The Elect* regarding their satirical lambasting of religious charlatanism. In *The Elect* this is embodied in the wholly vulgar figure of the American-trained Indian evangelist Pastor Goberdan. Sharlow's satire carries with it an additional element of bawdy humour that only sharpens the author's unsparing attack on religious dogma. *The Elect* can be said to continue the tradition, so deftly crafted in *The Mystic Masseur* (and differently echoed in such works as *Cereus Blooms at Night* or Cyril Dabydeen's *The Wizard Swami*) of revealing the relationship between literacy, power, and religious leadership in Caribbean communities.

In her study of the development of Indo-Trinidadian literature, from oral to print culture, Kris Rampersad provides a helpful explanation of the inextricable relationship between religious instruction and community leadership in the diaspora: 'Initially, leaders in the new society arose from among those who were versed in the Indian languages, Sanskrit, Hindi and Urdu. They were, or became, the pundits and imams. Later, those versed in English were the ones who held the leadership positions. Demystification of book learning, once held to be the domain of the Brahmin castes, with access to education, levelled the playing field between castes.'[46] The idea that literacy, 'book learning,' and caste status were indelibly linked is, of course, echoed in the guise of Naipaul's memorable character, the self-proclaimed pundit of higher learning, 'Ganesh Ramsumair, B.A.,' the 'mystic Masseur' whose double validation as a self-appointed pundit is contingent upon a body of learning which encompasses sacred Hindu texts and Indology, as well as a post-secondary education accredited by the hallowed institutions of imperial power. However, by the time we arrive in the post-independence setting of *The Elect*, it is the young educated people who are best able to discern the 'spiritual holocaust'[47] overrunning the Palmist community at the hands of a corrupt evangelical (himself a local convert) with the capitalist stamp of 'American' credentials.

Sharlow's satirical treatment of the relationship between religion, politics, ethnicity, and personal ambition speaks to a common theme across the body of Indo-Caribbean writing. Cyril Dabydeen's earlier novel, *The Wizard Swami* (1985), exposes such ambitions in the misadventures of Devan, an Indo-Guyanese family man who proceeds to dazzle the locals with what they mistakenly perceive to be his mastery of Hindu scripture and gifts of oration. Devan's personal ambition to become a member of the 'All India League,' a group of the country's wealthiest Hindus, propels his involvement in more selfless endeavours, such as teaching the local children to read and write Hindi when they are more interested in drawing 'trees and houses.'[48] Devan is sensitive enough to know that the destiny of the ethnic community lies in its reconnection to its spiritual centre: '"It about Hindus in dis part of de world. The New World, you know, Panditji. We been cut off from we roots when white people bring we from India."'[49] But, in true comic fashion, he is no less mortified when he is upstaged and outsalaried by a real 'Sanskrit scholar.'[50]

Sharlow's *The Elect* offers an interesting basis for comparison with Persaud's idyllic Tunapuna community on several levels: (a) whereas Persaud celebrates the strength of religious belief and custom as the

cornerstone of her predominantly Hindu community, Sharlow examines the effects of religious conversion along a historical chain of communal disruption, beginning with colonial civilizing missions such as
those embodied by the Canadian Presbyterian mission and now filtered
through the commercial allure of American evangelicalism; (b) whereas Persaud configures the family as the symbolic nucleus of the community's social and cultural cohesion, Sharlow reveals that this is an
extremely tenuous interrelationship that is predicated on both class
and caste privileges; and (c) whereas Persaud emphazises the patriarchal underpinnings of colonialism and Hinduism, Sharlow explicitly exposes the complicity of religious structures in the commodification and
deployment of female sexuality.

Conversely, the most notable similarity between the two texts is the
centrality of the interrelated and long-established institutions of family
and community among the descendants of Trinidad's formerly indentured peoples. Sharlow and Persaud project common tropes of
community and commonality as real and vital expressions of diasporic
identity. Even though both novelists write against the stereotype of 'East
Indians' as a homogenous entity, their novels are nonetheless structured
upon an overriding projection of community as the simultaneously limiting and empowering axis around which the diasporic subject's life revolves. A comparative look at Sharlow and Persaud's novels reveals that
these communities are neither static replicas of their originary cultures
nor an altogether exclusive or homogenous entity. These works echo
Peter Nazareth's and Farida Karodia's Africa-based novels insofar as they
consciously seek to reverse Afrocentric and Eurocentric stereotypes
alike, by first emphasizing the diversity of South Asian diasporic peoples,
even within the close quarters of an Indo-Trinidadian village such as
Palmist: 'A couple of shops, a mosque, a Hindu temple, and a Presbyterian
school and church met all Palmist's needs.'[51] In a more explicit gesture,
Persaud writes against the East Indian stereotype: 'Some may think that
because Pasea Villagers were East Indian, that there was amongst them a
uniformity of colour and culture. What we had, in reality, was a mosaic of
peoples.'[52] Moreover, Persaud debunks the coolie stereotype in her portrait of the extended Maharaj family as a symbol of the diversification of
the Indo-Trinidadian's professional and economic base.[53]

Though both novels consciously alert us to the relative heterogeneity
of the diasporic community, neither novel offers a convincing or complex consideration of the ethnic and/or religious minorities within the
South Asian diaspora itself. As Naipaul retrospectively testifies, religious

differences affected intracommunal relations as much as they kept Indo-Trinidadians segregated from other racial groups: 'We knew nothing of Muslims. This idea of strangeness, of the thing to be kept outside, extended even to other Hindus.'[54] In fact, both novels resort to what I shall term the 'Mrs Mohammed' archetype; that is, in each work there exists an elusive female character who sporadically slips in and out of the narrative as a flat representative of Muslim orthodoxy within the greater Hindu community.

One might conclude that the innocuousness of 'Mrs Mohammed' is a comment on the relative harmonization of religious differences in the diasporic context. In a wonderful passage from Naipaul's *The Suffrage of Elvira* (1958), perhaps the most elaborate treatment of Hindu-Muslim relations in 1950s Trinidad, a hopeful political candidate unwittingly recruits the son of a local Muslim tailor, Baksh, as his campaign manager. The political process in this small Indo-Trinidadian township principally revolves around vote solicitation from the leaders of the three major religious groups (Hindu, Muslim, and Christian) to ensure 'Indian' representation in the local elections. But religious difference functions comically as another kind of smokescreen for what are essentially personal ambitions and petty skirmishes, including marital disagreements, boyish pranks, shady economic transactions turned sour, neighbourly bickering, and so on. In other words, while the political process exploits religious and ethnic difference, the day-to-day lives of the community are hardly so rigidly delineated. As the narrator tells us,

> Things were crazily mixed up in Elvira. Everybody, Hindus, Muslims, and Christians, owned a Bible; the Hindus and Muslims looking on it, if anything, with greater awe. Hindus and Muslims celebrated Christmas and Easter. The Spaniards and some of the negroes celebrated the Hindu festival of lights ... Everybody celebrated the Muslim festival of Hosein.[55]

Persaud and Mohammed echo the above sentiment. As the narrator of *The Elect* tells us, in villages like Palmist 'differences of religion were no big thing.'[56] However, in the virtual absence of Muslim characters in works which otherwise consciously foreground a religio-centred diasporic consciousness, the absence of a round Muslim character leaves something to be desired. The Mrs Mohammed archetype becomes somewhat problematic when compared with more fully developed Afro-Caribbean characters. In *The Elect*, for example, the Rastafarian figure of James Wellington is shown to have a greater role to play in the goings-on of the Indo-Trinidadian community than does Mrs Mohammed. Even in her movements, Mrs Mohammed remains a furtive outsider who looks 'out of the window of her upstairs house' while Wellington lives at the 'cross-roads of the trace.'[57]

Persaud does set aside a few brief paragraphs to comment on Muslim-Hindu relations: 'Moslems were not invited to our *kathas* and *pujas* and we were not invited to their mosques. So side by side we walked the dirt roads not knowing anything about the deeper feelings of the other.'[58] However, her investigation of interreligious difference is restricted to a handful of such cursory observations. This is typified in Kamla's recollection of her neighbour Mrs Hassan's refusal of Kamla's mother's dinner invitation (she will not dine where the meat is not *halal*). Though Kamla points out that Mrs Hassan's standoffishness is the result of cultural misunderstanding, she nonetheless simplifies the latter's position as an unbending orthodoxy which contrasts radically with the more accommodating Hindu doctrine. It is not her presence as a minor character that renders Mrs Mohammed a problematic archetype, therefore, but the deployment of her character and values as contrast and foil.

The treatment of Mrs Mohammed is in part a symptom of Persaud's larger project to articulate the diaspora's cultural and ideological cohesion when held up against other sociocultural groups. Kamla's idealized version of communal wholeness is later confirmed in her observations on Indian independence and its significance for the diaspora writ large. Here, the globally felt effects of Indian independence underline James Clifford's assertion that the diaspora's political and other links usually exceed the country of settlement.[59] Thus, Kamla witnesses the decolonization of the Indian subcontinent as a catalyst for more politicized assertions of cultural autonomy in the diaspora, including the opening of independent schools, the resurgence of native language learning and religious teachings, and greater financial investment on the part of Indian organizations, particularly religious-based movements such as Arya Samaj. Kamla poignantly celebrates the direct impact of Indian independence on the diaspora in the image of Indo-Trinidadian school children singing the Indian national anthem and commemorating Indian Independence day. It is interesting to note, however, that the rebirth of a specifically 'Indian' cultural consciousness is, in Kamla's eyes, an unambiguously shared point of identification. Though Kamla poetically refers to Indian independence as a symbol of the Trinbagonian's shared struggle against European hegemony, her unqualified celebration of Indian nationalism glosses over its dominant Hindu discourse. As

Brinda Mehta states, Kamla's Hindu community is shown to look toward religion not only as a method of self-preservation but as a monolithic paradigm for an 'Indian way of life whereby cultural monopoly compromises the scope for hybridity and a plurality of cultural experiences.'[60] This can be seen in the following description of the Sanatan Dharam Maha Sabha, a doctrinal movement to which Kamla's family is shown to belong:

> Throughout the 1940s and 1950s the East Indian population in Trinidad grew rapidly. At this time came the Mahasabha Movement, men and women concerned that Trinidad Indians should become more fully conscious of the educational facilities on the island and of the rich inheritance of Indian classical dance, music, song and literature. It was felt that the more traditional, difficult and profound aspects of Indian culture were being neglected and their place taken by both Indian and Western popular culture displayed on our cinema screens.[61]

Indian independence as a symbol of a new era of national pride is not, in and of itself, as problematic as Kamla's matter-of-fact treatment of Indian nationalist rhetoric as a unifying force.[62] In other words, the prevailing impulse in Kamla's retrospective is her insistence on a spiritual unity reminiscent of the *jahaji-bhai* principle, which, when applied indiscriminately to contemporary Indo-Trinidadian society, oversimplifies an otherwise complex group of stratified religious, political, ideological, and class interests. This idyllic portrait of the Indo-Caribbean community is rendered as a Manichean binary between cultural outsider and cultural insider. For example, when Kamla is outraged over a gender-biased Hindu morality (symbolized by the community's indifference toward a local elder's adulterous behaviour), she judges the transgressor's self-imposed exile in Tobago among an alien black race to be an unduly severe punishment: 'As the years went by, I sometimes thought of him: living on a small, thinly populated island with his son, growing greyer amongst strangers, outside his own East Indian village community. What would the few black fishermen there know of him?'[63] For Kamla, therefore, the issue of Baboo's cultural alienation in the neighbouring island underscores the extent to which the corrosion of cultural values is shown to be located in the racial other.

Despite some of the obvious critical limitations of *Butterfly in the Wind*,[64] Persaud marks a turning point in Indo-Caribbean literature by countering the long-standing tradition of '*orhni*-covered' (*orhni* refers to a traditional covering worn by women in the subcontinent) minor female characters found in her male counterparts' works. Ramabai Espinet's examination of this phenomenon reveals female characters to be either happily or unhappily circumscribed by 'a largely peasant, village culture, firmly attached to the traditional values of the home and seeking no active combat with the external, non-Hindu world.'[65] Moreover, Espinet confirms that even in more fully conceived characters such as Shama in Naipaul's *A House for Mr Biswas*, there is no attempt at casting a deeper look at the internal life of these female characters or the kinds of anguishes and desires that drive and motivate their actions. Here, even Sharlow's *The Promise* falls short, for though the character of Rati is set up as the ostensible heroine of the indenture narrative, her heroism is couched in Hindu patriarchal discourse, for she is typecast as a spiritually chaste devotee to father, husband, and Brahma.

For her part, Persaud writes against the 'myth of the "eternal feminine" in which women have been marginalized by a particular strategy of "narrative petrification" ... as passive receptacles of the male writer's unconscious.'[66] She gives voice to women of three generations, each of whom embodies the gradual liberation of the subaltern female from the confines of a tightly reined plantation estate community that is further subject to the proscriptions of Hinduism. Though Kamla's conservatism confirms Partha Chatterjee's argument that, as the primary bearers of tradition, women are central to the upkeep of the community's cultural and spiritual core,[67] the women of Tunapuna are also shown to be the unacknowledged economic backbone of a community that is ravaged by alcoholism and material hardship. In communities for which alcoholism has historically served as a means of escape from the drudgery and toil of plantation labour, particularly among its male constituency, Persaud reveals that it is women who are often left to shoulder the various responsibilities of family:

> Daya had good Fridays and bad Fridays. On the good Fridays, her husband came to the gate, called out to her and brought her his wage. She, in return, handed him enough for three more drinks ... Her bad Fridays were when she had to hurry to the rum shop before he spent it all.[68]

Kamla's astute perception that women bear the brunt of an economically disadvantaged community is nonetheless compromised in the text's uncritical portrait of the family's own hierarchized place in the economic structure. The alcoholism and attendant patterns of behaviour, such as domestic violence or economic bankruptcy, besieging the male members of the community are shown to affect those employed by her family, yet the family's complicity as the well-to-do proprietors of a local rum shop in these continuing patterns of social dysfunction is never addressed. This bittersweet irony – one that is further reinforced by the fact that rum drinking would have 'gone against proscriptions of both Hindu and Muslim religious practice'[69] – seems altogether lost on the protagonist: 'I couldn't understand why the police were upset if people wanted to purchase a bottle to drink at home on a Sunday and my father was prepared to sell it.'[70]

As Indo-Caribbean women scholars such as Brinda Mehta seem to suggest, Indo-Caribbean women have had to confront the tenuous task of giving voice to a marginalized ethnic community without betraying its intrinsic value systems, particularly as they pertain to its ascribed gender roles: 'Caught in the impasse between cultural conformity and the right/write to free expression, Indo-Caribbean women writers have to negotiate the slipperiness of interstitiality through a careful crafting of their work that has to remain respectful to cultural dictates without compromising the writer's personal integrity.'[71] However, I would suggest that the awkward silences in Persaud's text do not merely function as acts of self-censorship for fear of communal reprisal; rather, they might also be apprehended as honest expressions of her characters' own orthodox upbringing.

Indeed, the manner in which Kamla addresses the sexual and gender politics of her community is itself a telling reflection of a Hindu ethos and cultural sensibility that the principle character seeks not so much to reject, but rather to reform (much like Rooplall Monar's Data) within the context of the wider colonial community and her more immediate social reality. In this sense, Kamla's assertion of selfhood is negotiated through the strictures of Hinduism and its caste system rather than as an outright repudiation of religious orthodoxy and its teachings. This is without a doubt a tentative coming-of-age within a governing ethnic and religious framework, one that does not resonate with the spirit of abject rebellion, particularly against mother figures, that is characteristic of the protagonists in Afro-Caribbean female Bildungsromans, such as Annie in Jamaica Kincaid's *Annie John* or Sophie in Edwidge Danticatt's *Breath, Eyes, Memory*. Instead, she calls attention to a subject-position that is differently anchored in the competing discourses of colonial Caribbean life. It is interesting that while Afro-Caribbean female characters usually see the complicit discourses of Christianity and colonialism as inhibitors to their sexual, intellectual, and personal freedom, Kamla sees in the 'Western' practices underlying both institutions the source of spiritual degradation and sexual corruption. Religion also serves as the primary basis for discrimination when Kamla is denied access, by the Catholic school system, to higher level exams because of her 'pagan' Hindu practices. Conversely, even the missionary schools of Trinidad become the source of contamination of female purity (insofar as they violate the gendered precepts of Hindu orthodoxy).

The journey to Europe that marks the end of Kamla's narrative is a wonderfully nuanced case in point of the ways in which female empowerment is often manifested within the customary framework of patriarchal order and vice versa. Kamla's journey appears to be an unusual reversal of the diasporic female's typecast role as the upkeeper of tradition in the face of creolization and assimilation. Ironically, then, Kamla's educational path is facilitated by her mother whose own position as the preserver of a heteronormative and patriarchal Hindu Brahmin moral code is also shown to be the outspoken champion of female autonomy. In fact, Kamla's mother reveals a complicated mixture of feminist and patriarchal attitudes. In her role as the bearer of tradition, the mother is complicit in the structures that delimit her daughter's choices within the repeated precepts of custom; on the other hand, as the insurer of individual and collective forms of empowerment in the face of assimilative colonial practices, the mother is, for Kamla, a model of female empowerment: it is Mrs Maharaj who passes down the knowledge systems of the subcontinent within an oppressive colonial environment while also passing down invaluable life skills, such as the day-to-day management of the family business. In other words, though Kamla's mother is rarely seen to move beyond the acceptable physical parameters of the home, the yard, or the temple, she is nonetheless Kamla's primary influence as a strong-willed woman of colour. This is because female empowerment is often manifested in discreet models of resistance, just as traditional patterns of gender conformity and gender roles often betray other avenues for resistance as much as they might expose class and other hierarchies.

Like Edward Said's claim that the immigrant can transform the anxiety of exile into a critical vantage point between 'mass institutions,' the diasporic subject's exposure to other discursive practices carries with it a similar potential for 'scrupulous subjectivity':[72] on the one hand, religious and other forms of indoctrination are shown to be an ideological assault on the South Asian diasporic subject's sense of cultural autonomy; on the other hand, the exposure to multiple belief systems functions as a critical disruption of an inward-looking community. Though Kamla and Tom are steeped in the institutions of their cultural and political communities, the extreme ideological disjunctures inherent in these conflicting models – in social, political, and religious terms – help each character cultivate a degree of critical distance. It is at such an intellectual crossroads that Kamla comes to directly challenge the Rama-Sita paradigm that anchors the Hindu construction of female identity in terms of religious devotion, filial piety, and wifely duty. In her reflections on the unequal punitive measures meted out to male and female adulterers in Hindu society, Kamla comes to the realization that a woman's passive acceptance of such gender biases is directly related to religious upbringing, such as the moral lessons on female conduct to be found in the *Mahabharata* and *Ramayana*. It is significant that Kamla directs her interrogation at her mother rather than the male members of the community, for she not only makes the correlation between storytelling and religio-cultural instruction but also recognizes these to be female-centred activities. When Kamla asks her mother why Sita was put through the ordeal of fire after her abduction by the demon-king Ravana, and why the woman's 'word' was not enough for her liberator, Rama, 'one of the avators of God,' she is wholly dissatisfied with her mother's response that Sita is answerable not only to a king but to all of his subjects. Kamla's realization that her 'understanding of female morality was formed – by the interpretation of the *Ramayana* by my mother and by my father and the pundit and others,'[73] is the first sign of a feminist sensibility that is directed outward against forms of colonial injustice as well as inward to those seemingly inviolable mores that the female diasporic subject is meant to hold sacred in the ensurance of cultural self-preservation and communal integrity.

Kamla's 'scrupulous subjectivity' is often compromised by an internal conflict driven by an overriding impulse to outwardly 'project a coherent world.'[74] These nostalgic overtones notwithstanding, the uneven and seemingly contradictory set of practices embedded in the two major belief systems to which Kamla is exposed opens her eyes to her status as a marginalized ethnic and religious minority. Kamla's discovery of her particular ethnocultural status in wider Caribbean society is underscored in the image of her discomfort at a school dance. Here, she perceives in Western society a level of permissibility with respect to the interaction between the sexes as 'contrary to [her] upbringing.'[75] While another individual in her position might see in the event an opportunity for rebellion or at least experimentation, Kamla's reaction is as credible a response for one whose tutelage and realm of experience has been circumscribed within an insular model of community; thus, the school dance only compounds her sense of alienation as 'a displaced person between two worlds whose rules of etiquette were foreign one to another.'[76]

Persaud's Trinidad-based novels incorporate, like numerous other post-colonial novels set in the era of decolonization, the recurring motif of departure to the Western metropolis. Kamla's departure is a natural extension of her colonial destiny: 'But there was a built-in assumption, never questioned, that going' abroad by its very nature meant a transformation of self, a dramatic improvement of one's status.'[77] Though Mehta rightly suggests that Persaud's female protagonists' journeys abroad serve as a viable means of escape from the strictures of Hinduism, I would argue that Kamla's journey functions less as a rejection of Hindu orthodoxy than as a paradoxical conformity to communal expectations. This is because traditional apprehensions that might have otherwise restricted a woman's social mobility are often forfeited in the diasporic community which looks to each member's economic and social advancement as a form of collective empowerment. In this sense, individual mobility is seen as a vehicle for collective strength. Kamla's university training is simultaneously a break with tradition and a symbol of the family's elevated place in the social hierarchy, for now the Maharaj family patriarch can 'finance not only his son but also a daughter.'[78] Moreover, Kamla's higher education further ensures the community's cultural survival since it will provide her with the necessary credentials with which to teach in one of the new 'Indian-run' schools. As such, Kamla's departure is grounded in the discourse of indenture history, as a process of migration, labour, enterprise, and eventually, material and social advancement. To this end, Kamla's aunt comments, '"Who would have thought of a day like this when our grandmothers and great grandmothers left India, not knowing where they were going? All they were told was that there would be work. They came in good faith; they placed themselves in God's hands. And look at this now, look at this success story."'[79] Moreover, as the first female in her community to travel overseas, Kamla marks a turning point in the multigenerational history of South Asian diasporic women: 'a female child, disadvantaged by custom – an untold of freedom and privilege – at much personal sacrifice to themselves. They were sweeping aside time-honoured ways of thinking of their own volition.'[80]

Kamla's bold step into the unknown simultaneously recalls and reverses the life histories of an earlier generation of *jahaji-bhain* (ship-sisters) whose own infinitely more perilous journey across the *kala pani*, without the financial, familial, or communal support that Kamla enjoys, signalled not only a courageous act but also the arrival into a new form of bondage under the dictates and hardships of indenture. As the recipient of familial and communal support as well as the spiritual insurance of her elite Brahmin caste, Kamla's journey reverses several of the tropes associated with the initial crossing of the *kala pani*, including the loss of caste in the seemingly irreversible distancing from the sacred Ganges. As a symbol of a transcendent and ascendant immigrant experience, Kamla's anticipated participation in one of the new 'Indian-run' schools suggests the extent to which her individual success is equated with collective empowerment in the struggle for ethnic self-determination. As the extended family comes to send off their prodigal daughter on her historic journey, therefore, the event is described as a collective triumph, commemorated with readings from the *Ramayana*. Similarly, in being one of the first to afford the modern amenities of travel, the community is about to witness a reversal of the historical scar produced by the dehumanizing and perilous ship voyage across the *kala pani*: 'Others talked about how different travel was now – the days of six months from India were over; of how bad it had been in the old ships and how many had died. Things had changed for the better; they were so happy for me.'[81]

Though Sharlow might not give voice to the female diasporic subject as vividly as does Persaud, he offers a more even-handed critique of the community's sites of female repression. Indeed, *The Elect* exposes the hypocrisies of communal solidarity in light of its gaping gender inequalities. In such an equation, the women of Palmist are shown to be the most easily targeted casualties of religious doctrine, both in their deployment as the bearers of tradition and in their own search for alternate conceptions of female identity. For instance, the evangelizing pastor capitalizes on the Palmist women's shared desire to resist their community's 'male-prescribed cultural mandates for Hindu women.'[82] As such the pastor easily convinces Sorijini that the church will afford her a degree of autonomy not found in her own religion: 'She say the church going to be she own, an' she done with this blasted *ka, ka, ja, ja, wa, wa,* an' with wearing *orhini*.'[83] Conversely, in a thematic echo of Kamla's realization of a gender-biased Hindu morality, Shanti, Sorijini's mother, feels vindicated by the pastor's condemnation of her husband's transgressive behaviour:

> 'It's about your husband I've come to speak, Shanti … The Lord will not tolerate drunkenness and fornication. It's your duty as a Christian woman to make your husband stop drinking and committing adultery.'
> 'But Pastor, he doh listen to one word ah say …'

'... Your husband's ... drinking is offensive to the Lord. You are the chosen, you know. And no matter what you do, your place in Heaven is secure.'[84]

The pastor's religious piety camouflages racist and imperialist aims in the doctrine of 'salvation.' Here, Sharlow underscores the seamless transition from colonial to neocolonial practices in the 'corrupt and exclusive church'[85] and its civilizing mission. However, Sharlow also casts an inward eye on internal forms of corruption in the Hindu pundit's extortionist drive for 'tithes.' In a society that is paradoxically held together and torn asunder by religious beliefs and customs, Sharlow enshrouds his younger female characters in a trinity of religious archetypes; the three women who vie for the youthful protagonist Tom's attention are Indrani, the temptress; Sorijini, the chaste; and Mary, the virgin. To a certain extent, the 'Mrs Mohammed' character found in Sharlow's text falls in line with these religious archetypes. However, Tom's indifference to Mrs Mohammed and her Muslim daughters stands in contrast to his visceral dissatisfaction with the restrictions imposed on other women in this tightly controlled socioreligious environment. Tom, himself, is shown to harbour chauvinistic tendencies, for though he seems fed up with 'stereotypical' female behaviour, he is unable to fully accept the assertions of female autonomy that challenge his own gender constructs. Indeed, though it is his intellectual female companion, Mary, who convinces him to attend university, Tom's frustrated sexual desires thwart an otherwise promising romance with a potential equal. Moreover, Tom is unable to partake in the villager's unspoken admiration for Shanti's metamorphosis from a brow-beaten housewife to an independent thinker who single-handedly brings about the pastor's downfall.

In her study of the pejorative positioning of Indo-Trinidadian subaltern women in Trinidadian nationalist discourse, Shalini Puri points to the centrality of the 'douglarization debate' which erupted in the 1990s. Referring to the Hindi term for 'bastard,' 'dougla' entered the Trinidadian vocabulary to apply to peoples of mixed Indian and African descent. Puri argues that conservative Afro- and Indo-Caribbean nationalist discourse had posited in symmetrical ways the image of the 'dougla' and that of the chaste 'Indian' woman to maintain racial demarcations in contemporary Caribbean society.[86] As was seen in Rooplall Monar's *Janjhat*, an older generation is suspicious of the 'ruinous' influence of the western jukebox and radio on female youth; in other words, deviant forms of Indian female subjectivity are attributed to the effects of creolization, and therefore seen as a corruption of the model Indian girl's strictly controlled codes of morality and conduct.

This reflects a common depiction in Indo-Caribbean literature of creolization (or cultural hybridization) as an assimilative force steeped in dominant Western cultural models. In this regard, then, the female 'dougla' in particular becomes the epitomy of the creolizing process as an assault on Indian female sexuality. Sharlow critically approaches the issue of hybrid identities in his thematization of the 'douglarization debate' by making explicit not only the pejorative connotation of the 'dougla' among the Indo-Caribbean population, but also the perceived relationship between transgressive sexuality and hybrid identities. In the pastor's subservient accomplice, Brother Samuel, and Tom's love interest Mary, each of whom is of ambiguous racial ancestry, Sharlow takes the self-righteous Palmist community to task for its prejudicial attitudes. Mary's genealogy, for one, is a matter for local speculation and gossip: 'And when Tom asked how come Mary was Indian and Mrs Penco was Portuguese, Lal had just chuckled over his beer: "People mix-up like callalou all over the place, oui."'[87] Moreover, even though Mary claims to identify herself with the Indo-Caribbean members of Palmist insofar as her brother is 'a labourer,' her ambiguous genealogical ties to the local estate owner's family (the remnants of the European plantocracy) relegates her to its margins, so that even her romance with Tom transpires in the form of clandestine meetings on the village outskirts. Mary's association with the European plantation owner's family further mobilizes indenture history insofar as the connection resurrects the prevalent fears, among early generations of male migrants, of promiscuity not only in light of the female subaltern's greater sexual freedom as a gendered minority or as an autonomous (wage-earning) being, but also in her heightened commodification as an object of the white master's desire.

But Sharlow comically inverts the racial stereotype of dougla/female promiscuity in Mary's vow of abstinence until marriage; moreover, Mary's chastity comes across as a seemingly informed, independent decision rather than as an act of passive conformity to religious or social norms. Consequently, Sharlow can be said to rewrite the pejorative connotations of the 'dougla' not only in terms of its endorsement of racial purity but also in its representation of female sexuality as the site of cultural and racial contamination. Sharlow's exposure of the marginalization of dougla identities illustrates, in turn, the extent to which racist thinking facilitates external forms of economic and cultural predation. Indeed, institutions such as those set up by Pastor Goberdan are shown to continue the long-standing tradition of seeing in the Indian subaltern woman the most vulnerable, because most fiercely protected, aspect of the community itself.

A comparison of these novels reveals that community and commonality are as much projected fictions as they are realistic articulations of diasporic identity as an alignment of shared experiences in the face of displacement, diversity, and a racially divisive history. To this end, each novel highlights the centrality of a shared sense of community that is 'family and kinship oriented.'[88] Moreover, in the process of settlement and acculturation, religious practices are shown to be a stabilizing element which counterbalances feelings of alienation and displacement. For these diasporic communities, the Muslim Hosay festivals or Hindu rites such as *jharaying* do not signify alien ways of life but local practices which have as central a place in Trinidadian society as Obeah practices and church congregations. To return to Naipaul's *Suffrage of Elvira*, it is the shared belief in, or at least deference to, the power of Obeah that spurs on local political intrigue, so that both the candidate and his main rival deflect waning public opinion by suggesting the local American Jehovah's Witnesses are using Obeah to sway the community in their favour. Conversely, in Sharlow's Palmist community, the character of James Wellington embraces Hindu-Muslim customs, such as renouncing 'unclean foods like pork,' in exchange for the Palmist lifestyle of 'clean, natural living'[89] either because as a Rastafarian he is at home in these religious practices,[90] or because of his greater reaction to what he perceives to be the excesses of contemporary Trinbagonian society.

While Persaud's text emphasizes the integrity of religious practices and customs as a necessary prerequisite to greater assertions of cultural autonomy in a dominant Christian, Afro-Caribbean environment, Sharlow's text serves as a self-directed cautionary tale against doctrines of exclusivism: 'The church of the chosen had divided the villagers ... Pullbassie's and Lal's families had their Bhagavan; James his Jah; Mrs Mohammed her Allah; Shanti her Deo; and the chosen had their own exclusive Jesus.'[91] Though Sharlow hints at religious belief and custom as one of the unifying features of the diasporic community, he simultaneously rejects the over-reliance on religious doctrine as its primary building block. Moreover, in the post-colonial setting of Palmist, Sharlow articulates the shift from colonial to neocolonial forms of cultural imperialism. In Palmist, this transition is not merely expressed as a site of cultural conflict represented by the likes of Kamla's feeling that she is a 'displaced person between two worlds whose rules of etiquette were foreign, one to another';[92] rather, Sharlow's protagonist identifies the Palmist community's subjection to foreign 'investment' – typified by Pastor Goberdan's acquisition of local property, local women, and local trust – as the more insidious neoimperial reality, in which even the vaunted Hindu *bhajan* is no match for the television and the pastor's resounding microphone.

Diasporic consciousness accordingly develops within the framework of an imagined community that is principally anchored in the language of faith and spiritual belonging at the private and public level. Religious and spiritual activities are disseminated by means of formal functions (such as ritual ceremonies, *panchayats*, and town meetings) as well as by informal social interactions (such as the free-flowing exchange of news and gossip) and offer critical channels of dialogue and debate which sustain the community's autonomy in the face of increasing assimilation. The spiritual community is thus the centripetal force around which the diasporic community revolves. The question of 'whose' faith to turn to is continually put to the test in each of these texts, but the centrality of faith in the formation of diasporic subjectivity unites these otherwise strikingly different fictions of community.

PART FOUR

Asia-Pacific

7 The Politics of (the English) Language in Malaysia and Singapore: K.S. Maniam's *The Return* and Gopal Baratham's *A Candle or the Sun*

Asian Tigers of Many Stripes: Multiracial Malaysia and Singapore

The majority of South Asian peoples to have permanently settled in South-East Asia by the nineteenth century followed the common patterns of migration under the colonial administration, as indentured labourers or free passengers. South Asian immigrants came to the Malaysian peninsula as estate labourers who quickly dominated the dense rubber plantations. In contrast, such plantations were scarce on the small island colony of Singapore (which was primarily used by the British Empire as a major naval base). Here immigrants were essentially employed as civil servicemen/women and for public services such as policing and sanitation. In both regions, a large proportion of immigrants also came in the spirit of entrepreneurship, opening up wholesale and retail trades that have come to mark South-East Asia with the colours, textures, and tastes of the Indian subcontinent. One need only enter the bustling avenues of Singapore's 'Little India' to find oneself enamoured by the kaleidoscopic colours of hand-embroidered silk saris, the glint of gold and glass bangles, the enticing aromas of South Indian cuisine, the blaring beats of the latest Bollywood soundtrack, and, of course, the multiple tongues – Tamil, Malayalam, Gujarati, Urdu, and so on – of South Asia.

South-East Asia is unique insofar as these immigrants were not venturing into alien territory; they were going to a land that had already been indelibly marked, for over a millennium, by the religious imprints of Hinduism, Buddhism, and Islam. Well before European colonization, South-East Asia was a vital crossroads in the transmission of the ancient belief systems, goods, and cultural resources of Asia's major civilizations. As historian Milton W. Meyer states, 'The Indic Culture, in both Hindu and Buddhist forms, began to manifest itself strikingly by the second century A.D. in both mainland and insular areas. The Indian legacy was perhaps the most significant feature of this period in Southeast Asian history.'[1] In addition, Islam made its presence felt by the thirteenth century, and by the fifteenth century the Malaysian peninsula was flourishing as a heterogeneous, commercial, maritime community where 'Javanese, Sumatrans, Persians, Chinese, Arabs, Parsees, Bengalis, and Gujrats rubbed shoulders.'[2] In fact, under the Islamic sultanate, Malacca (an important historical region on the southwestern coast of the Malaysian peninsula) housed the most influential port in South-East Asia.

The South Asian diaspora in this part of the world is part of an ancient chain of historical, cultural, and religious ties between the Indian subcontinent and South-East Asia.[3] Consequently, the exodus of South Asian peoples to South-East Asia by the mid- to late nineteenth century was not a complete severing of the cultural cord but a subsequent impression in the flesh of what was already existent in South-East Asian spirit and culture. For example, shared cultural values of family and community, together with the centrality of religious practices in daily life, helped ease intercultural tensions in the process of adaptation. Sociologist Sinnappah Arasaratnam says of Singapore and Malaysia:

> The movement of people and ideas before modern times may in a sense be said to have made the more intensive modern movement of people less painful. It may be argued that short-term migration and settlement in Malaya was already part of Indian history and tradition ... It certainly explains the ease with which the Indian settled down, since the country was not far different from his own ... The Indian in Malaya, unlike the Indian in the West Indian islands or the colonies of East and South Africa, did not feel himself so completely alienated from his environment or so drastically separated from the indigenous people.[4]

Of course, the historic umbilical cord connecting South-East Asia to the Indian subcontinent did not eliminate the itinerant hardships of colonial rule. Rather, the intimate historical ties between these two regions, underscored by their geographic and cultural proximity, presented a far less alienating environment for its South Asian inhabitants. Diasporic Muslims, for instance, have tended to integrate quite comfortably into this society so embedded in Islamic civilization. This process of accommodation came full circle when post-independence Malaysia became an Islamic Republic, bringing Muslim South Asians even closer to greater Malaysian society, immersed as it is in Islamic practices and beliefs.[5]

As each of the previous chapters points out, however, such observations must be considered in light of the diverse nature of the South Asian diaspora itself.[6] Unlike the other regions under study, the diaspora in Malaysia and Singapore is dominated by South Indian and Ceylonese (or Sri Lankan) Tamils who represent around 77 per cent of ethnic South Asians. The remainder is comprised of Punjabis, Bengalis, Gujaratis, and Sindhis.[7] Moreover, as elsewhere in the South Asian diaspora, numerous factors have strained group dynamics, such as 'occupational specialization,'[8] stratified group interests, ties to the motherland, the eruption of Indian nationalist discourses, and the internal political climate, to name only a few.[9]

In post-independence Malaysia and Singapore, language has come to constitute one such major infrastructural and cultural factor of differentiation. In Malaysia, the turn to indigenous Malay as the national language necessarily ushered the former colonial tongue to the back door of the political and social arena. However, unlike other minority languages such as Tamil and Mandarin, English has continued to boast of a certain degree of elitism in its 'internationality.' Nonetheless, more than a hundred million people now 'speak the local and national language, Malay, with greater ease than they did English.'[10] Yet to the diasporic subject who is often neither completely 'at home' in the mother tongue (be it Tamil, Hindi, Urdu, etc.) nor the 'step-mother tongue'[11] (English), the most obvious signifier of the irreversibility of change and irrecoverability of the past can be said to manifest itself linguistically.

A cursory glance, such as the scope of this study will permit, at the complex linguistic and cultural context of South-East Asia is indispensable to an understanding of Singaporean and Malaysian literature in English. Suffice it to say that one of the most striking features in the content and criticism of Malaysian and Singaporean literature in English is the polemics of language itself. In the multilingual South-East Asian context, a literary work's linguistic medium says much about a writer's orientation to his/her community. Though the English language carries its by now familiar resonance as a colonial tongue in this region, it has come to occupy considerably different positions in its 'minority' or 'official' status in post-independence Malaysia and Singapore, respectively.

The English-Language Novel: The Discursive Medium of a Minority Elite?

The prominence of present-day Malaysia's linguistic minorities in the production of English language literature is itself a conspicuous reminder of the linguistically aligned politics of identity therein. In fact, it would seem that among South Asian diasporic writers in Malaysia, it is writers of Hindu background who produce the majority of English language literary texts.[12] Although he seems to overstate the case, T. Wignesan rightly foregrounds the distinct correlation between a writer's religious background and his/her language of choice in the context of this Islamic republic: 'Where race is synonymous with religion, it is hardly surprising that language remains the point of contention of both ... In a land where the national and living tongue is Malay, the English language offers a refuge: it is the religion of he who chooses to write in it.'[13]

Singapore tells a very different story than its parent Malaysian society. In the island nation's official policy of multiracialism, sociologist John Clammer states that there is a 'deliberate heightening of ethnic aware-ness through the imposition of a scheme of social classification that re-quires every citizen ... to have a race, and to have it in what is officially expected to be an unambiguous way.'[14] In Singaporean taxonomy, 'race' combines ethnicity and language, so that, officially speaking, there exist Mandarin-speaking Chinese, Tamil-speaking Indians, Malay-speaking Malays, and English-speaking 'others' (that is, Europeans, Eurasians, Arabs, and so on). Tamil is identified as one of the four official languages in Singapore because, as in the Malaysian context, it is the language spoken by the dominant Tamil community.

In what has proved to be a relatively harmonious multiracial state, it is fair to say that cultural and linguistic marginalization is less acutely manifested in Singaporean society than it is elsewhere. Nevertheless, the emphasis on one language group over another necessarily creates exclu-sions and gaps in Singapore's 'quadratomy' or 'four-races' model.[15] For instance, the Chinese-dominant body politic has, according to most ob-servers of Singaporean society, tended to privilege Mandarin over and above other Chinese languages as well as the other officially acknow-ledged linguistic groups. In this regard, Clammer speaks of 'a basically Chinese cultural bias'[16] in Singaporean society.

While Clammer foregrounds the Chinese cultural bias prevalent in Singapore, literary critics foreground the English cultural bias in the literary arena. This cultural bias has appeared in what is the relatively nascent stage of Singaporean English literature itself.[17] For instance, the Singaporean establishment had traditionally envisaged English as a tech-nical medium or one of international finance, which was to be kept sep-arate from the Asian-based languages of cultural expression. Though English has pervaded most public spheres of communication, it occupies a tenuous hold on Singaporean cultural consciousness. Shirley Geok-Lin Lim, for one, speaks of the hierarchical register of English as a language that 'is not in actuality either a neutral or a bridge language except in a rather simple-minded use of the terms.'[18] When it comes to English language literary production in Singapore, Lim asserts that one must take into consideration the fact that the majority of writers who use English as a literary medium 'belong to the small English-educated elite whose interests are inextricably bound up with governmental, bureaucratic aims.'[19]

Conversely, Lim convincingly suggests that literary critics have thus far 'overlooked' the Singaporean English-language literary tradition itself because it is most often assessed by 'Western ideals of aesthetic and grammatical standards, stylistic and formal achievements derived wholly from the canon and traditions of British and American Literature.'[20] There is an interesting debate here where Lim (herself a creative writer and scholar) and Peter Hyland stand on opposite sides of the fence. While Lim argues that Singaporean English literature needs to break free from Western-imposed standards of canonicity, and forge its own literary identity, Hyland argues that Singaporean literature can only achieve such a status if it is 'evaluated by non-Singaporean critics' and if the 'voices of Singaporean critics be heard more widely beyond the national boundaries.'[21] Hyland's underlying assumption that a wider readership, like a wider base of criticism, takes local literatures out of small, self-reflexive literary circles stands to reason. In fact, as I have expressed in my introductory chapters, it is precisely the desire to facilitate such a process (widening our own base of criticism to include other local literary traditions) that motivates this study. However, Lim's suggestion that Singaporean English literature can and should come-of-age on its own terms does not preclude the possibility of international exposure; rather, Lim's concern, rightly so, is that what underpins Hyland's argument is the notion that only those local works that are subject to the critical scrutiny of a Western readership and its evaluative methods will garner or even merit international recognition. For Lim, as for other post-colonial writers, such a prospect is necessarily fraught with irony since it is by now a truism that anglophone writers from regions where English is a vestige of colonial rule in an otherwise polyglot society are, at the very least, wholly self-conscious about the aesthetic and other trappings of writing in a borrowed language at the expense of one's mother tongue.

What the two very different contexts of Malaysia and Singapore invariably reveal, therefore, is that English is hardly a neutral language in either national context. To complicate matters, English is often the preferred literary medium not simply for those writers seeking to reach an international audience, but also, as Wignesan suggests, for those wishing to make a local statement that often runs counter to national interests. Maniam himself seems determined to change local attitudes to English-language writing: 'For those of us who are involved in this business, the task seems to be ... to produce more literature in English, so that students in the Malaysian education system can realise that being a writer in this language and in this country is not a foreign thing.'[22] In other words, though the colonial resonance of English is common to both regions, the different ways in which English is institutionalized and deployed in Malaysia and Singapore speaks as much of each national culture as it does of their shared histories of British rule.[23] Highlighting a further delineation between the rural and urban populace, Wong Ming Yook's 2000 survey of Malaysian English fiction draws the following portrait of English-language usage in the country:

> The move downward from a common administrative language to a language used by an urban minority has meant that users and writers of English have become increasingly marginalized; simultaneously, English has contributed to an increasingly fragmented context in which it stands alongside other local (and limited) vernaculars such as Tamil and Chinese. Most speakers of English are educated and middle-class urban dwellers. Many, though not all, of them are non-Malays who may have little access to their own native tongues, or most probably prefer instead the internationality of English as a means of effective communication, though they are familiar enough with Malay as the medium of communication locally.[24]

Critics concur that Malaysian and Singaporean English literature began in the 1940s and 1950s, prior to the region's political split in 1965. Authors Catherine Lim, Shirley Geok-Lin Lim, and Kirpal Singh refer to the nascent stage of Singaporean English literature not so much in chronological terms but in terms of its recent distancing from Western canonical standards and also in terms of its recent emergence in novel form. While Sino-Singaporean Catherine Lim's short story collection *Little Ironies: Stories of Singapore* (1978) was popular among local readers, Philip Jeyaratnan's *First Loves* (1987), a short story collection, and the novel *Raffles Place Ragtime* (1988) were the first works of fiction by an Anglo-Indian to achieve commercial success. Jeyaratnam would eventually settle in Canada, and author a second novel, *Abraham's Promise*

(1995). In Malaysia, too, the first novel by and about the South Asian diaspora was penned by the Eurasian writer Lloyd Fernando (who was born in
the Ceylon of the 1920s). The author of two novels, *Scorpion Orchid* (1976)
and *Green is the Colour* (1993), Fernando, unlike K.S. Maniam, focuses on
the volatile era of the 1950s and 1960s which saw numerous outbreaks of
interracial conflict, rather than on the historical genesis or cultural realities of the diasporic community itself. Both Jeyaratnam and Fernando's
works attempt to capture the multiracial spectrum of contemporary
Malaysian and Singaporean society, respectively.

Though one cannot as yet speak of a growing tradition of novel writing
by women of South Asian origin (as one can in the Caribbean and South
African context), it is worth noting that the Malay-language novel can
boast a long and active tradition of novel writing by women, such as Salmi
Manja's *Hari Mana Bulan Mana* (1960; *Which Day, Which Month*), Abidah
Amin's *Seroja Masih di Kolam* (1968; *The Lotus Is Still in the Pond*), and
Khadijah Hashim's *Merpati Putih Terbang Lagi* (1979; *The Last Days of an
Artist*), or Fatimah Busu's Kepulangan (1980; *Homecoming*). In terms of
English-language novels, Rani Manicka's *The Rice Mother* (2002) is the first
published by an Indo-Malaysian woman, and certainly the first to chronicle female diasporic experience through the structure of a multigenerational saga. The novel also bridges Ceylon and Malaysia, which speaks of
Manicka's own Tamil-Ceylonese ancestry. In the trope of an arranged
marriage which sends a young girl, Lakshmi, away from her homeland,
the novel charts her development in a multiracial Malay society in the first
half of the twentieth century, including the witnessing of a young daughter's rape by occupying Japanese troops during the Second World War. A
common feature found in diasporic novels is the tribute to the grandmother figure. Manicka's description of her own grandmother as a woman
with 'indomitable energy'[25] seems to be the main source of inspiration for
her first novel, which received the prestigious Commonwealth Writers'
Prize in 2003 for South-East Asia and the South Pacific region. Manicka
has since penned a second novel, *Touching Earth* (2004).[26]

Kirpal Singh, a scholar and poet of considerable repute in his native
Singapore, has also authored several works of short fiction. Interestingly,
Singh reveals the same kind of insistence on ethnic and religious diversity among diasporic South Asians that one finds across the diaspora (one
remembers Nazareth's insistence on Goan difference, as well as Persaud's
description of local ethnic diversity in her native Indo-Trinidadian township). Similarly, in his short story 'Jaspal,' Singh complicates the quadratic axis within which Tamils are favoured in Singapore, at least in terms

of official government policy, by foregrounding the Sikh minority: 'His parents had instilled in him the fundamental belief that he was very different from the Malays, Tamils, Seranees, Chinese, and others of all description that lived in the same kampong.'[27] As Singh suggests, though drama and poetry have preceded the diasporic South Asian's penchant for creative writing, 'it is in the fiction that Indianness has most manifested itself.'[28]

The Power of the 'Word-Wallah': The Way Out of Servitude

Both K.S. Maniam and Gopal Baratham are third-generation diasporic subjects whose grandparents made the initial migration overseas and whose parents were born in British-ruled Malaya. Both also belong to the majority Tamil community of diasporic South Asians. Born in 1942 in Bedong, Kedah, West Malaysia, Maniam continues to reside in his country of birth. He has produced a multigenre corpus of poetry, short stories, plays, and novels. His three novels to date are *The Return* (1981), *In a Far Country* (1993), and *Between Lives* (2003). Born in 1935 on the island of Singapore, Baratham continued to reside in his country of birth until his recent death in 2003. He has also had a prestigious literary career as the author of several short story collections and three novels, including his first work *A Candle or the Sun* (1991), *Sayang* (1991), and *Moonrise, Sunset* (1996). As the most prolific English-language authors of Malaysia and Singapore to date, Maniam and Baratham thematize the issue of language in their respective polyglot societies. In Maniam's *The Return*[29] and Baratham's *A Candle or the Sun*,[30] the English language takes centre stage in the protagonist's growing understanding of his own place as an ethnic 'other' in his multiracial world.

In Maniam's Bildungsroman, the process of anglicization by means of a colonial education has a paradoxical effect on the protagonist, Ravi. On the one hand, it affords him a way out of caste divisions and the economic privations of an immigrant family whose beginnings can be traced back to one brave soul who appeared 'suddenly out of the horizon, like a camel, with nothing except some baggage and three boys in tow.'[31] On the other hand, his vocation as an English teacher implicates him in the dissemination of imperial ideology and ironically marginalizes him from the indigenous population and the Tamil-speaking community simultaneously.

In Baratham's *Kunstlerroman*, the writer-protagonist, Hernando Perera, discerns that language is quickly turned into a discourse of power when deployed (be it as a political tool or an aesthetic product) to hem in the complex fabric of individual and cultural identity. This realization assumes greater significance for the Singaporean writer who resides in a city-state[32] where 'the voice of government is loud and clear, the hand of government strong and perceived to be authoritarian and omnipresent.'[33] For both Maniam and Baratham's first-person narrators, therefore, a meaningful articulation of selfhood and nationhood necessitates a twofold approach to language: first by divesting the colonizer's language of its hierarchical systems of representation; and second by pushing the limits of language to more fully represent a cross-cultural imagination that is 'capable of both responsible and creative dissent.'[34]

Maniam's first novel draws heavily on several autobiographical elements, such as the central symbolic figure of Ravi's grandmother and his own profession as an English teacher/university professor. As Margaret Young states, 'While Maniam has refuted the view that his work is "autobiographical," attributing affinities to "coincidences" rather than "events," his writing is clarified in incalculable ways by an understanding of his life.'[35] Indeed, the semirural setting of The Return and its focus on a caste- and class-stratified Tamil community whose livelihood was once closely tied to the rubber plantation estates not only reflects Maniam's childhood in western Malaysia but also speaks of indentured existence in the region. His first novel sets the stage for much of his fiction in characterizing diasporic experience as an often uneasy tension between the tightly woven social patterns and cultural codes of a relatively segregated community and his protagonist's desire to enter 'a larger area of consciousness ... so as to emphasise the common bonds and concerns that illuminate the large and often bewildering impulse to be human.'[36]

Maniam's short story 'Arriving' helps preface his first novel in bringing to the fore the complex relationship between language and diasporic identity in the process of self-definition.[37] In this story, Maniam's central character, Krishnan, must come to terms with the exclusionary labels of indenture/migrancy that continue to alienate him from wider Malaysian society in a post-colonial era. In the following passages, for instance, Krishnan attempts to reckon with the fact that his friend has resorted to calling him a *pendatang*, a pejorative Malay word used to classify non-Malay peoples as permanent outsiders:

> What did it mean, *pendatang?* Arrivals? Illegals? ...
> He tried to recall his father's memories of his voyage out to Malaysia but his mind was choked with some strange obstruction ... Yes, it had been his determination that had kept him innocent of his father's experiences. He

had decided, when he became aware of his budding consciousness, not to
be influenced by other people's memories and nostalgia. He clawed at familiarity. But he only floated, set adrift by this new uncertainty ...
    He struggled against the dark waters of uncertainty for a long time.
Many times he was sucked into a fathomless fear, but, finally, he rose to the
surface, strengthened ...[38]

In grappling with the meaning of the word, Krishnan is forced to confront his immigrant history and, by extension, to immerse himself in the
alienating metaphors of the indentured labourer's arduous journey
across the *kala pani* (alluded to as the 'dark waters'). In so doing, Krishnan
reenvisions his Malaysian identity as one which is connected to the 'elsewhere' of his ancestor's homeland, without the incumbent stigmatiza-
tion of the 'outsider.' Krishnan thus reinvents the term in turning the
image of cultural displacement into a transcendental mobility of spirit
and mind: '*Pendatang*. One who arrives. One who goes through different
experiences to reach the most enlightening knowledge, he thought.'[39]
This revisionist process parallels his attempt to make the 'word,' like the
new world itself, his own, and to participate in reevaluating and reshaping its systems of meaning production.
    Published over a decade before the above story, *The Return* is the au-
thor's first novel-length attempt to give voice to the proverbial *pendatang*.
The protagonist Ravi similarly embarks on an imaginative return to the
moment of his ancestor's arrival on foreign soil. Interestingly, for Ravi,
the attempt at memorialization does not begin with the anxiety of loss
(signified by the loss of one's mother tongue or the other markers of
ethnic identity) but with a conscious reckoning of the discursive stronghold of the vocabularies of indenture on diasporic consciousness. In this
regard, the Malay construct of the *pendatang*[40] is once again decoded and
divested of its connotations of cultural and racial outsidership, a deconstructive gesture that includes the decontamination of language from its
racist markers and the subsequent reformulation of the genealogy of
migration in the self-defining coda of a newly adopted language.
    Ironically, Ravi's narrative is constructed in the language (that is, the
colonial 'stepmother tongue') that has come to rigidly define him as
another kind of cultural outsider, a colonized subject. The protagonist's
orientation to the colonial language and culture is further problematized by his diasporic identity as an ethnic and linguistic minority. As the
product of a colonial education, Ravi has to struggle to articulate a
heterogeneous Malaysian identity in a language that 'speaks' neither of

his Tamil roots nor of his Malaysian cultural reality. Ravi's connection to the past has therefore been doubly compromised by what Ngũgĩ describes as the two-pronged aim of the 'colonialist imposition of a foreign language ... as the destruction or deliberate undervaluing of a people's culture, their arts, dances, religions, history, geography, education, orature and literature, and the conscious elevation of the language of the coloniser.'[41] Maniam's first novel is thus quintessentially post-colonial in its critical assessment of assimilationist colonial practices. Maniam's protagonist's initial response to English is reminiscent of Frantz Fanon's apprehension of the colonial language as an assault on the cultural psyche – an assault, as he states, on 'local cultural originality' by 'the language ... that is, the culture of the mother country.'[42]

Consequently, the first casualties of Ravi's uprooting from a Tamil to an English school system are the folkloric and religious narratives of his grandmother, the pioneering family member, the first to arrive on foreign soil. Referred to as 'Periathai, the Big Mother,'[43] Ravi's grandmother assumes mythic proportions because of the courageous nature of her migration; she exemplifies the early stages of indenture during which women often migrated independently and at great personal risk. She is further mythologized for her connection to the sacred ancestral language, one which brings to life the gods and goddesses, folklore, and sacred texts of Hinduism and the oral history that animates the individual's journey. Indeed, like the indigenization of the signs and symbols of South Asian culture in the Caribbean landscape, Periathai's 'saffron-scented, death-churned memories, stories, experiences and nostalgia' are shown to have infused the foreign 'fringes and foothills'[44] of the Malaysian jungle with 'the thick spiritual and domestic air she must have breathed there, back in some remote district in India.'[45]

The increasing distance between Ravi and his grandmother's generation, like his increasing distance from his mother tongue, severs the physical and psychic link between the originary homeland and country of settlement. Ravi's English education is accordingly described as a violent uprooting from all that is familiar. Consequently, he is thrust into a state of culture shock as jarringly as 'the thunder and lightning that ripped the sky and destroyed a calm evening.'[46] This is because Ravi's early Tamil education immersed him in a script that made accessible the strangely familiar symbols of his South Asian heritage as well as the immediate landscape of his 'knowable world' of 'shopkeepers, goldsmiths, newspaper-vendor, *chettiar* and labourer he saw daily.'[47] Tamil functions as both a mythic and a living language because it evokes the diasporic subject's double consciousness, one in which the signs of loss and continuity co-exist.

In contrast, English appears to him as 'strange, squiggly marks' which paint an entirely foreign landscape that 'bewildered and fascinated.'[48] English language acquisition renders him twice-removed from the homeland, a process of separation which first began with his ancestor's historic migration, and continues as a figurative voyage into the wholly alien/ alienating terrain of a new people and, with them, a new language community. Indeed, the more infused Ravi is in the discourse of 'Englishness' and its attendant symptoms of anglophilia, the more alienated he becomes from the language, customs, history and identity of the country's numerous other ethnic populations. This double alienation positions Ravi within an awkward, anxiety-ridden third space that configures his identity within the semantics of negation: he is neither English nor indigenous Malay, nor fully recognizable to himself and others as a Tamil, for even the most familiar cultural signs, such as his mother's face or his peers' boyish banter, begin to seem unrecognizable, if not 'savage.'[49]

Most profound, perhaps, is the process of deracination brought about by English-language immersion. Maniam likens the colonial education and its discursive assault on ethnic identity to the lingering effect of the fairy tale on a child's impressionable mind. Like the child in the throes of suspended disbelief, Ravi and his school-going peers are frightened into a kind of speechless submission given their willing acceptance of the school mistress's imperial authority. Ravi's English teacher, Miss Nancy, is treated as a sadistic mouthpiece for the civilizing mission in her terrifyingly realistic renditions of the fairy tale. In her sinister flare for animating the grotesque, Miss Nancy reads the fairy tales to a captivated audience, thus whipping into submission 'the savages' in her charge: 'Miss Nancy reasoned, cajoled, jolted, mocked, "feruled" and commanded. The boys, touched, persuaded, pampered and compelled, obeyed and changed.'[50]

Ravi finds himself trapped in the language that symbolizes his peculiar predicament as the excluding subject who gradually dissociates himself from family and friends (his recognizable world), as well as the excluded subject among a European elite, a majority indigenous Malay population and an increasingly incomprehensible Tamil community. Ravi's condition reflects Maniam's own predicament as an English language writer. This is because, as Wong Ming Yook rightly suggests,

> In fact, English serves quite well as the language to carry the ideas and metaphors of alienation occurring within migrant communities. Its alienness

lends to its use a peculiar suitability, a deliberate dissonance and distancing between text and reader that only emphasises the extent of alienation experienced. For the Malaysian writer in English, this is amplified in the content of the writing itself, which is usually to do with the migrant consciousness struggling for integration and authenticity.[51]

However, Ravi's discomfort arises not only from the gradual loss of his mother tongue but also from his growing awareness that cultural discourse carries with it the exclusionary signatures of group identity. Maniam deftly juxtaposes his childhood English teacher's sinister tones with the equally discriminatory vernacular of his Tamil schoolmates. In other words, be it in his peers' mockery of Ravi's 'English' affectations in what is their own 'broken English,' in Miss Nancy's verbal assaults, or in his community's recourse to Tamil to abuse or alienate him, Ravi states: 'I wasn't comfortable in all the talk that stormed over my head.'[52]

Kirpal Singh's observation about the diasporic writer in Singapore applies equally to the Malaysian context: 'Though not frequently bitter or even cynical, many of the new literary works indicate a growing need to break free from bonds brought over from India through direct, intimate contact.'[53] As Maniam's novel demonstrates, however, India represents only one of the many cultural/historical narratives which inform the diasporic writer's consciousness in the process of self-definition.[54] Here again, language is the primary symbol of a heterogeneous identity that speaks of the multiply positioned diasporic subject whose cultural and historical points of reference are as numerous as the speech registers that constitute his heteroglossic world. As Anne Brewster suggests, *The Return* evokes Mikhail Bakhtin's concept of heteroglossia as a 'multiplicity of voices' which are 'engaged in an internal "dialogue" with each other. Because these voices are drawn from variously stratified groups, the novel is the site of struggle among socio-linguistic points of view.'[55]

In keeping with the motif of imaginative returns to the moment of the immigrant's arrival on foreign shores, a poem titled 'Full Circle' punctuates Ravi's narrative. The journey motif and the alienating effects of a foreign language combine to produce the diasporic narrator's acute sense of disconnection from his past and the simultaneous impulse to break free from the repetitious cycles of history and its master narratives (be they in the alienating voice of the colonial culture, the host culture, the diasporic community, or the motherland). In Maniam's oeuvre, motifs and metaphors are overtly or indirectly overlaid with the complex religious symbols of the author's Hindu-Tamil heritage. The journey motif is steeped in the Hindu principle of reincarnation, 'the eternal story of arrival and departure.'[56] Though many critics have interpreted Maniam's journey motif as a spiritual reconnection to 'Mother India,' Maniam seems less interested in hearkening back than in calling attention to 'how Indian religious belief can be ... modified to suit new lands, peoples and customs.'[57] Moreover, he employs Hindu symbols as they pertain to the shared fabric of human experience. In this sense, reincarnation metaphorically evokes the continuous nature of identity-formation as a 'motioning' toward new contexts that continually accrue meaning in the ongoing process of human contact, cultural exchange, and a person's own materially changing circumstances.

Ravi's dispassionate process of dissociation from family, community, and culture seems to situate him on the side of the dominant colonial power. However, Ravi's insertion of his ancestors' narrative of migration and survival into the 'master narrative' counters the hegemonic effects of the step-mother tongue. On the one hand, then, the poem that signals the end of Ravi's narrative of 'return,' brings the protagonist 'full circle' to the realization that 'words will not serve' the 'cultureless.'[58] On the other hand, Ravi's diasporic poetics of identity formation as a continual process serves to break the cycle of hegemony that 'imprisoned [his] flesh, [his] thoughts.'[59] In contrast, Ravi's father's attempt to transplant India, in the form of land ownership and the obsessive construction of a house designed to resurrect the signs and symbols of the originary culture, ends on a tragic note. As Ravi comes to witness his father's obsession with the past, he sees that the new land calls for alternate ways to 'belong,' not through repetition but renewal. In this endeavour, Ravi fully acknowledges his father's impassioned struggle 'to drive some stake into the country.'[60] However, he simultaneously releases his ancestors' understanding of permanence through the signs of nostalgia and loss, arriving instead at an understanding of diasporic consciousness as a 'series of narratives, sets of metaphors with which to begin dismantling concepts of permanence as the desirable condition of being.'[61]

Unlike Maniam's familiar diasporic setting of a relatively close-knit community, Baratham's South Asian diasporic characters are unique insofar as they are citizens of the world's most urbanized nation, who consequently function as detached metropolitan beings. In fact, Baratham himself can be said to write from 'the consciousness of an English-educated, and to some extent detribalized, Tamil-Singaporean.'[62] In his case, the absence of community in his novels not only reflects the anonymity inherent in city life, but also appears to be an implicit critique of the Singapore establishment's drive to manufacture an alternate national 'community' through state-sanctioned policy. As noted in Sharon Siddique and Nirmala PuruShotam's study, *Singapore's Little India*, 'one of PAP's main alterations of geopolitical space has been to attempt to racially integrate otherwise segregated communities in public housing estates.'[63] In *A Candle or the Sun*, the process of deterritorialization is alluded to in Perera's domicile within one of the many 'state-subsidized housing estates.'[64] The interrelated effects of deterritorialization and 'detribalization' on Baratham's (South Asian) characters is reinforced in the character of Alaga (a product of the hopeful author-protagonist Perera's creative imagination), who not only prefers voyeurism over actual human contact but also finds that his Chinese neighbour knows more about his South Asian heritage (ironically represented in her touristic dalliance with Yoga and Sanskrit) than he does.

In Baratham's subsequent novels, it is possible to see not only more explicitly 'South Asian' characters, but also a more scathing satirization of the cultural hypocrisies prevalent across Singapore's multiracial communities. Indeed, by *Moonrise, Sunset* (1996), Baratham thematizes and critiques the more fundamentalist strains of religious discourse imported by such organizations as Arya Samaj to Singapore's Hindu community. In *Moonrise, Sunset*, Baratham even offers a partial glimpse into the famous 'Serangoon Road' community of Singapore's Little India. As Philip Holden asserts, the particular divestment of a racialized subjectivity in much of Baratham's fiction is in and of itself, a politicized reaction to a nationalist policy that quantifies identity in fixed racial and ethnic terms.[65]

The above observations notwithstanding, the absence of explicitly South Asian diasporic themes in Baratham's first two novels could also reflect what some critics refer to as a common pattern of self-censorship in Singaporean writing. Catherine Lim, for one, points out, 'Any topic that could be construed as even remotely touching upon the sensitive issues of race, language and religion in this multiethnic society is likely to be self-censored out at the manuscript stage.'[66] If this is true of *A Candle or the Sun*, it is only true in the most ironic sense, for the novel is itself an unabashed critique of the mutually reinforcing patterns of self-censorship and state censorship. According to Peter Hyland, Baratham was himself at the centre of controversy when he publicly denounced the Singapore National Development Council for denying *A Candle or the Sun* its due recognition because of what he deemed its unease with the novel's political content.[67] What Baratham's novel foregrounds, then, is the monopoly that the state implicitly holds over cultural discourse.

While Maniam writes in a minority language and from a minority perspective, Baratham writes in the language that has come to express a national literature from his relatively integrated position in contemporary Singaporean society. In *A Candle or the Sun*, the English language is shown to be used at every level of communication, both in its official capacity and as the local lingua franca. In fact, Baratham's first-person narrator-writer, Hernando Perera, takes great liberties with language, engaging in word play and poking fun at those whose speech patterns betray even the slightest traces of artifice or mimicry. The pre-eminent status of English notwithstanding, Baratham is also aware of the obvious colonial import of English, both in cultural and literary terms – at least insofar as it presupposes external standards at the expense of local ingenuity and creolized expression.

Baratham accordingly attempts to stretch the cultural parameters of English beyond its privileged and politically enshrouded function. To this end, *A Candle or the Sun* (1991), *Sayang* (1991), and *Moonrise, Sunset* (1996) explore the seedy underbelly of Singapore's officiously run establishment, while also raising culturally taboo subjects, such as AIDS, homophobia, illicit sexual behaviour, the inflexibility of moral codes, and the question of censorship. *A Candle or the Sun* immediately exposes its author's Foucaultian reading of the complicit discourses of power in contemporary Singaporean society. Indeed, in a work that is set within a city-state – which is, itself, an artifice of sorts, at least as a community born out of the imperial machinery, it is not surprising that *A Candle or the Sun* invariably evokes a post-modernist reading of identity as a highly mutable construct.

In this regard, it is also of little surprise that Baratham is the most experimental novelist among the authors under study; drawing on postmodern techniques such as metafiction, Baratham strives to draw parallels between the writer's manipulation of language for aesthetic ends and the state's deployment of language for ideological ends. In fact, Perera's development as an artist unfolds as a self-conscious acknowledgment of the way language can apprehend the complex fabric of experience as much as it can flatten cultural and national identities. Baratham's most poignant attack on the dissemination of state ideology is found in the guise of his protagonist. In struggling to come to terms with his role as a writer in Singaporean society, Hernando Perera questions the point at which creative expression is hindered by a state in which culture/ cultural production is part and parcel of governance and state policy. It is significant, then, that Perera keeps his creative interests separate from his professional life in the awareness that an 'official' writing career could be compromised in the service of state interests. Baratham thus relies heavily on speech patterns as expressions of character development. Moreover, his multiracial cast of characters is often rendered through linguistic rather than ethnic variation, since they are shown to comprise a polyvocal portrait of accents, lexical affectations, and semantic idiosyncrasies that are unique to Singaporean society. For example, Perera's Chinese-Indian wife, Sylvie, is said to talk in 'mismatched clichés which gave her conversation a jokiness and ambiguity.'[68] In other words, Sylvie's linguistic hybridity mirrors her ambiguous racial lineage. Perera favours Sylvie's speech as its uncontrived brand of interlingual mixing is a symbolic extension of her sympathetically hybrid character. As Baratham himself comments on the issue of cultural and racial hybridity, 'I would like everybody to be multi-ethnic ... My ex-wife is Chinese and my children are mixtures. I do find hybrids softer because I think they are more uncertain.'[69] Indeed, while Baratham is keenly aware of the different social registers of English across class and ethnic backgrounds, his fiction celebrates the diverse cultural composition of Singapore's multilingual population. While this is evident throughout Baratham's oeuvre, it is particularly pronounced in *Moonrise, Sunset*, in which the narrator goes so far as to provide an etymology of the particle 'lah' (an abbreviation of 'Allah') – an interlingual trait that is echoed across the Islamic-influenced Malaysian peninsula. In Baratham's oeuvre, therefore, linguistic hybridity is most expressive of a creolized population and culture that is nonetheless contained in distinct categories of ethnic identity.

Conversely, the discourse of officialdom as a discretely compartmentalized hierarchy of language groups is exposed as a vestige of imperial ideology and power. Echoing Lim's critique of scholarly practices steeped in imported Western standards, Baratham also throws a direct punch to the establishment's favouring of 'a version of British English over local, Singlish versions of the language.'[70] Though 'Singlish' (the local hybridized version of English) is relatively absent in this first novel, the multilingual, syncretic character of Singaporean society that the novel brings to life stands in direct contrast to speech patterns that betray an individual's engagement in colonial mimicry. Perera's parents, for instance, second-generation Singaporeans who grew up during the colonial heyday, speak in a language that smacks of cultural artifice and affectation. For one, Perera is irritated by his mother's habit of imitating the melodramatic scenes of 1950s Hollywood films and by his father's brand of intellectual showmanship. Indeed, Perera perceives his father, a retired school teacher given to quoting Shakespeare, as a 'long-winded, somewhat pedantic phoney.'[71] Perera's parents' speech is little better than pastiche, an empty, almost farcical signifier of a colonized mindset, a legacy of Empire that Perera himself perceives to be the white elephant in the new national culture.

In a racially and linguistically delineated society, Baratham reveals the extent to which discourses of power are quite literally embedded in other kinds of accents and linguistic affectations. Perera's Chinese boss, Chuang, speaks in Confucian aphorisms that reflect a Chinese education system of rote learning in the 'teaching of ancient ways.' Perera further exposes the distinct ideological rift between Chuang's Confucian teachings and the language of corporate profiteering, or the globalized context of late capitalism to which they are applied: 'We must flung [sic] out Western values leading to moral decay, unemployment and social welfare. No more imitating falsity. Right here in furniture department ... we install traditional Asian values ... Here we recommence true Asian spirit of co-operation and co-prosperity. Vanquish cut-throat competition from Manila, Jakarta and Thailand.'[72] Furthermore, Chuang's anti-imperialist/ nationalist discourse of Asian fraternity is rendered suspicious in light of his racially and socially dominant position as a member of the Chinese-Singaporean 'management': 'In Chuang's manner this morning was the conviction not merely that he spoke the truth but that he spoke the truth over which he had been given proprietary rights.'[73]

Baratham's characterization of Samson Alagaratnam, one of the few explicitly ethnic Indian characters in his first novel, is the object of satire given his unquestioning subscription to state rhetoric. Samson's cultural and intellectual hypocrisy is first made evident in the footnote Perera provides about what he perceives to be his friend's apostasy, for Samson is a Christian convert who rejected his Hindu faith 'to be part of what he saw as the established order.'[74] As the now established 'authority' in English literature and in his high-ranking position in the Ministry of Culture, Samson's rise to the top is attributed to his ability to mimic the appropriate manners of speech/discourse required for the job at hand, rather than any self-proclaimed talents as a 'word-wallah.'[75] Perera deftly describes Alagaratnam's profession using the Hindu/Urdu suffix 'wallah' (the equivalent of the English '-ist'), playfully drawing attention to the same ethnic background that his friend has tried to erase. Referring to Alagaratnam as a 'word-wallah,' the one who specializes in words or language, Baratham aligns Samson's 'wordmanship' with the establishment's attempt to control cultural production.

Since Perera is himself a word-wallah (as a writer of fiction), Samson is an obvious foil to the narrator-author, whose unique ability to shift effort-lessly across different language registers (which might be likened to the notion of the 'Creole continuum' as a form of linguistic code-switching from Creole to Standard English) counters the establishment's desire to control the outlets for expression of its polyglot population. In contrast, Samson's terse, colourful phraseology echoes the establishment's ability to bedazzle the masses with catchy slogans. Thus, his jingoistic jargon ranges from the materialistic and banal – '"It's like you got bad breath, man, and nobody will get near you till they know you're chewing double mint"' – to the official party line – '"Multiracial harmony's the beat, right?"' As Perera explains, in Samson's world, creative expression 'had become a habit with which he disguised the intentions of his words, and the nastier these were the more colourful did his affectation become.'[76] Baratham's own linguistic flare can be seen in his skilful manipulation of the subtle shifts in tone – from the comical to the sinister or from the innocent to the vulgar – that mirror the almost imperceptible shifts be-tween the two levels of state discourse: the public and the 'classified.' When Perera presses his friend on the subject of police brutality, for example, Samson's usual idiomatic phraseology is couched in vulgar analogies and sadistic undertones which betray the more sinister side of a police state: '"Ain't this modern Singapore? We got electricity, boyyo, and ... refrigeration ... Once we stick a cat's wick into an ice-block it rarely lights up again."'[77]

To a great extent, Baratham struggles with the question of the public and private function of writing itself. The novel's 'frame-tale' structure mirrors the delineation between public and private spheres, just as Perera divides his own narrative between autobiography and fiction. For Perera, creative expression serves as a private outlet for a more or less conserva-tive imagination. His employment in the furniture section of a depart-ment store – a metonym for the highly structured social fabric of the nation itself – mirrors his personal credo to compartmentalize experience in the neurotic desire to manage the 'ungainly contours of events.'[78] Like the wintery 'Christmas dinner tableau' that Perera creates to please a tropics-bound clientele, Perera's writing is equally stilted by archetypes and artifice. In fact, Perera's evolution as an artist is contingent upon his eventual acceptance that the public and private, like imaginative and lived experience, cannot be so neatly separated: 'I had decided to compart-mentalize my life, to live in sealed rooms that had no communicating doors. But words made this impossible. They crept like mildew upon the walls, spreading from one room to the other, connecting them.'[79]

In this sense, the novel's metafictional quality stylistically evokes not only the tension between the public and private spheres of national discourse but also the delineation between the aesthetic and the social function of art. *A Candle or the Sun* thematizes the assertion by Singaporean author/scholar Shirley Geok-Lin Lim that the Singaporean novelist has traditionally restricted his/her writing to universal themes because of 'the writer's ideology of "art for art's sake" ; from the ideology of English as a world language, with its own set of Western, cosmopolitan values and removed from Asian identity.'[80] Ironically, then, there is some truth to Samson's criticism of Perera's pandering to an international, Western market at the expense of a local audience: '"Your stories make waves on the BBC, you group into anthologies of Asian writing, yet back in homesville you're Mr Unknown."'[81] Baratham appears critical of this trend, but is equally conscious of the fact that the turn away from the international toward the local is not an easy transition for the Singaporean writer. As Kirpal Singh notes, 'In a small tightly-knit society like Singapore, expression and exploration of sensitive issues ... is bound to encourage provocation ... The writer, therefore, always conscious of his role and more so of his duty, hesitates, and becomes necessarily cautious.'[82] Subsequently, Baratham questions the particular dilemma of the Singaporean writer as caught between the often unattainable expectations of the international marketplace and the implicit pressures at the local level to conform to national cultural standards.

When Perera is confronted by the very real consequences of intellectual honesty, he becomes aware of his own ineffectuality as an 'impressionistic and esoteric'[83] writer. Up to his encounter with the Children of the Book, a subversive youth-led Marxist organization, Perera is shown to be unaffected by the political import of language and communication: 'I have never felt inhibited by the censorship prevailing in Singapore, nor have I felt the urge for mass communication. However, the possibility that other people might miss what I did not require was not something that escaped me.'[84] True to his word, it is only when his own writing goes 'public' that Perera is able to see both the ideological deployment of language and its potential for agency and change.

It is in terms of the post-independence context that Malaysia and Singapore have so obviously parted ways. In Malaysia, the official language of communication is reflective of its Malay-dominant population. On the other hand, Singapore has adopted English as its lingua franca among a Chinese-dominant though multilingual population, a linguistic ploy that has certainly had its material benefits in a globalized economy but one that has caused considerable anxiety in the expression of Singaporean cultural consciousness. And it is within this complex and divergent linguistic, cultural, and political framework that Maniam and Baratham's novels emerge. Both writers were born during the tail-end of British rule and so are necessarily sensitive to the ideological underpinnings of the English language. Both writers are also of Tamil background and therefore enjoy a majority status among South Asian diasporic communities in the Malaysian peninsula. However, each writer has spent the bulk of his life in a post-colonial era which, as I have outlined above, signals the contrasting positions of peoples of Tamil/South Asian background in the Malaysian and Singaporean contexts as well as that of English language usage in each country.

The political import of language immediately comes to the fore as the common thematic thread that ties Maniam and Baratham's otherwise wholly different first novels together. Both writers are keenly aware of the historical and actual uses of language in the management of the polyglot and culturally diverse societies of Malaysia and Singapore. For Ravi, returns are not linear or reverse journeys to an ancestral past but a transhistorical motioning toward a more plural expression of nationhood, where an individual's mode of expression does not become the yardstick against which his or her emotional investment in and connection to land, people, and place is assessed. For Baratham, the call for a more honest expression of individual, cultural, and national identity seems worth the risk of admission if the alternative is to err on the side of caution in the illusive separation of political and creative life into discreet entities.

Indeed, both writers have attempted to push the limits of language in responding to the multiple and often conflicting demands of their cross-cultural backgrounds in which the borders of the mind, like the borders of the world, are increasingly porous. In this sense, Maniam and Baratham echo other post-colonial writers for whom cultural discourse is often weighted by the accumulative 'sighs of history'[85] and, conversely, for whom literature is the 'attempt to increase the sum of what it is possible to think.'[86] While I am not suggesting that either Maniam or Baratham experiment with the English language to the degree found in other post-colonial works, most notably that of their contemporary Salman Rushdie, I do think that they nonetheless subvert the potential of their 'step-mother tongue' to impose a diglossic or hegemonic cultural discourse over these pluri-ethno-linguistic national environments. Maniam does this thematically and symbolically, while

Baratham does so more explicitly in the interlingual mixing and obvious delight in word play that colours his writing.

For the diasporic subject/writer, language is both the most visible sign of loss (in its severance of ties to the originary culture) and the primary vehicle for self-definition. In a heteroglossic and multiracial environment, both Maniam and Baratham evoke a multiply positioned identity that sees in language a reflection of a collective, syncretic identity that is no less expressive of its richly varied and unique speech communities.

8 From the Ganges to the South Seas: Fiji as 'Fatal Paradise' in Satendra Nandan's *The Wounded Sea*

The Oriental Other in the 'South Seas'

Officially ceded to Queen Victoria as late as 1874, Fiji, one of the youngest colonies of the Empire, was also the last to receive indentured labourers from the Indian subcontinent. The first wave of labourers arrived on board the *Leonidas* in 1879, four decades after Mauritius received the very first group of *girmitiyas* in 1835 on the *Shah Allum*. Of course, Fiji, like other islands in the Pacific Rim, had seeped into the British imperial imagination as early as 1768, through the writings of Captain James Cook in his numerous expeditions across the Pacific Ocean. The colonial writing and travelogues of the period produced a relatively consistent ethnographic portrait of island societies. The islands captivated British readers over a century later, through the South Sea stories made famous by Robert Louis Stevenson. Non-fictional and fictional writing, including ship-board journalism, sailor's yarns, Robinsonades, and missionary tracts, combined to flavour the genre known as the South Sea adventure tale, which presented 'an idyllic island in the South Seas where the flower of English youth thwarts both cannibalism and savagery and exemplifies in their own loves Evangelical morality and the "message of empire."'[1] In fact, Stevenson's personal testimonies on the regenerative properties of life in the secluded archipelago, as well as his sympathetic accounts of the Pacific islanders' struggle for self-preservation against the licentious materialism of the European trader, rekindled romantic sensibilities.[2]

The infantilization of indigenous groups and the concomitant image of the tropical island as 1) either an Edenic playing field onto which imperial fantasies – sexual, spiritual, or material – could be easily projected, or 2) as a dystopic countersite to modernity, industrialization, and European ascendancy was itself the product of imperial cartographic and ethnographic practice. Anthropologist Gananath Obeyesekere notes that the 'South Seas' was, much like the Orient, a category of the European imagination rather than an oceanographic one.[3] Similarly, Michelle Keown notes, in *Postcolonial Pacific Writing*, that the British were not alone in their imaginative invention of Pacific island cultures. For example, French navigator Jules-Sebastien-César Dumont d'Urville 'introduced a systematized distinction between Polynesian and Melanesian races on the basis of skin colour.'[4]

Pseudoethnographic reportage of cannibalism and ritual human sacrifice, such as William Endicott's *Wrecked Among the Cannibals in Fiji* (penned between 1829 and 1832) or John Jackson's 1899 novel *Cannibal Jack*, usually vilified those seen to be engaged in anti-imperial aggression such as the Maori or Samoan, while those who gave themselves more readily to Christianity reinforced 'the pacific versus savage' binary, which has remained a caricature of indigenous peoples in the Americas as well. Obeyesekere exposes the persistence of colonial myths in contemporary anthropology and their overreliance on dubious 'empirical' data, such as quasi-ethnographic reportage or semifictional autobiographies, which forms the bulk of colonial accounts of the region and its peoples. Though Obeyesekere does not dispute the existence of ritual and symbolic forms of anthropophagy, he believes that cannibalism, like other predominant typologies about Pacific islanders, is an ideologically motivated imperial myth. Mel Gibson's cinematic epic *Apocalypto*,[5] which imaginatively depicts the tail-end of Mayan civilization, is a sad reminder of the extent to which indigenous societies are still filtered through imperial racial typology, pitting savagery-as-sadism against docility-as-prelapsarian innocence.

As social historians suggest, however, the latter vision of native islanders as spiritually untainted inhabitants of a paradise-on-earth resulted in a paternalistic protectionist colonial policy in Fiji. Brij V. Lal, in one of his numerous studies on the history of indentureship in Fiji, provides a critical rereading of the colonial climate and imperial mythos around which the indentured labourer came to form the backbone of the Fijian economy:

> The new colony, remote and reluctantly acquired, needed rapid economic development to sustain itself, but the conditions for it were lacking ... And Fijian labour had been effectively prohibited from commercial employment by Fiji's first governor, Sir Arthur Gordon, whose native policy required the Fijians to remain in their own traditional surroundings under the leadership of their chiefs, protected from the harmful effects of external contact. Bold

and imaginative and impressively connected to London, Gordon decided on a line of action that was to set the foundations of modern Fiji. Having settled on the plantation system as his preferred mode of economic development and sugar as the main crop ... Gordon chose Indian indentured labour whose success he had seen in Trinidad and Mauritius, where he had been governor before his Fiji assignment. European capital, Indian labour and Fijian land underpinned the Fijian economy in the century between cession and independence.[6]

This is the imaginative and administrative South Seas toward which the comparatively disfavoured colonized unit of the Oriental other, comprised of the incoming labour force, set sail in the late nineteenth century.

Subaltern Others and Native Paramountcy

In the first Indo-Fijian anthology (Subramani's *The Indo-Fijian Experience*), published to commemorate the centennial anniversary of Indian settlement in Fiji, the celebratory moment is tempered by the sentiment in the opening essay by Ahmed Ali that European imperial deception, betrayal, and the ensuing assault on the Indo-Fijian male *izzat* underline this diaspora's historical consciousness. As Ali argues, Indo-Fijian history is predicated on imperial deceit. Echoing Lal's rereading of colonial policy in the Pacific Rim, Ali suggests that though Fiji's first governor was the proponent of native paramountcy, he was equally attuned to imperial economic interests. In an attempt to balance protectionist policies and the need for labour if Fiji was to be turned into a viable plantation economy worthy of the Crown's investment, the colonial administration embarked on a campaign of empty promises designed to encourage Indian support for emigration to Fiji:

Indians saw equality as only possible through common franchise. For Fijians, Europeans and the colonial regime, common franchise spelt insecurity through a likelihood of Indian domination, and a menace to their own security. The origin of the problem lay with the inherent nature of colonialism, its double standards. When Indians were brought to Fiji they were promised equality ... So to obtain labour crucial to their Fijian policy and economic needs, the British were prepared to make promises on the assumption that the indefinite duration of their empire would enable them to manipulate situations in a manner making possible accommodation and adjustments that maintained law and order and simultaneously satisfied imperial needs.[7]

One such 'accommodation' was the practice of leasing out land to those who had served their *girmit* or contractual period of bonded labour. But unlike the Caribbean, where ex-labourers were able to assume legal ownership of land, here the Indo-Fijian was not offered similar privileges. And so the bitterness of betrayal began.

Ali and Lal suggest that the post-indenture period ushered in professional and commercial diversification, which included the arrival of free passengers of Gujarati and Punjabi origin at the turn of the century.[8] The once-bonded labourer now 'freed' only to occupy a subordinate position as a tenant farmer became the prevailing image of the diasporic Fijian. The growing sentiment became one of anxiety and bitterness in those who were encouraged to settle permanently in the new land by the very same regime that had denied them a sense of permanence, security, and belonging therein. Land rights and land ownership thus assume particular significance for people who live in the awareness that they are seeding, fertilizing, and harvesting a borrowed land for the patrimonial benefit of others. Referring to Raymond Pillai's Hindi-Fijian play *Adhuuraa Sapnaa* (*Shattered Dreams*), Vijay Mishra writes: 'The idea of permanence via ownership of land/house is a crucial signifier of diasporic lives.– a piece of earth that one can claim/reclaim as one's home is an enduring motif.'[9]

The concept of the 'reserve' has a very different meaning in Fiji than it has in North America where the 'reservation' is a reminder of racial apartheid and violated land treaties. In Fiji, land 'reserve' refers to the reverting of land to its original native chieftains at the end of a predetermined period of tenancy implemented in the colonial period; '83% of the land is native-owned.'[10] In Satendra Nandan's first and only novel to date, *The Wounded Sea* (1991), it is the protagonist-narrator's grandmother who, because of her status as a freed labourer, is shown to become the first to experience the anxiety brought about by the practice of land 'reserving.' Rather than see in her lush and plentiful orchard a thing of prosperity, pride, and beauty, the grandmother cautions: '"Too many cocknuts mean Fijian reserving the land one day," she explained. "Reserving" meant the reverting of land to the native Fijian owners, leaving the indentured labourers and their children landless."'[11] Moreover, the practice of reverting land to native chieftains is also shown to carry itself forward, where it marks an equally uncertain future for subsequent generations: 'Being the eldest, he had taken over the family inheritance – ten acres of native land on lease to my father until 1992.'[12]

The expiration date attached to land tenure not only creates an acute sense of dispossession in the adoptive land, but also becomes a form of emasculation within a patriarchal structure that is grounded in patrimonial laws. While the policy of 'reserving land' is one that surely has prevented in Fiji the kind of continued disenfranchisement meted out against indigenous groups in European settler societies, one can also see why it has created a feeling of betrayal among Indo-Fijians who have cultivated the greater portion of Fijian land for well over a century, where they have also raised families who span several generations. Where indenture has already involved an uprooting, the state of landlessness for a labour force whose raison d'être is intimately connected to the earth compounds the anxiety caused by the original displacement to the point of despair. This is certainly reflected in Nandan's poetry where the speaker usually mourns, through a haze of nostalgia for an idyllic motherland, the certainty of belonging that is denied to subsequent diasporic generations:

only the tree so deeply rooted
seems so loving, so infinitely free.[13]

In Fiji, then, the post-colonial paradigm of colonizer/colonized is most radically overturned, not only because the dyadic axis pits two historically subordinated groups against each other but because these groups had been, in imperial discourse and policy, constituted differently along a complex trajectory of pseudoscientific race theories. This radical rereading of post-colonial society is made all the more poignant in the Fijian context where an indigenous group, often infantilized and caricatured by imperial discourse as 'God's best – at least God's sweetest works,'[14] becomes the primary obstacle to the Oriental subaltern's assurance of political and social equality in the absence of the Mother Empire. Indeed, it is when the dyadic axis is activated to produce an exclusionary power dynamic that the fate of the Indo-Fijian is rendered tragic. Moreover, it is in the rude awakening of political and racial dispossession that the wound of colonial betrayal becomes most viscerally entrenched. So deep is the wound left in the wake of real or imagined dispossession that two hundred Indo-Fijians are said to have committed suicide since the 2000 coup which, in the ousting of the first democratically elected Indo-Fijian prime minister, violently doused the optimism of a population hoping for interethnic solidarity.[15]

Here, the 'coolie' finds himself living uneasily alongside the paternalistically protected indigene. In 1884, a colonial administrator remarked that 'the Fijians and Indians regard each other with unconcealed contempt and disgust.'[16] However, as Pio Manoa cautions, colonial and Western accounts of ethnic and native Fijian hostility and mistrust have typically reinforced the image of racial division without a concomitant assessment of its historical genesis, much less of the many instances of interethnic solidarity in Fiji's sociopolitical life. From his self-conscious perspective as the sole native Fijian voice included in Subramani's commemorative anthology, Manoa counterbalances his reading of Western bias with his own critical self-reflection on interethnic rivalry:

> The institutions within Fijian society, imposed, accepted or inherited, were meant to protect. In many ways, they overprotected, imposed a false security that the overprotected child is only now beginning to question because in his new awareness he feels they have hindered his development. The Fijian also needs to understand himself, and to be understood ... His fate as an individual and as a group is implicated in the fate of those who live on the other side of the fence, and he must enter with good will and imagination into their living reality.[17]

Sadly, individual and group solidarity has not readily translated itself into sound political action. Satendra Nandan's *The Wounded Sea* (1991) was written between the infamous coups in 1987 and 2000: the two coups of 1987 derailed multiracial collaboration and what was perceived to be an Indian-dominated body politic under the newly elected Timoci Bavadra government, and the third 'millennium coup' ousted Indo-Fijian Prime Minister Mahendra Chaudry who came into power following the constitutional reforms of 1997. Nandan's novel is not only the first English-language Indo-Fijian novel but also the first to provide a full-length study of the events leading up to the 1987 coup. Nandan himself is personally embroiled in the country's political history. He was the newly appointed Minister of Health in the first multiracial government led by Bavadra, whom Nandan refers to as 'the most beloved PM of Fiji,'[18] He also went into exile in Australia (settling into an academic career at the University of Canberra) as part of the larger exodus in the years that followed the 1987 coup. Twenty thousand Indo-Fijians left their island home during this period. This is a very large number for a modest national population of some 715,000.[19] In Nandan's novel, then, the poetics of permanent exile, though rooted in the history of indenture, is further reinforced in the dyadic axis represented here by the dystopic post-colonial era.

Drawing on the story of Rama's exile at the hands of his stepmother as the definitive textual representation of the Indo-Fijian predicament, Nandan refers to the coups as the 'second banishment' to be endured by the diasporic Fijian.[20] Here, it is the long-departed British Empire which stands in as the wicked stepmother, since Indo-Fijian settlement is, by and large, seen to be waylaid by 'imperial machinations' and its legislative groundwork. This is the elegiac poetic of betrayal, trauma, and exile that Nandan puts into motion in his oeuvre as a poet, storyteller, and political essayist. Echoing Peter Nazareth's Ugandan post-colonial dystopia *In a Brown Mantle*, Nandan's protagonist-narrator finds his dream of a multiracial state blindsided by a nativist discourse and 'the butt of a gun.'[21] Nandan's novel also begins and ends in the no-man's land of the open sky, his forlorn protagonist peering down from the departing plane's cabin at the receding horizon of another adoptive homeland. Indeed, like Nazareth and countless others of the old South Asian diaspora, Nandan too writes from the space of the double diaspora, and the wound of multiple separations. As another 'bastard son' of both Empire and his fellow subaltern, Nandan identifies most viscerally with the forced or private exiles of his contemporaries Salman Rushdie and V.S. Naipaul: 'Salman, our brave brother is still alive.'[22] This point of identification is overtly referenced in the section of the novel that is culled directly from Nandan's memoir, which is based on his personal experience of house arrest during the 1987 coup, and at the brink of his own second banishment. For Nandan, then, the greater betrayal comes from the banishment brought on by kith and kin, represented by the ethnic and native Fijian's historical bond of colonization. In the absence of that bond, Fiji is characterized as a 'fatal paradise,' and the Indo-Fijian its primary casualty.

Revisiting *Girmitiya* Ideology

It is in the Indo-Fijian context that the experience of indenture seems to have produced the most lingering metaphysical and psychological scar of victimhood. Consequently, it is the Indo-Fijian writer who has looked most philosophically at the historic moment of arrival on foreign shores as the definitive impetus for a new kind of collective consciousness, a new coda of affiliation and survival. Vijay Mishra looks to g*irmitiya* experience as the defining feature of Indo-Fijian consciousness, beginning with his early surveys of Indo-Fijian writing and culminating in his 2007 monograph, *The Literature of the Indian Diaspora*.[23] In her seminal survey,

'History and Community Involvement in Indo-Fijian and Indo-Trinidadian Writing,' Helen Tiffin also confirms that indenture history was the central mythos that underpinned Indo-Fijian writing, leaving a far more indelible imprint on the Indo-Fijian imagination than it did on the early generation of Indo-Caribbean writers. This is a conclusion that is repeated across the body of Indo-Fijian literature, at least for its major writers, consisting of Raymond Pillai, Subramani, and Satendra Nandan. Even writers such as Subramani, who appear more optimistic about interethnic integration and acceptance, throw a backward glance at the *girmit* past as a necessary step for ethnocultural and individual self-actualization in the present: 'Indo-Fijian destiny lies in integration with the native Fijian population after an acceptance of the *girmit* past, and a revivification of a sense of self-worth.'[24]

As Mishra suggests, the *Ramayana* is the textual and spiritual foundation of *girmit* ideology. The *Ramayana* offers images of triumph and heroism where there is only the drudgery of labour and its vicissitudes, together with the fragmented status of the diaspora as the politically disenfranchised and racially subordinated other in the new world:

> The *Tulsidasa Ramayana*, of course, had everything in it for the girmit experience: fourteen years banishment for the epic hero and God incarnate Rama, trials and tribulations in the black forest of Dandak, symbolic ravishing of his wife by the demon-king Ravana, Rama's victory over Ravana, and his return to the utopian metropolis of Ayodhya … Although the *Tulsidasa* text omitted a key episode – Rama's subsequent rejection of Sita after returning to his kingdom – this part of the narrative was generally known and is a crucial structure for our understanding of the rejection of Mother India (Sita incarnate) when the diaspora actually returns to the motherland.[25]

For the predominantly Hindu majority, the *Ramayana* came to be the spiritual anchor of the diasporic community, as it was for Indo-Mauritian Deepchand Beeharry and Indo-Trinidadian Lakshmi Persaud. However, it is Nandan who provides the most explicit references to the epic hero Rama's story in his poetry and fiction.

Indeed, in one of his most anthologized signature poems, 'The Ghost,' Nandan conflates the speaker's experience with that of Rama, drawing directly on the imagery and currency of the sacred antecedent:

> In the blind eyeball's swollen veins
> *I've carried the ganges;*

... I have lived this exile
more gloriously than rama
and built kingdoms, you may find,
nobler than ajodhya,
in my ancient eternal mind.[26]

The poet's conceit – namely, that his suffering and endurance has been greater than that of Rama – is one that is carried over into his first novel. Not only does the narrator draw heavily on the stories and precepts of the *Ramayana* when describing the young protagonist's spiritual and philosophical upbringing – one which notably falls outside the purview of colonial indoctrination – but he also didactically draws parallels between his personal and communal plight with that of Rama: 'We lived by such stories, our ancient epics – first our grandparents, then our mothers and fathers, now our political leaders. Our fate in Fiji had echoes of the *Ramayana*: exile; suffering, separation; battles but no return.'[27]

Chevla Kanaganayakam, in his interview with Nandan shortly after the publication of *The Wounded Sea*, picks up on the ideological conceit implied by the unquestioned primacy of the Hindu epics in Nandan's oeuvre. Kanaganayakam makes the point that the epics may be perceived as 'hegemonic' texts that 'valorize the Aryan race.'[28] To this Nandan responds that it is precisely the 'colonizing' narrative embedded in the *Ramayana* that functions as a cautionary subtext in his own work: 'It gives us the Aryan view of the world and pushes the Dravidian people down. I wanted people to know that my sensibility was fragmented and shaped by some of these metatexts ... I am not glorifying the events of the *Mahabharata*, what I am saying is that it shows us that every epic grows out of a local quarrel.'[29] However, given the narrator's explicit identification and repeated insistence on the spiritual centrality of Rama's plight for the Indo-Fijian male, it is difficult to take the author's comment at face value.

Moreover, the *Ramayana*'s metatextual primacy circumscribes Nandan's poetics of exile within a somewhat chauvinistic world view. Even though the novel is a Bildungsroman that traces the protagonoist-narrator's coming-of-age, women in the novel are cast as minor characters who are usually objects of male desire or fascination. In fact, the most glaring omission in the novel is the entire chapter of the narrator's married life. His marriage is offhandedly mentioned as a mere afterthought. In this regard, one might suggest that the narrator's deeply felt identification with Rama, though necessarily drawn from a religio-centred consciousness, evokes a specifically Indo-Brahmin ethos that predicates the spiritual guardianship of Mother India on a male-centred narrative of trauma, trial, and triumphant return. Unlike Rama, who returns home to an adoring people, however, the feeling of trauma for the diasporic male is, at its core, an emasculating experience. The relinquishment of authorial control is made all the more visceral where returns seem impossible and endings are thrown open to revision in a foreign land that threatens to recast the role of men and women alike in unexpected and unpredictable ways.

As Mishra comments, the *Ramayana* that serves as the Indo-Fijian's metatext is faithfully reproduced in all of its original splendor, with the exception of the glaring omission of Rama's mistrust of Sita, his wife, upon his return and the subsequent subjection of his wife to a number of trials designed to test her fidelity and chastity.[30] Mishra poses but does not quite develop the ideological dissonance or potential male bias to be found in the selective use of the Rama story in Indo-Fijian male writing. In contrast, Shaista Shameem, in her vitriolic feminist critique, provides a far less celebratory reading of the heretofore unrivalled centrality of Hindu symbolism in Indo-Fijian fiction:

> One cannot expect us to praise the significance of Indian Vedic 'images' or to identify with 'displaced' Indian males. We are too much preoccupied … with our own refugee status as women. The regaining of the Indo-Fijian male 'izzat' has for far too long been conditional on our female chastity, on our lack of freedom, and we have to come to terms with that.[31]

The only other Indo-Fijian novel to date, *Veiled Honour* (2001) by Satya Colpani, problematizes with irony (given the thrust of the title alone) the male-centred *izzat* that has so often served as a justification of violence against women. As Lal states, 'Men evaluated women's roles on the plantations in stereotypes. Some measured them against the ideal of Sita, the paragon of Hindu womanhood, who gave up everything to accompany her husband Lord Rama, into exile.'[32] Indeed, it is just such an ideal that Mala, the female protagonist of *Veiled Honour*, is attempting to reconcile with her individual hopes and dreams. Her story aptly begins with her arranged marriage, which soon collapses into an empty bourgeois lifestyle that offers little fulfilment outside the parameters of material comfort and motherhood. In the interim, Mala passively witnesses the gradual rise of a gender revolution in a younger generation of women, including her daughter, who wrestle themselves free of the Sita paradigm. Unlike this new generation of women, Mala recollects her girlish fantasies on the eve of her wedding distilled through the Rama-Sita story of abduction and rescue. In Mala's mind, the Rama-Sita story is further distorted through her schooling in colonial and Hindu teachings, each of which renders female subjectivity in the image of dependency and subordination. What is significant here is the rendering of the Rama-Sita story in the narratological coda of the Western fairy tale or romance, which is itself little more than a distorted patriarchal myth.

> She imagined herself being rescued by Rama, flying down and lifting her up with one sweep to take her to the mythical garden of Brindavanam ... The forest was abundant with every imaginable fruit and vegetable. Everything was so green and lush, and everyone appeared happy. There she would live in perfect harmony with Rama and his people, and become their queen. Suddenly Rama turned to Raj.[33]

The textual centrality of the *Ramayana* is also contested in other parts of the diaspora, insofar as it is seen to be at odds with an emerging feminist consciousness. For example, in Indo-Guyanese novelist Arnold Itwaru's *Shanti*, the protagonist is bemused by the significance of *Divali*, the festival which commemorates Rama's return. Her response indicates not only the corrosion of religious teachings for subsequent generations schooled within the colonial curriculum, but also the waning impact of scriptural lessons that seem divorced from daily struggles: 'Where was Ram returning, to where was he returning and what did that have to do with her ... or anyone here in this village so far away from Ram's kingdom? ... it was preposterous that Ram was called here where her father and mother worked from dawn to the dusk ... without his aid or presence.'[34]

Although I would suggest that both Raymond Pillai and Subramani attempt to address patterns of male violence and domestic abuse in stories such as 'The Celebration' and 'Marigolds,' respectively, the emphasis on male suffering more often than not results in a mutually exclusive dialectic of gender-specific destinies. Echoing the Indo-Caribbean women writers' challenge to the male-dominated literary tradition that projected the image of the 'orhni-covered' woman through the Indo-Caribbean male gaze, Shameem goes a step further in suggesting that Indo-Fijian women have been rendered invisible through the imaginative and material arena of the Indo-Fijian elite. Here she provides the example of female author Prem Banfal whose emergence, in the 1970s, alongside the 'trinity' of male writers, continues to be eclipsed in discussions of Indo-Fijian literature and criticism.

Both figuratively and literally, then, the exilic perspective is as much a construct of poetic conceit as it is a lived experience. Though the predominant sense of exile and dispossession is created by an exclusionary body politic, the relative geopolitical positioning of Fiji within the oceanic systems of continental Asia has also situated Indo-Fijians closer to the motherland left behind. Unlike their Caribbean counterparts, for whom the idea of return would prove inconceivable given the sheer distance and expense of the journey, Indo-Fijians have enjoyed a greater degree of mobility and connection with the Indian subcontinent, maintaining familial, cultural, and other ties to the motherland. Victor Ramraj suggests that these ties are reflected in the greater frequency of allusions to Indian literature and myths in Indo-Fijian cultural discourse, its spectrum of religious rites and ceremonies, and Hindi language usage within this part of the diaspora.[35] This is also reflected in the development of Indo-Fijian writing itself, which began with Totaram Sanadhya, in his account of his life as an Indian migrant in Fiji during the years 1893–1914.[36] Moreover, Hindi and a locally creolized form of Hindi called Fiji *baat* (the Hindi/Urdu term for talk or speech) are active linguistic mediums in the island's literary culture, including Sudesh Mishra's poetry collection *Tandava*, also published between the 1987 and 2000 coups. Literature written in Hindi or its creolized variant includes several plays, such as Sudesh Mishra's *Ferringhi* (2001) and Pillai's *Adhuuraa Saapnaa* (1993), and an active body of written poetry (Hindi and English) that dates back as early as 1916.[37] In fact, publication in Hindi continues to thrive in the island. As Jogindar Singh Kanwal suggests in his 1996 survey of Indo-Fijian poetry, 'As the facilities to print books in Hindi are now more readily available in Fiji, many books are being published ... Another salient feature is that in spite of the ... dominant position of the English language in Fiji, the younger generation are still interested in Hindi literature.'[38]

Nandan, in his personal and creative life, has illustrated this interconnection on various levels: as a visiting student, as a prospective marriage suitor, as a boy enamoured by the village beauty for her uncanny resemblance to a Hindi film actress, or as a disgruntled or bemused pupil of Indian-imported teachers and religious charlatans. In *The Wounded Sea*, personal and professional credentials are validated in terms of Indian contact; for example, the protagonist says that his father is 'reassured because Dr. Ponia had got his medical degree in India in a college called Gurukul';[39] and the opportunistic character of Gautam becomes the envy of his fellow male villagers when he finds an Indian bride from New Delhi: 'A daughter in-law from the land of Gandhi Mahatma ... a real *bahu*.'[40] Similarly, Nandan's contemporary, Subramani, speaks of contact with India 'through Bombay movies, visiting cultural troupes and occasional package tours to the holy places.'[41]

Though one might expect that greater proximity to the originary homeland might alleviate the burden of the engulfing shadow of 'authenticity' represented by Mother India, the migrant's overriding sensibility – namely, that return is impossible – is the pronouncement found in Nandan's work. And Nandan is certainly not alone in the formidable shadow that the subcontinent has cast across the diasporic imagination. In Indo-Guyanese poet Cyril Dabydeen's 'Elephants Make Good Stepladders,' the speaker takes the reader on a journey through the 'hinterland of memory,' describing the peculiar condition felt by those diasporic subjects who find themselves within a new world geography that seems to reflect the ancestral homeland at one moment only to betray its difference in the next:

It isn't the same growing up
on a different side of the tropics
after all they're worlds apart
... How I wished for more than youthful
visits to circuses in a colonial town
to hear a real elephant's grunt
to watch its trunk come alive.[42]

In Dabydeen's imaginative landscape, the speaker often confuses the signs and symbols that connect geography with cultural topography, resulting in an inability to distinguish between the imagined and the real distances between the 'new' and the 'old' world. When he finally finds himself vacationing in the ancestral homeland, where he meets 'the elephant, eye to eye,' he finds the empirical evidence he has been searching for to confirm that the two 'tropical' states of being are indeed two distinct realities, each of which has nonetheless come to shape his own cartography of being.

In an uncanny echo of Dabydeen's elephant motif, Nandan, in his own strangely familiar tropical landscape, invests in the elephant a similar degree of symbolic potency. Here, too, the elephant is the umbilical cord that keeps the narrator's imagination tied to the sacred land. As a boy who receives images of India through the already fragmented imagination and nostalgia of his father, however, he is not comforted by the elephant; rather, the sacred animal signals the finality of the disconnection between past and present. This reaffirms the feeling of insecurity and displacement in the new land: 'Elephants, he said, couldn't live on our island. The land was soft and they would sink into the ground. I believed him and dreamed of elephants often. Huge and mighty creatures ... From fragments of fragmented lives, this is the dream that the old man, my Baba, gave me: to see elephants where there were none.'[43]

A Water Elegy to the 'Cannibal Sea'

Interestingly, Mishra glosses over *The Wounded Sea* in his discussion of *girmitiya* ideology as the defining ethos of the Indo-Fijian collective, suggesting that Nandan's novel, like much of his oeuvre, is too 'romantic' and 'elegiac.'[44] Indeed, Nandan is offered a scant few pages of passing comment in a text that otherwise offers a comprehensive discussion of Raymond Pillai's and Sudesh Mishra's works. What Vijay Mishra objects to in Nandan's reading of *girmitiya* is the shift of emphasis away from the material experience of labour 'into a belief system that is sustained through a prior memory in which history is constructed in an "ancient eternal mind."' Thus, the elegiac thrust of Nandan's poetics is fossilized within the language of mourning, given the writer's 'inability to capture the original pain.'[45]

The overly romanticized if not solipsistic tone found in Nandan's poetry is transposed into his first novel. On the one hand, the novel offers a compelling study of contemporary Indo-Fijian life as a continuing struggle for survival in the political morass of the Fijian body politic; on the other, it offers neither the possibility of redemption nor the triumph of survival that one finds in other works, obsessed as it is with the poetics of exile, mourning, suffering, and loss. Though it is obviously not the task of the author to provide a definitive vision of indenture experience, the novel conflates testimony and memoir with the concomitant desire to speak for the collective in a way that is both unconvincing and dogmatic. This is reinforced by the emphasis on suffering and betrayal of the self-made Indo-Fijian man who, through a vaguely represented collusion of individual and collective will, pulls himself out of his inherited colonial condition only to find that he is not up to the task of recovering from the wound of native Fijian betrayal in the post-colonial moment. What we are left with, then, is a highly selective representation that, in its glossing over of women's lives, entire episodes of the narrator's adult life, and even the daily interactions of native Fijian and Indo-Fijian peoples produces a series of gaps and omissions that are neither self-consciously nor self-critically addressed. This in turn produces a level of dissonance that undermines the reader's sympathy for what is ostensibly a semiauto-biographical work.

This narrative dissonance speaks to some of the formal limitations of this first novel. As a piecing together of various fragments of Nandan's writing, including, as the acknowledgments page highlights, the short stories 'The Guru,' 'A Pair of Black Shoes,' 'Bro's Funeral,' and excerpts from the author's political writings, the novel presents itself as an oddly hybrid genre of fictional autobiography, memoir, and Bildungsroman. Syd Harrex, in his afterword to Nandan's (2000) memoir, considers the novel 'quintessentially post-colonial in being a hybrid text.'[46] Though Harrex is not wrong in suggesting that the text defies generic classifica-tion, the assumption that hybridity and post-coloniality are unproblem-atic corollaries (insofar as the latter is typified by generic schizophrenia) is rather far-reaching. Similarly, Kanaganayakam suggests that the 'multi-plicity that gives the novel its particular texture, its mixture of autobiog-raphy, realism and artifice' is a formal reflection of the author's desire not to resort to 'a narrow nationalist response through fiction.'[47] Contrary to the above readings, I would suggest that *The Wounded Sea* echoes the kind of generic hybridity found in Lakshmi Persaud's *Butterfly in the Wind*, which rather clumsily gropes with the kind of partiality of memory created by the double diaspora's multiple frames of reference. Each work is driven by a highly personal and urgent desire for individual and ethnic self-assertion rather than by the self-conscious or ironic desire to aesthetically encode the narrative and other slippages that might arise in the experience of diasporic displacement or migration. In the case of Nandan and Persaud's texts, autobiography and testimony, like the para-doxical currents of individual self-reflection and public statement em-bedded in each genre, are the governing aesthetic principles that propel these narratives forward.

Where realism fails and autobiographic impulses eclipse a holistic rep-resentation of community, Nandan's poetic voice becomes the means by which he ties together the disparate threads of a seemingly irreparable identity and an equally fragmented narrative. Though little has been said of the imagery and poetic synergy underpinning the novel, it is here that Nandan offers not merely a poetics of mourning and trauma, but also an alternate poetics of cultural belonging and kinship. Specifically, water imagery, symbolism, and metaphors are unifying forces in the otherwise seemingly competing currents of native Fijian and Indo-Fijian life. A consideration of the way water imagery is interwoven throughout the narrative reveals not only the *girmitiya* ideology propounded by Vijay Mishra, but also a dialogic impulse that at least symbolically situates the narrative within the poetic and historical archipelagraphy of the Pacific.

The water imagery or archipelago motif found in Nandan's first novel lifts the narrative out of its seeming chasm of nostalgia, regret, and despair. It conveys a gesture of inclusiveness and identification with the narrator's island home through an island subjectivity that subtly undercuts the overarching exilic poetics of the twice-displaced diasporic subject. On the one hand, water is a symbol of rupture and dispossession in the devouring 'cannibal sea.'[48] Water imagery simultaneously activates and debunks the colonial mythology that has stripped the islands and native islanders of agency and complexity. The persistent and often contradictory allusions to the 'cannibalization' of the islands make for a complicated delineation between the diasporic subject and the indigenous Fijian. At certain times the protagonist appears to expose cannibal imagery as imperial fallacy, and, at other times, to don the perspective of the imperilled traveller, subject to the potential savagery of the islands. The following passage offers a striking example of the latter: 'In Fiji the thin curtain – as thin as a page of the holy Bible – between cannibalism and Christianity is torn asunder.'[49] References to the 'cannibal sea' function as a cautionary subtext that resurrects the imperial mythos of the 'savage' nature of the island/er.

But Nandan quickly derails this association in the overarching conflation of the 'cannibal sea' with the ravages of imperial history itself. Fittingly, the author rewrites the Middle Passage paradigm in his reference to the historic shipwreck of the *Syria* in 1884,[50] which littered the Indian Ocean with the ghosts of those indentured labourers who died in the sea voyage in the same way that the Atlantic is strewn with the ghosts of African slaves. The reference to the shipwreck not only suggests that colonial migration history has spawned into a haunting *narak* or nightmare existence from which the labourer cannot awaken, but also serves as a metaphor for the exilic condition, particularly for the present generation, who are now left in a state of spiritual limbo as 'girmit grandchildren shipwrecked.'[51]

But water is also a regenerative bridge that symbolically links the River Ganges to the 'wounded sea,' and reminds the narrator that as the 'mother of all life' the ocean is not merely a conveyor of rupture and loss, but a unifying and healing principle.[52] This carries even greater import in the religio-centred consciousness of the Hindu practitioner, who realizes that the Pacific is a fluid extension of the Indian Ocean and the Indian Ocean is itself sustained by the Ganges and its many tributaries: 'The Pacific Ocean, part of the Indian Ocean, part of the holy Ganga ... it was comforting. The sea is one, I thought.'[53] The Middle Passage becomes the *kala pani*, the *kala pani* transmogrifies into the 'cannibal sea,' which in turn becomes the 'wound-womb' out of which 'new life bleeds and is born.'[54]

Though the underlying sentiment in his creative and non-fictional writing seems to suggest that the exilic condition best captures the state of political instability and disenfranchisement felt by Indo-Fijian peoples, the novel elegiacally mourns the casualties of the post-colonial island-state in an effort to expose the ghosts of the imperial past which still seem to devour or 'cannibalize' contemporary Fijian society. Though the novel does not offer a way out of the quagmire of political opportunism and individual disillusionment, Nandan's work is nonetheless steeped in an island subjectivity that Indo-Fijians have come to share with their indigenous counterparts. The transformation of a continental identity (that stands like a shadow over the island-bound diasporic subject) into a distinctly water-bound islander is not one that should be underestimated. Though Nandan's exilic perspective seems to foreclose the possibility of arrival, the metaphorical bridging of the ethnic and indigenous Fijian consciousness in the predominant water imagery that unites continental and island identities offers at least the possibility for an alternate poetics of being and becoming in the cross-cultural currents of the inherited seascape.

Nandan's work is necessarily a highly personal expression of diasporic subjectivity written at a time of extreme personal anguish. It remains to be seen what such a horizon will hold for a new generation of writers who, unlike Nandan and the 'pioneering trinity,' have never left their island-home. Instead, they have braved the various tides of Fijian history on the home front, which has sadly experienced another coup in 2006, the fourth in twenty years. In the most recent coup, led by Commander Bainimarama, the tides of history, at least in the currencies of political rhetoric, have been recast again, given the military leader's call to a multiracial Fiji.[55] For the new generation of Indo-Fijian writers, then, the story of settlement has come to span well over a century. This is an investment in history, space, and time that cannot be so easily summed up in the exilic condition, and gives the lie to Nandan's contention that only trees are rooted in Fiji's native soil.

Conclusion

As a body of writing that has developed in the lap of indenture history, the narratives of the old diaspora invariably offer a specialized critique of the systems and institutions of European imperialism. These novels necessarily evoke and nuance, from their variously positioned geopolitical perspectives, the tropes, themes, and concerns of post-colonial literature. However, they explore not simply the relationship between race and power across the colonial and post-colonial era but also the particular experience of migration, settlement, and belonging of colonized people among other colonized groups.

This unique aspect of the old South Asian diaspora has greatly shaped the poetics and concerns of its novelists, as writers respond to the particular axis of interrelation in which they, and their diasporic communities, find themselves. When these writers are among the first to give voice to their diaspora, they often endow their narrators with a certain prophetic omniscience, so as to project into the unpredictable future of the post-colonial state the collective anxieties, hopes, and fears of a community whose socio-political fate has yet to be sealed. But in simultaneously turning a critical eye to the ideological baggage that the diaspora brings to the new land, these writers also turn to realism and satire in an effort to counteract the exploitation and festering of old historical wounds in the struggle for political and cultural self-representation.

They also share a common desire to draw attention to the diversity of the diaspora itself, not in idyllic but in interrogative terms. This accounts for the ethnic and class prejudices, caste hierarchies, gender inequalities, and religious differences that appear in these novels. For instance, the object of satire for many novelists in the old South Asian diaspora has often been the figure of the religious charlatan who capitalizes on the vulnerability of a community whose belief systems are threatened by colonial missionary practices and further compromised by the lack of access to formal instruction on its own religious teachings. This is, of course, particularly true of the dominant Hindu community for whom the Indian subcontinent is the source not just of ancestral and cultural pride but also of Hinduism and its spiritual topography. Colonial mimicry thus transmogrifies into 'ancestral mimicry,' that is, a kind of willed gullibility in the desire to project an uncontaminated spiritual centre.

Even the most cursory glance of the diaspora in its various post-colonial contexts suggests that diasporic peoples are not only positioned *within* and *by* the narratives of the past, but they also become an agential body politic which radically alters and influences the new land. This is most poetically brought to view in Lakshmi Persaud's semiautobiographical story of the Maharaj family's immigrant success story. The narrative of upward (socio-economic) mobility that is enjoyed by the young female protagonist is made all the more poignant by its validation of the struggle, endurance, and spiritual resilience of an earlier generation of Maharaj women, indentured labourers who toiled under the heat of a tropical sun that never set on the seemingly invincible Empire. The immigrant success story as another feature of the collective saga of the indentured labourer and his/her descendants also considerably rewrites the poetics of victimhood associated with the coolie stereotype, suggesting that both the free passenger and the indentured labourer saw, to differing degrees, horizons for self-betterment in the cartography of Empire. The immigrant's dream is, of course, terribly ironic where the colonized subject's catalyst for migration to the Empire's colonies was driven by the devastating impact of the policies and practices of the British Raj on the homeland itself, particularly in the aftermath of the 1857 rebellion.

The feeling of betrayal and rejection is echoed in other regions where a minority diaspora lives alongside a majority indigenous population and other minority ethnic groups, but in all of its variations the dyadic axis of diaspora/indigene seems to exacerbate, most acutely, the diaspora's anxiety over questions of citizenship and belonging. Indeed, it will be interesting to see how Maniam and a younger generation of writers respond to the eruption of race riots in Kuala Lumpur which made international headlines on 25 November 2007, where some 20,000 Indo-Malaysians (mainly composed of ethnic Tamils, the descendants of indentured labourers) petitioned their former colonial master for compensation for 150 years of exploitation and subsequent abandonment to a 'Malays-first affirmative action policy instituted after independence in 1957.'[1] And how a younger generation of Indo-Fijian writers might respond to the 2006 coup, or challenge the anti-Indian rhetoric that has clouded the island-nation's political horizon since the first 1987 coup against a newly elected multiracial government.[2] Or, for that matter, how will Ugandans, rechannel their energies[3] into a shared grassroots struggle against globalizing forces which have compromised the national collective writ large, as much as its ethnic contingencies?

Though Deepchand Beeharry's sociohistorical novel's depiction of servitude at the hands of an exploitative and dehumanizing system appears to contradict the more optimistic portrait of the old diaspora, the real-life saga of the Indo-Mauritian population as the political guardians of the island's national destiny is perhaps the most obvious narrative of collective empowerment. The indenture narrative therefore often brings to bear the lessons of history while affirming that even the most seemingly helpless figures carry the potential for transformative action. All of the writers under study illustrate the extent to which the experiences of migration or of the particular hardships of indentured labour have created a resilient ethnic community that is driven by a history of struggle and resistance against past and current hegemonies. As such, the diasporic subject's seemingly commonplace struggle for survival, in the often painful awareness of a fractured identity, is celebrated as an intrinsically heroic act. The diasporic novel accordingly sets the stage for an epic imaginary that unfolds as an ongoing quest to triumph over both the external and self-imposed limitations of the human condition, in the poetics of possibility that is subtly embodied in the multiply positioned or plural identity of the diasporic subject.

Where novelists of the old South Asian diaspora have since come to form part of the double diaspora in the Western metropolis, one still has to be careful not to conflate their experiences 'as first-generation immigrants' with those of the new South Asian diaspora. For one, the latter may be said to pivot around a binational axis that, even in its hybridity and heterogeneity, does not speak of the kind of distance, thrice-removed, from the ancestral motherland that is particular to the double diaspora. Moreover, for writers of the old South Asian diaspora who remain within the new adoptive homeland, the 'twilight' or 'in-between' condition of the migrant's split perspective is greatly complicated for people whose links to the Indian subcontinent have long been severed, or for those who have experienced the painful reality of dispossession and relocation within their adoptive homelands. Thus, for the first-generation immigrant of the new diaspora, ties to the motherland are often reinforced by extended family networks, by the recent memory of personal and historical landmarks, and by the likelihood of travel and communication with those who have remained behind – ties which are not always available to the descendants of the old South Asian diaspora.

A comparative consideration of these texts and contexts also cautions against a reading of South Asian diasporic identity that does not take into consideration the historically specific and simultaneously processual nature of diasporic experience, as it is embodied and transformed in individuals, communities, and nations. In the same vein, the local conditions which produce these novels, including textual production, national funding, cultural discursive practices, and critical reception, are themselves indispensable areas for future inquiry. Indeed, each diasporic axis has come to determine the writer's relative access to publication and self-expression in a given language.

The comparative framework of this study affords a few final observations or, perhaps, modest predictions about the unfolding development of the diasporic novel in these regions. As already indicated, the Caribbean is home to the longest and most vigorous tradition of novel writing. The Indo-Caribbean writer has played an integral part in the shaping of the Caribbean novel, not only in giving voice to the diasporic community but also in adding to the genre's spectrum of stylistic features, thematic concerns, and formal innovation. The once male-dominated literary genre has been overturned by a new generation of women writers who challenge the numerous fallacies projected in earlier fiction, including the depiction of subaltern women as passive foils to male agency and self-authorizing power. Women writers also address a range of topics traditionally considered to be off-limits or taboo, such as the prevalence of domestic violence, patterns of alcoholism and abuse, and, conversely, a more complex consideration of female sexuality and the gendered experiences of diasporic women within a plural, creolized collective. Women's voices are also central to the new South Asian diasporic novel in South Africa; in fact, Karodia's own predominantly women-centred narratives reveal the extent to which female bonds carry the potential for ideological and revolutionary change where coloured men find themselves emasculated by colonial and apartheid policy. Women's stories have necessarily widened the thematic and formal parameters of the diasporic novel in many ways: their feminist or gendered readings of indenture and migration history; their critical rereading of the intertextual and metatextual frames of reference that inform diasporic subjectivity; and their representation of the historic participation of women in the struggle for social equity, cultural self-preservation, nation building, and so on. The new gendered frontiers of the diasporic novel have considerably enriched the diasporic imaginary, suggesting that in those regions where women's stories are still not part of the cultural conversation, the saga of the old South Asian diaspora will remain incomplete. This is most certainly apparent in regions where the English-language novel has proved to be at its most fledgling state, and where the diasporic novel has tended to remain in the hands of a small cross-section of society that consists of a university-educated cultural elite.

The small population of ethnic South Asians in East Africa carries the weight of its own implications. Though a few novelists have emerged since Nazareth's foundational portrait of Asian expulsion from Uganda, they, too, have done so as part of the double diaspora, and it is up to a new generation who might never have set foot on the African continent to continue telling their stories. Moreover, it has yet to be seen how those born in East Africa might respond to their subject-position as Indo-Africans. Will they speak from the perspective of an indigenized group, as their Indo-Mauritian counterparts do, or as a conspicuous and potentially ever-dwindling minority? Conversely, where populations have stabilized or continued to grow (Fiji, Singapore, South Africa, Malaysia, the Caribbean), a new generation of writers, born well after the initial seeds of betrayal or discontent were sown at the birth of the nation, stand to greatly impact the development of a national literature. However, in the case of Fiji and Malaysia, the question of which language this story might be told in is harder to predict. It is not clear yet whether Malaysia might increase its national funding of English-language literature, not only for its minority diaspora but also for a younger generation who might see in the 'Malays-first' policy a relic of an earlier day. Similarly, the Tamil-dominant South Asian diaspora of both Singapore and Malaysia might not feel the kind of colonial alienation experienced by an earlier generation schooled in the colonial curriculum. Instead, they might foreseeably opt to write in their inherited mother tongue. This might not be so difficult to imagine in Singapore where Tamil language-training has been a part of government policy. Similarly, in Fiji, younger writers are showing greater signs of interest in recuperating their mother tongue, and there has been a modest resurgence of Hindi-language writing there. In other words, though the diasporic novel might very well continue to evolve in these regions, it might not do so in the English language. Mauritius confirms the possibility of this trend in the increasing production of francophone novels by Indo-Mauritians, where French remains the linguistic medium of choice, and Kreol the language of daily communication.

This brings us to the related question of when the 'diaspora' paradigm is no longer a useful qualifier or descriptor. Indeed, in the process of indigenization or increased identification as equal partners in the national culture, the 'diasporic' label itself might become increasingly redundant, if not wholly counterintuitive to people who identify themselves as firmly rooted in the new land over what will soon be a bicentennial history by 2034. Whether this suggests that diasporic experience is itself predicated on the anxiety of being and belonging is also not entirely clear. Does the codification of the novel as a diasporic body of writing necessitate a community's continuing need to mythologize or, for that matter, realistically confront its ethnic migration history? Does the process of indigenization or naturalization neutralize that desire? Recent trends in the Indo-Caribbean novel seem to suggest otherwise: here, the greater the process of indigenization in the new land, the greater the impulse to map the diaspora's historical trajectory onto the national imaginary. Is this the last rite of passage that will signify the diaspora's reconciliation with its own cultural and historical difference? Of course, the sheer breadth and diversity of the old South Asian diaspora alone suggests that such patterns can never be so uniform. The increasingly specialized focus on the diaspora's ethnic, religious, and gendered minorities indicates that a considerable portion of the diasporic imaginary has yet to be mapped; for example, the little-discussed Muslim contingent of Indo-Caribbean peoples (and the growth of Islam in Trinidad itself) might very well become a new frontier for diasporic expression and scholarly interest.

The resurgent focus on the policies and practices of immigration and citizenship in our present global economy has been accompanied by an effort in North America to look beyond the borders of Euro-American nation-states and also to the untold histories of the past. To equitably participate in the intersecting debates of statehood and globalizing practices, it is imperative that we continue to cultivate an awareness of the interconnectedness of our individual and collective histories and identities. What is certain about the old South Asian diaspora and its multiply positioned identities is that this interconnectedness is nowhere more pronounced than in its globally scattered imaginative landscape, where concepts such as home/homeland, citizenship, ethnicity, migrancy, and even indigeneity are continually remapped along an ever-shifting axis of interrelation.

Notes

1 The Multiple Voices of Indenture History

1 This book is limited to overseas communities (the diaspora), and does not consider countries of the Indian subcontinent, such as Sri Lanka, where en masse migration also occurred for the purposes of plantation labour.
2 As early as the 1820s, a group of Punjabi-Sikhs migrated to the southwestern United States, where many of these migrant labourers eventually established prosperous farming communities. At the turn of the twentieth century, Punjabi-Sikhs also formed the first major South Asian community in Canada, settling in British Columbia where they worked mainly as agricultural labourers.
3 In her demographic overview of overseas Indians, K. Laxmi Narayan attributes the change to the passage of the 1976 Immigration Act, which institutionalized less racially selective admission practices. See Narayan, 'Indian Diaspora.' See also Thomas Sowell's discussion of the shift in migration policies in the western hemisphere in *Migrations and Cultures.*
4 The western hemisphere's history of South Asian immigration is as old as the British Raj itself. South Asians have populated Britain for almost three hundred years both as domestic servants and professionals schooled in law and medicine.
5 The British presence in the Indian subcontinent lasted for a period of over 400 years. The first permanent trading post was established in 1612 in Gujarat. Imperial rule began much later in the aftermath of the 1857 rebellion. In 1858, the East India Company was transferred to the British Crown and by 1876 Queen Victoria proclaimed herself Empress of India. British imperial rule in the subcontinent lasted until 1947, the year of Indian and Pakistani independence.

6 Tinker, in *A New System of Slavery*, notes that free passengers were often called *khula* and indentured labourers *girmit-wallahs*. Both are Hindi terms.

7 This definition of 'indenture' is found in the *Concise Oxford English Dictionary* (10th edition, 1999).

8 Tinker, *A New System of Slavery*, 179.

9 South Asian immigrants came mainly from the northern region of Bihar, though there was also some immigration from the southern region of Madras. The majority of immigrants were Hindus; the remainder were primarily Muslims and Christians.

10 Since Sharlow has come to refer to himself by first name only, he will be referred to that way in reference to his novels.

11 Sharlow, *The Promise*, 32.

12 The South Asian officers and personnel of the British colonial military rebelled against the British Raj in 1857. British historians continue to refer to this event as a mutiny, while South Asian historians refer to it as anticolonial resistance.

13 See Northrup, *Indentured Labour in the Age of Imperialism*. This phenomenon is explored in chapter 3 on Mauritius.

14 *Rama's Voyage* by Ron Ramdin is also an excellent example of the indenture narrative, since it is based on the journals of a British colonial sea captain written during the ship voyage across to the plantation colonies. Sharlow's *The Promise* is another example.

15 Sharlow, *The Promise*, 32.

16 Narayan, 'Indian Diaspora,' 5.

17 Subramani, *The Indo-Fijian Experience*, x.

18 Lal, *Crossing the Kala Pani*, 15.

19 Shepherd, 'Indian Indentured Women in the Caribbean,' 68.

20 Tinker, *A New System of Slavery*, 38.

21 Bowman, *Mauritius*, 23.

22 Historians state that many indentured labourers were promised not only a free passage to the colony but also a return passage upon completion of the contracted period, though the contractual promise of a return passage was not always honoured.

23 Mishra, *The Literature of the Indian Diaspora*, 2–3.

24 On 5 November 1972, Ugandan President Idi Amin Dada called for the expulsion of South Asians from Uganda. Idi Amin's edict was an extreme manifestation of prevalent African–South Asian tensions in post-colonial East African nations.

25 After several thousand years of a Muslim South Asian presence in East Africa, the population of South Asians in Tanzania has dwindled to .17 per cent in a post-independence era. See Clarke et al., *South Asians Overseas*.

26 See Nandan, *Fiji: Paradise in Pieces.*
27 Mira Nair, director, *Mississippi Masala* (Sony Pictures, 1991; Columbia TriStar, 1992).
28 Rushdie, 'Imaginary Homelands,' 15.

2 New Approaches to an Old Diaspora

1 See, for instance, Nelson, *Reworlding,* and Vijay Mishra, *Literature of the Indian Diaspora.*
2 Nelson, *Writers of the Indian Diaspora,* x.
3 Crane and Mohanran, 'Constructing the Diasporic Body,' vii.
4 Sharlow, *The Promise,* 42.
5 Lavie and Swedenburg, 'Displacement, Diaspora, and Geographies of Identity,' 14, 15.
6 See Radhakrishnan, *Diasporic Mediations.* Radhakrishnan correctly affirms that only in the interpenetration of post-structural and post-colonial theories can we arrive at a better understanding of diaspora.
7 See Dubois, *The Souls of Black Folk.*
8 See Braziel and Mannur, 'Nation, Migration, Globalization.'
9 Lavie and Swedenburg, 'Displacement, Diaspora, and Geographies of Identity,' 14.
10 Glissant, *Caribbean Discourse.*
11 Vijay Mishra, '(B)ordering Naipaul,' 190.
12 Hall, 'Cultural Identity,' 402.
13 See Vijay Mishra, *Literature of the Indian Diaspora,* for a discussion of *girmitiya* ideology.
14 Sudesh Mishra, *Diaspora Criticism,* 104.
15 Ibid.
16 See Shepherd, 'Indian Indentured Women in the Caribbean.'
17 Sam, *Jesus is Indian,* 130.
18 Vassanji, *The In-Between World of Vikram Lall,* 17.
19 Clifford, *Routes,* 258.
20 Shameem, 'The Art of Raymod Pillai, Subramani and Prem Banfal,' 30.
21 Here I am referring specifically to the Indo-Mauritian context where French and Creole are the dominant languages of cultural and literary production. Deepchand Beeharry, for instance, writes in English, French, and Hindi.
22 Mukherjee, *Postcolonialism,* 33.
23 Aijaz Ahmed, quoted in Mukherjee, *Postcolonialism,* 33.
24 See Vijay Mishra's compelling theorization of Naipaul's novels as 'diasporic allegories' in '(B)ordering Naipaul.'
25 Chetty, 'Exile and Return in Farida Karodia's *Other Secrets,*' 149.

26 Mohammed now publishes under the name of Sharlow. Two of his works, *The Promise* (1995) and *Colour of Pain* (2001) are self-published; *When Gods Were Slaves* was republished in 2004 by Sirens Publications in Lincoln, Nebraska. The novel studied here, *The Elect* (1992), is published by Peepal Tree Press in Leeds, U.K. The novellas *Requiem for a Village* and *Apartheid Love* were first published in 1982 by Imprint in Port of Spain, Trinidad.

27 Jameela Siddiqi is a freelance producer, broadcaster, and writer living in Great Britain. Her first novel, *The Feast of the Nine Virgins*, was published in 2001 by the London-based Bogle L'Ouverture Publications. Her second novel, *Bombay Gardens* (2006), was published by an on-line press www.lulu Press.com but is currently available in print.

28 Ramchand, 'Coming out of Repression,' 225.

29 Persaud has since written three other novels: *Sastra, For the Love of My Name*, and *Raise the Lanterns High*.

30 Karodia's first novel has since been reworked as the first of a trilogy titled *Other Secrets*, published by Penguin in 2000, and was nominated for the International IMPAC Dublin Literary Award.

31 Achmat Dangor lives and works in New York. He publishes in many genres, though his first novel appeared in the 1990s with the publication of *The Z Town Trilogy*. An earlier first novel, *Waiting for Leila* (1981), has long been out of print.

32 Chetty and Piciucco, *Indias Abroad*, 7.

3 The Indenture Narrative of Mauritius

1 Mauritius is one of two major islands in the Mascarene archipelago situated in the southwestern Indian Ocean, off the East African coast. The other major island is Ile de la Réunion, which is still a department of France. The two smaller islands are Rodrigues and Diego Garcia. The archipelago was named after Pedro Mascarenhas (the Portuguese navigator who discovered present-day Réunion). Mauritius gained its independence in 1968, after approximately 150 years of British rule. Its first prime minister was an Indo-Mauritian, Seewoosagur Ramgoolam. Mauritius became a republic in 1992. Prime Minister Navinchandra Ramgoolam came into power in 2005.

2 See Bowman, *Mauritius: Democracy and Development.*

3 Tinker, *A New System of Slavery*, 56.

4 South Asian immigration to Mauritius stemmed mainly from the northern region of Bihar, but there was also some immigration from the southern region of Madras. The majority of immigrants were lower-caste Hindus,

though there were also a number of Muslims, Christians, and upper-caste Hindus. See Bowman, *Mauritius*, and Carter, *Servants, Sirdars and Settlers*.

5 Carter, *Servants, Sirdars and Settlers*, 6.

6 Tinker, *A New System of Slavery*, 38.

7 All parenthetical references to *That Others Might Live* will be abbreviated as *TOML*. I am using the only existing Orient Paperback edition of the novel, which is sadly out of print.

8 The novel is based on a shipwreck that occurred in 1744. Jacques Henri Bernardin de St Pierre's *Paul et Virginie* is core reading for Mauritian students. The writer/philosopher wrote the story during his brief stay on the island.

9 Naipaul, 'The Overcrowded Barraccoon,' 292; emphasis added.

10 Pratt, *Imperial Eyes*, 5.

11 Ibid., 6.

12 Deloughery, '"The litany of islands,"' 24.

13 I am borrowing the term from Benitez-Rojo, *The Repeating Island*.

14 Naipaul, 'The Overcrowded Barraccoon,' 287, 270.

15 Foucault, 'Of Other Spaces,' 27.

16 Ibid., 24.

17 Deloughery, '"The litany of islands,"' 26.

18 I borrow the term from Deloughery's discussion of the Caribbean/Pacific Rim in the article cited in note 17, where '*i-landness*' (coined by poet Marlene Nourbese Philip) foregrounds the subjectivity of the islander as a poetic reclamation of history and identity.

19 Lionnet, '*Créolité* in the Indian Ocean,' 104.

20 Ibid., 106.

21 Burton, *Mauritius: The Problems of a Plural Society*, 28.

22 Slaves from the subcontinent were brought to Mauritius by French planters as early as the eighteenth century. They constituted 13 per cent of the population prior to British colonization. (See Tinker, *A New System of Slavery*, 44; Northrup, *Indentured Labour*, 60; and Bowman, *Mauritius: Democracy and Development*, 15.)

23 By the 1930s, Creole and Indo-Mauritian demands were more effectively conveyed in the emergence of what would become permanent political organizations, such as the Indian Cultural Association, the Hindu Cultural Revival Movement, the Mauritian Agricultural Labourers' Association, and the Mauritian Labour Party. The other major party, Parti Mauricien, represents primarily Franco-Mauritian/Creole interests, while further divisions arose in the formation of a Muslim organization, the Comité d'action Musulman, and another Hindu-dominated party, the Independent Forward Bloc. Despite the obvious ethnic delineations in Mauritian

politics, Creole and Indo-Mauritian interests were more often than not in alignment. In fact, ethnic confrontations have been few and far between. (See Bowman, *Mauritius: Democracy and Development*, and Lionnet, '*Créolité* in the Indian Ocean'.)

24 Bowman, *Mauritius: Democracy and Development*, 151.

25 Fabre, 'Mauritian Voices,' 124.

26 Quet, 'Mauritian Voices,' 305.

27 For a discussion of anglophone writing, see Smith's survey, 'Mauritian Literature in English,' and Fabre, 'Mauritian Voices.'

28 Fabre, 'Mauritian Voices,' 123.

29 Bhautoo-Dewnarain, 'Mauritian Writing in English,' 21; emphasis added.

30 There is very little scholarship on this body of writing. I have found only four surveys of Mauritian literature in English (those of Quet, Fabre, Smith, and Bhautoo-Dewnarain). Individual authors have enjoyed even less critical attention to date. As brief as it is, Arthur Pollard's review appears to be the only other examination of the novel to date.

31 Smith, 'Mauritian Literature in English,' 77.

32 Bhautoo-Dewnarain, 'Mauritian Writing in English,' 24.

33 Issur, 'Le roman mauricien d'aujourd'hui,' 115. My translation of the quoted passage is as follows: 'The new generation of novelists have completely changed their tone and themes and, far from perpetuating stereotypes or expressing the false optimism of the young nation, dare to point out the bankruptcy of the system and give voice to the desires and aspirations of individuals.'

34 Beeharry, *Never Goodbye*, n.p.

35 Beeharry, 'Why Do I Write?' in *The Road Ahead*, 2. Given Beeharry's faithful documentation of the material conditions of Mauritius's downtrodden, his oeuvre lends itself to a Marxist reading. However, I have resisted such ideological pigeonholing, for I believe that Beeharry is, above all, a humanist responding to the most urgent avenues for reform in an agriculturally based economy, and whose championing of human rights extends as much to the injustices of race, caste, and gender as to class and labour.

36 Danielle Quet conducted a follow-up survey to that of Michel Fabre. Both studies are restricted to literature produced between 1920 and 1980. The most current survey of Mauritian writing in English remains that of Nandini Bhautoo-Dewnarain.

37 Fabre, 'Mauritian Voices,' 132.

38 Tinker, *A New System of Slavery*, 46.

39 Vijay Mishra, *The Literature of the Indian Diaspora*, 12.

40 Beeharry, *That Others Might Live*, 38.

41 Beeharry, *Never Goodbye*, 1.
42 See Barbadian novelist George Lamming's *In the Castle of My Skin*.
43 I borrow this term from Ngũgĩ wa Thiong'o's seminal article, 'The Language of African Literature.' Ngũgĩ loosely defines 'colonial alienation' as the process of linguistic and, by extension, intellectual and cultural distancing that occurs in the gradual identification with the colonizer through the ideological and cultural precepts of a Eurocentric education system. This term will be further contextualized in later chapters.
44 See specifically Naipual, *The Mimic Men*, Persaud, *Sastra*, and Maniam, *The Return*.
45 See Bowman, *Mauritius: Democracy and Development*, for a discussion of the significance of the OAU Conference to Mauritius's presence in the continental African and international arena.
46 In fact, this novel in particular exposes Beeharry's affinity to other Indo-African writers. We shall see this affinity in chapter 4, which discusses Peter Nazareth's portrayal of Uganda's exiled citizens of South Asian origin.
47 Vijay Mishra, 'The Diasporic Imaginary,' 429.
48 This term appears in Rudyard Kipling's 1906 address delivered at the Royal Academy, although it can be traced back to Mallarmé's sonnet, 'Le tombeau d'Edgar Poe': 'Donner un sens plus pur aux mots de la tribu.' See Bernstein, *The Tale of the Tribe*.
49 See Pollard, 'Beeharry's *That Others Might Live*.'
50 Bernstein, *The Tale of the Tribe*, 8.
51 Beeharry, *TOML*, 9–10; 16; emphasis added.
52 This is borrowed from the title of Hugh Tinker's foundational study of indentured labour as 'a new system of slavery.' Subsequent scholarship (such as that of Marina Carter) attempts to nuance further the history of indentured peoples as a more variegated experience, though few would argue with Tinker's view of the dehumanizing conditions of the plantation system.
53 I am thinking primarily of the haunting metaphor of the sea in Derek Walcott's epic poem, *Omeros*.
54 Benitez-Rojo, *The Repeating Island*, 20.
55 Beeharry, *TOML*, 16.
56 See entry for 'trans-' in the *Concise Oxford English Dictionary*, 10th ed.
57 Beeharry, *TOML*, 29.
58 Ibid., 20; emphasis added.
59 Mishra, '(B)ordering Naipaul,' 198.
60 Beeharry, *TOML*, 286.
61 Northrup, *Indentured Labour*, 66.

62 Manish's narrative seems inspired by Beeharry's short story titled 'Le Nouveau Venu' found in a multilingual collection of his short fiction, *The Road Ahead.*

63 Beeharry, *TOML*, 131.

64 Carter, *Servants, Sirdars and Settlers*, 30.

65 Ibid., 200.

66 See Tinker, *A New System of Slavery*, and Carter, *Servants, Sirdars and Settlers*, for an in-depth study of the genesis and reform of the contractual system of indenture. As both historians state, the number of years of bondage were constantly under revision, fluctuating anywhere from two-to five-year periods. All historians concur, however, that the 1870s ushered in major reform. The system of indenture officially lasted until 1917. By 1922 labourers were finally free to work wherever they wished.

67 Beeharry, *TOML*, 216–7.

68 In 1871 Adolphe de Plevitz forwarded such a petition, signed by approximately 10, 000 labourers, to the governor of Mauritius, Sir Arthur Hamilton Gordon (1871–4). For a more detailed study of de Plevitz's role in labour reform, see Mookherji, *The Indenture System in Mauritius (1837–1915).*

69 Mookherji, *The Indenture System*, 54.

70 Beeharry, *TOML*, 72.

71 Mookherji, *The Indenture System*, 53.

72 A *baitka* is a Hindu socio-religious association. Throughout the novel, various community activities are shown to revolve around *baitkas.*

73 Fabre, 'Mauritian Voices,' 129.

74 Beeharry, *TOML*, 76, 74.

75 By 1844 women comprised 17 per cent of the Indo-Mauritian population. This ratio increased once labourers were permitted to emigrate with their families, but it was a gradual change which left women vulnerable to abuse by planter and labourer alike.

76 Carter, *Servants, Sirdars and Slavery*, 182.

77 I am referring, of course, to Thomas Hardy's *Tess of the D'Urbervilles.* Hardy has most certainly had a major influence on Beeharry, which can be seen in the social realism (though without the latter's overly deterministic view) that pervades his oeuvre.

78 Tinker, *A New System of Slavery*, 88

79 *Malagash* is the term used to describe the descendants of African slaves from Madagascar.

80 Beeharry, *TOML*, 77.

81 Bernstein, *Tale of the Tribe*, 9

82 Beeharry, *TOML*, 304.

4 'Passenger Indians' and Dispossessed Citizens in Uganda and South Africa

1 South Asian trade and, to a lesser degree, settlement, along the East African coast dates as far back as the first century AD. Upon their arrival in Zanzibar in the nineteenth century, British officials must have noticed the ease with which South Asian and Arab settlers conducted their daily trade under the sultanate's authority, a trade which included slavery. As I have indicated in the previous chapter on Mauritius, South Asians were also used as slaves alongside their African counterparts in French colonies. See Twaddle, 'East African Asians through a Hundred Years,' Tinker, 'Indians Abroad,' and Sarvan, 'Ethnicity and Alienation.'

2 See Ocaya-Lakidi, 'Black Attitudes to the Brown and White Colonizers of East Africa,' Twaddle, 'East African Asians,' and Nazareth, *Literature and Society in Modern Africa.*

3 Carter and Torabully, *Coolitude,* 118.

4 Indian independence has exerted a considerable impact on group dynamics and realignments throughout the diaspora. In the African context, many migrants also retained Indian citizenship.

5 Ngũgĩ wa Thiong'o, *Weep Not Child,* 7–8.

6 Ocaya-Lakidi, 'Black Attitudes,' 82.

7 Nazareth and Ngũgĩ became acquainted while they were students at the Makerere University in Kampala, Uganda. See Simatei, *The Novel and the Politics of Nation Building in East Africa*; for a discussion of the Ngũgĩ-Nazareth connection, see Bernth Lindfors's interview with Peter Nazareth in Lindfors's *Mazungumzo.*

8 Nazareth, *In a Brown Mantle.* This will be abbreviated as *IBM* throughout this chapter. Unfortunately, the novel is out of print.

9 'Asian' was the official racial category created by the British East Africa Protectorate to refer to people of South Asian descent. 'Indian' was the equivalent classification in South Africa. Nazareth and Karodia resist these labels in their insistence on South Asian ethnic pluralities.

10 Ocaya-Lakidi, 'Black Attitudes,' 82.

11 The population deemed of Asian or Indian descent has plummeted from approximately 100,000 each in Tanzania, Kenya, and Uganda to less than 1 per cent of the greater population since each nation's rise to independence in the early sixties. Uganda became independent in 1962 under the leadership of Milton Obote. (Nazareth's figure of Robert Kyeyune in *In a Brown Mantle* is a thinly veiled fictionalization of Obote and his ascension to power.)

12 Twaddle, 'East African Asians,' 150.
13 These figures are from the 2001 South Africa census. See http://www
.statssa.gov.za/census01/html/RSAPrimary.pdf.
14 Coovadia, *The Wedding*, 105.
15 Ngũgĩ wa Thiong'o's *Weep Not, Child* depicts the Gikuyu-led Mau Mau armed
rebellion against British imperial rule in the author's native Kenya.
16 One only has to think of the repeated stereotypical images of the servile
Indian or usurious merchant in such works as Joyce Cary's *Mister Johnson* or
Isak Dinesen's *Out of Africa*, not to mention Hollywood's perpetuation of
these stereotypes.
17 Gregory, 'Literary Development in East Africa,' 440.
18 For example, Ugandan literature has been graced by the 2001 publication
of Jameela Siddiqi's first novel *The Feast of the Nine Virgins*. Siddiqi resides in
England but her novel is set entirely in her native Uganda. See Peter
Nazareth's review of her first novel in *World Literature Today*.
19 In 1991, President Yoweri Musevini officially invited the exiled 'Asians' to
return to Uganda, a few years after the overthrow of Idi Amin.
20 Rastoji, 'From South Asia to South Africa,' 549.
21 Ibid., 549–50.
22 Nazareth, 'Waiting for Amin,' 8.
23 See Simatei, 'La question asiatique.'
24 Ibid., 21. My translation of the Simatei citation: 'They have attempted to
evaluate the forces that created homogenous nations to the detriment of
minorities of foreign origins and have, above all, tried to evaluate the
responsibility of all parties involved.'
25 Rubadiri, *No Bride Price*, 105.
26 Siddiqi, 'Uganda: a personal viewpoint on the expulsion, 30 years.'
27 Sam, 'The Well-Loved Woman,' in *Jesus Is Indian*, 45.
28 Ibid.
29 The Goan community is a diaspora in and of itself. Located on the southeast-
ern coast of the Indian subcontinent, Goa was a Portuguese colony for
450 years, only becoming part of post-independence India in 1961. Goans are
known to reject the label 'Indian,' and are considered to be the most
Europeanized of South Asians, perhaps if only because of colonial Portugal's
stringent policy of conversion to Roman Catholicism. Goans are almost 40 per
cent Roman Catholic. Gujratis are a particularly important immigrant group
given their ancient history of trade along the East African coastal regions.
Chinese artefacts such as blue and white porcelain are said to have been
transported on Gujrati ships during the medieval period. Gujrat is a major
state in the northwestern Indian subcontinent; it is a majority Muslim area.
30 Kuper, *Indian People in Natal*, xv.

31 Shinebourne, *Timepiece*, 12.

32 Lindfors, 'Sites of Production in African Literature Scholarship,' 167.

33 Versi, 'Not at Home, At Home,' 40.

34 Apartheid came into being with the election of the National Party in 1948.
    South Africa repealed its apartheid laws in 1991. See Davenport, *South
    Africa*, and Ormond, *The Apartheid Handbook*.

35 Nazareth states, in his interview with Bernth Lindfors, that he completed
    the novel in January 1970; it was published in 1972.

36 The only other novels focusing on the South Asian diaspora in East Africa
    produced at this time were David Rubadiri's *No Bride Price* (1967) and
    Behadar Tejani's *Day After Tomorrow* (1971).

37 The factors contributing to Idi Amin Dada's expulsion edict are the source
    of much debate among scholars and critics. See Twaddle, 'Was the Expul-
    sion Inevitable?' Most agree, however, that the seeds of discontent were
    sown well before his military-backed coup against President Milton Obote in
    1971. Amin's regime lasted from 1971 to 1979. See Jorgensen, *Uganda*.

38 See, for instance, Max Dorsinville's discussion of the 'mad king' in Haitian
    literature in his critical edition of Roger Dorsinville's novels, *The Rule of
    François ('Papa Doc') Duvalier in Two Novels by Roger Dorsinville.*

39 Salman Rushdie, 'Imaginary Homelands,' 19.

40 Ibid., 15.

41 Ibid., 19.

42 Elder, 'Indian Writing in East and South Africa,' 138.

43 See Arun Mukherjee's 'Whose Post-Colonialism and Whose Postmodernism?'

44 R. Radhakrishnan, *Diasporic Mediations*, xxiii.

45 Karodia, *Daughters of the Twilight*, 35–6.

46 Coovadia, *The Wedding*, 189.

47 Lindfors, 'Love in Oppressive Times,' 66.

48 Marina Carter suggests that Gandhi's legal interventions on behalf of the
    'South African Indian' were qualified in the delineation between the Indian
    merchants and the '[lower caste] coolies' (Carter and Torabully, *Coolitude*,
    118).

49 Rajendra Chetty, 'Exile and Return in Farida Karodia's *Other Secrets*,' in
    Indias Abroad, 144.

50 Karodia, quoted in Versi, 'Not at Home, At Home' 39.

51 Chetty, 'Exile and Return in Farida Karodia's *Other Secrets*,' 145.

52 Nazareth, *IBM*, 101.

53 By 1985, 91.3 per cent of Indians had been evicted from their businesses;
    similarly, those classified as 'coloured' constituted the highest percentage of
    families that were moved from their homes (66 per cent), followed by
    Indians (32 per cent). (See Ormond, *The Apartheid Handbook*.)

54 Ormond, *The Apartheid Handbook,* 33.

55 Karodia, *Daughters of the Twilight,* 24.

56 A great many indentured labourers in South Africa remained behind after the termination of their contracts. They came to be known as 'freed labourers' (see Kuper, *Indian People in Natal*). It is unclear whether Karodia's character Abdul arrived as a labourer or as a free passenger who worked alongside the labourers. In either case, it is significant that his lot was thrown in with the labourers he worked among.

57 Karodia, *Daughters of the Twilight,* 20.

58 Carter and Torabully, *Coolitude,* 62.

59 Karodia, *Daughters of the Twilight,* 93.

60 Ibid., 92.

61 Flockemann, '"Not-Quite Insiders and Not-Quite Outsiders,"': 38–9.

62 Karodia, *Daughters of the Twilight,* 73.

63 Ibid., 38.

64 Ibid., 41.

65 See Kuper, *Indian People in Natal.*

66 See Fanon's *Black Skin, White Masks,* and Ngũgĩ wa Thiong'o's 'The Language of African Literature.'

67 See Spivak's 'Can the Subaltern Speak?'.

68 See Nazareth's discussion of Behadur Tejani's *Day After Tomorrow* in 'Waiting for Amin.'

69 Two of the first laws to be established under the apartheid regime were The Immorality Amendment Act and Prohibition of Mixed Marriages Act, which 'forbade "unlawful carnal intercourse" or marriage between a white person on the one hand and an African, Indian or Coloured on the other' (Ormond, *The Apartheid Handbook,* 26).

70 See Bhabha, 'Signs Taken For Wonders,' 112.

71 Wicomb, 'Shame and Identity,' 93.

72 Karodia, *Daughters of the Twilight,* 77.

73 Ibid., 78.

74 Ibid., 83–4.

75 Boehmer, 'Endings and New Beginnings,' 50.

76 Nazareth, *IBM,* 150.

77 Rastoji, 'From South Asia to South Africa,' 556.

78 Karodia, *Daughters of the Twilight,* 119.

79 I borrow the term from John Skinner's *The Stepmother Tongue.*

80 Nazareth, 'Waiting for Amin,' 9.

81 Kiyimba, 'The Ghost of Idi Amin in Ugandan Literature,' 129.

82 Nazareth, *IBM,* 109.

83 Lindfors, Interview with Peter Nazareth, *Mazungumzo*, 90.
84 Nazareth, 'The Asian Presence in Two Decades of East African Literature,' 17.
85 Nazareth, *IBM*, 128.
86 Elder, 'Indian Writing in East and South Africa,' 118.
87 Nazareth, *IBM*, 23.
88 Ibid., 119.
89 Ibid., 74.
90 Simatei, *The Novel and the Politics of Nation Building in East Africa*, 113.
91 Kuper, 'The Goan Community in Kampala,' 58.
92 Nazareth, *IBM*, 2–3.
93 Lindfors, Interview with Peter Nazareth, *Mazungumzo*, 92.
94 Vijay Mishra, 'The Diasporic Imaginary,' 423.
95 Ahmed Virjee, quoted in Nazareth, 'The Asian Presence in Two Decades of East African Literature,' 20.
96 Nazareth, *IBM*, 110.
97 Ibid., 112.
98 Kiyimba, 'The Ghost of Idi Amin,' 131.
99 Nazareth, *IBM*, 150.
100 Young, *Colonial Desire*, 20.
101 Simatei, *The Novel and The Politics of Nation Building in East Africa*, 117.
102 See 'Ugandan-Asian Tensions Are Century Old' in *New Vision* (posted on the web 13 April 2007) by John Kakande, a Kampala journalist. The article discusses the 2007 riot in which one ethnic Indian was killed and many injured. Kakande contextualizes the event as one in a long series of interethnic rivalries which have continued well beyond the colonial era.

5 New Configurations of Identity for the Indo-Guyanese 'This Time Generation'

1 Hall, 'Cultural Identity,' 395.
2 Selvon, 'Three Into One Can't Go,' 10. Selvon writes in English Creole.
3 South Asian migrants also inhabit other parts of the Caribbean, including the French colonies (now departments) of Guadeloupe and Martinique, and Dutch Surinam. In the late nineteenth century, a community of migrants formed in Belize while it was a British colony.
4 See chapter 3 for a discussion of the Pass System.
5 See Brereton, 'The Experience of Indentureship,' and Singh, 'East Indians in the Larger Society,' for a discussion of the missionary school system and its impact on the indentured community.

6 See chapter 3 for a contextualization of the trope of the *jahaji-bhai.*
7 These statistics have been cross-referenced from Rauf, *Indian Village in Guyana,* and Carke et al., *South Asians Overseas.*
8 As Rauf contends, since its colonization by European powers, 'the unbroken account of Guyanese history … begins with the occupation of the colony by the English in 1831' (*Indian Village in Guyana,* 30).
9 Guyana is home to many different indigenous groups, most notably Caribs and Arawaks, natives of the Caribbean islands (the Caribs, of course, reminding us of why the archipelago was so-named). See Daly, *A Short History of Guyanese People.*
10 See, for instance, Cyril Dabydeen's short story 'Amerindians.'
11 See Rauf, *Indian Village in Guyana.* The 'six peoples' is a loose racial delineation which does not include 'Creole' as an official designation and yet distinguishes between Portuguese and European.
12 Selvon, 'Three Into One Can't Go,' 10.
13 Ibid., 11.
14 Email correspondence with author Cyril Dabydeen, 10 May 2003.
15 See Birbalsingh, *From Pillar to Post.*
16 Moore, *Cultural Power, Resistance, and Pluralism,* 306.
17 David Dabydeen, introduction to *Lutchmee and Dilloo,* by Edward Jenkins, 4.
18 See chapter 4 on East and South Africa for a discussion of the 'middleman' stereotype.
19 Birbalsingh, introduction to *Jahaji,* xi.
20 Das, 'They Came in Ships,' ll. 41–2, p. 289.
21 David Dabydeen, 'Coolie Odyssey,' ll. 122–6, pp. 11–12.
22 David Dabydeen, introduction to *Lutchmee and Dilloo,* by Edward Jenkins, 21.
23 Jenkins, *Lutchmee and Dilloo,* 34.
24 Itwaru, *Shanti,* 15.
25 Das, 'They Came in Ships,' 289.
26 Williams, review of *Corentyne Thunder* by Edgar Mittelholzer.
27 Shinebourne, interview by Frank Birbalsingh, *From Pillar to Post,* 148.
28 Ibid., Interview, 153.
29 See Poynting's overview 'Guyanese Literature (Peepal Tree Press Feature). Poynting is the founder and managing editor of Peepal Tree Press, which has been devoted to publishing Caribbean titles since its inception in 1985.
30 Mittelholzer, *Corentyne Thunder,* 9.
31 David Dabydeen, *The Intended,* 5.
32 Gafoor, 'The Depiction of Indo-Caribbean Female Experience by the Regional Woman Writer,' 56.

33 J.C. Jha notes that the majority of peoples came from the northern regions
of Uttar Pradesh and Bihar, while the minority principally came from
the southern region of Madras. The proportion of Hindus to Muslims was
85 per cent (Hindu) to 14 per cent Muslim by 1901. See Jha, 'The Indian
Heritage in Trinidad.

34 Samaroo, 'The Indian Connection,' 55.

35 The Hosay Festival was organized by the Shia Muslim community in
Trinidad, which sought to maintain the religious observance of Muharram,
in remembrance of Hussein's (Prophet Muhammad's grandson) martyrdom. Traditionally, an inclusive festival in the Indian subcontinent, the
Hosay Festival became a symbolic meeting ground of various religious and
ethnic groups in the plantation colony. See the special issue of *Indian Arrival
Day* 5.1 (2004), edited by the magazine's founder Kumar N. Mahabir. The
discussion of the Shia community in particular is taken from Daurius
Figueria's article 'The Islamic Realities of the Muharram Massacre of 1884'
(in the same issue, np).

36 Indeed, all of the contributors to the special *Indian Arrival Day* commemorative issue of the 120th anniversary of the Hosay Massacre of 1884 agree that
the incident had been virtually expunged from colonial records, and that it
is now up to the Indian community to resurrect the event so as to honour its
victims and ensure its recognition at the national level.

37 Kempadoo, *Buxton Spice*, 50.

38 Benjamin, introduction to *They Came in Ships*, 107.

39 Monar, *Janjhat*, 54.

40 Ibid., 38.

41 Poynting, introduction to *Backdam People*, by Rooplall Monar, 10.

42 Walcott, 'The Antilles,' 295.

43 The majority of indentured peoples in the Caribbean region came from
Eastern Bihar where the main language was Bhojpuri (a Hindi dialect).
In the mixed linguistic context of South Asian diasporic peoples, Indo-
Caribbeans cannot be said to speak only Creole, but a form of Creole that
incorporates South Asian languages, particularly Hindi, Urdu, and
Bhojpuri. See Brian L. Moore's comments about the creolization of
Bhojpuri with Afro-Guyanese Creole, in *Cultural Power, Resistance, and
Pluralism*.

44 Persaud, 'I hear a voice, is it mine?' 537.

45 The Barbadian poet Kamau Brathwaite spoke of the 'nation-language' in
History of the Voice in celebration, among other things, of the vibrant
influence of African oral culture on the English spoken in the Caribbean.
Braithwaite's nation-language looks to the creolized English in the West

Indies as an authoritative language of new world society, wrestling it free
from colonial perceptions of creolized English as dialects, as 'pidgin', or
merely as the bastardization of English. See also Nair, "Creolization, Orality,
and Nation Language in the Caribbean."

46 Monar, *Janjhat*, 10.
47 Schewcharan, 'Janjhat: Bhola Ram and the "Going Away Plan."'
48 For a more detailed look at Burnham's reign until the reelection of PPP
   (the first time since Guyana's independence from Britain in 1966), see the
   Guyana Human Rights Assocation's *Guyana: Fraudulent Revolution*. See Daly,
   A Short History of the Guyanese People.
49 Poynting, '"You Want to be a Coolie Woman?"', 101.
50 Suleri, 'Woman Skin Deep,' 246.
51 Trinidadian Lakshmi Persaud's *Butterfly in the Wind*, Antiguan Jamaica
   Kincaid's *Annie John*, Cuban-American Cristina Garcia's *Dreaming in Cuban*,
   and Guyanese Oonya Kempadoo's *Buxton Spice* are just a few Caribbean
   women writers whose first novels take the form of fictional autobiography.
52 Skinner, *The Stepmother Tongue*, 177. Skinner's categorization of the trends in
   anglophone Caribbean literature consist of the post-colonial dystopia, such
   as Shiva Naipaul's *A Hot Country* (1983), the fictional autobiography, such as
   George Lamming's *In the Castle of My Skin* (1953), experimental novels such
   as Wilson Harris's *Guyana Quartet* (1985), and, finally, 'other voices' under
   which all Indo-Caribbean writing would fall in its articulation of a 'new'
   ethno-Caribbean literary voice.
53 Gafoor, 'The Depiction of Indo-Caribbean Female Experience,' 129.
54 See Bacchus, 'The Education of East Indians in Guyana.'
55 Seenarine, 'Indentured Indian Women in Colonial Guyana,' 1.
56 See Mohammed, 'From Myth to Symbolism.'
57 Latif, 'Indo-Fijian Women – Past and Present,' 5
58 All subsequent references to Narmala Shewcharan's *Tomorrow Is Another Day*
   are from the Peepal Tree Press 1994 edition and will be abbreviated as
   TIAD.
59 Monar, *Janjhat*, 62.
60 Shewcharan, *TIAD*, 75.
61 Indeed, Monar is one of Guyana's leading literary voices. He is best known
   as a short story writer. *Backdam People* and *High House and Radio* are his two
   most important short story collections. There is very little biographical
   information on either Monar or Shewcharan. Any biographical information noted here has been taken from Poynting, 'Anglophone Caribbean
   Literature'; personal correspondence with Poynting (who published
   Monars' works) via email; Benjamin et al., *They Came in Ships*; and

Birbalsingh's introduction to *Jahaji*, as well as his collection of essays and reviews, *From Pillar to Post*.

62 Poynting, introduction to *Backdam People*, 9

63 Monar, *Janjhat*, 72.

64 Ibid., 14.

65 Shinebourne, *Timepiece*, 7.

66 The 'assimilationist versus traditionalist' debate is echoed across the South Asian diasporic context, from South Africa (see chapter 4) to the Caribbean, but it is a binary that needs to be better nuanced. At any rate, it certainly should not be generalized to the point that it is seen as the only response to diasporic identity.

67 See Partha Chatterjee's seminal work, *The Nation and Its Fragments*.

68 Monar, *Janjhat*, 18.

69 Ibid., 135.

70 Ibid., 122.

71 Shinebourne, 'Twin Influences,' 142.

72 Monar, *Janjhat*, 20.

73 Ibid., 13, 37 (emphasis added).

74 See Rauf, *Indian Village in Guyana*.

75 Monar, *Janjhat*, 110.

76 See Seenarine, 'Indentured Indian Women in Colonial Guyana.'

77 Monar, *Janjhat*, 83.

78 Ibid., 55.

79 Ibid., 8.

80 Ibid., 133–4.

81 Schewcharan, *TIAD*, 50.

82 Guyana Human Rights Association, *Guyana: A Fraudulent Revolution*, 84.

83 Schewcharan, *TIAD*, 17.

84 Rajan, *Real and Imagined Women*, 135.

85 Schewcharan, *TIAD*, 179.

86 Ibid., 185.

87 Ibid., 202.

88 See Samaroo, 'Two Abolitions.'

89 Schewcharan, *TIAD*, 183.

6 Indo-Trinidadian Fictions of Community within the Metanarratives of 'Faith'

1 Dr Kumar Mahabir, publisher and editor-in-chief of Chakra Publishing in San Juan, Trinidad, and chairman of the Indo-Caribbean Cultural Council,

has initiated a commemorative magazine called *Indian Arrival Day*. The national holiday and the magazine both mark the profound significance of this event to Indo-Trinidadian people.

2 The 2000 census does not provide ethnic ratios. These statistics have been taken from http://encarta.msn.com/fact_631504879/Trinidad_and_Tobago_Facts_and_Figures.html. Accessed 1 January 2008.

3 See Tinker, 'The Origins of Indian Migration to the West Indies,' and Narayan, 'Indian Diaspora.'

4 Walcott, 'The Antilles,' 294.

5 Lamming, 'The Indian Presence as a Caribbean Reality,' 47.

6 Ibid., 54.

7 See Dash, *The Other America.*

8 See Garcia, *Dreaming in Cuban* (1992), Kincaid, *Annie John* (1985), Jean Rhys, *Wide Sargasso Sea* (1966), and Ian McDonald, *The Hummingbird Tree* (1969), to name a few works in which the sea or water imagery are central to the novel's internal structure and themes as they pertain to issues of identity.

9 Glissant, *Caribbean Discourse*, 15.

10 Vijay Mishra calls this diaspora the old Indian diaspora of exclusivism or a self-contained 'little India.' See his numerous works on the subject.

11 Dash, *The Other America*, 5.

12 Since Sharlow Mohammed now self-publishes as Sharlow, I will refer to him as such in this chapter.

13 Sharlow, *The Elect*, 9.

14 See Ramraj, 'Still Arriving.' See specifically Naipaul, *The Enigma of Arrival* (1987), *The Mystic Masseur* (1957), *A House for Mr. Biswas* (1961), and *The Mimic Men* (1967).

15 See Robin Cohen's discussion of indentured peoples in *Global Diasporas*, and Vijay Mishra's '(B)ordering Naipaul.'

16 Tiffin, 'History and Community Involvement,' 96.

17 Birbalsingh, *From Pillar to Post*, xv.

18 V.S. Naipaul, quoted in Tiffin, 'History and Community Involvement,' 90.

19 Birbalsingh, *From Pillar to Post*, 141.

20 Khan, interview by Frank Birbalsingh, *From Pillar to Post*, 145.

21 Khan, interview by Frank Birbalsingh, 142–3.

22 Tiffin, 'History and Community Involvement,' 90.

23 Birbalsingh's reviews of Sharlow are found on the author's website sharlow.virtualave.net.

24 Ibid.

25 Sharlow, *The Promise*, 82. The appellation 'chinitat' recurs in Trinidadian writing. *Chini* is the Hindi/Urdu word for sugar. Chinitat, an interlingual

pun on Trinidad, refers to Trinidad as the land of sugar, in reference to the island's monoculture plantation economy, but more revealing, perhaps, of the early mythologization of a part of the world that the migrants would have known so little about.

26 Ibid., 70.

27 Both novels have been published locally, either by self-publication or by the Indo-Trinidadian publishing house Chakra, founded and run by scholar and author Kumar Mahabir.

28 The term is part of the title of Ramdin's non-fictional work *The Other Middle Passage*. The work provides a critical introduction and reprinting of the real-life journal of a British sea captain and his rare eyewitness account of the wretched conditions on board the 'coolie ship,' the *Salsette*, which made the journey from Calcutta to Trinidad.

29 Rampersad, *Finding a Place*, 2.

30 See Birbalsingh's *Jahaji: An Anthology of Indo-Caribbean Fiction*.

31 See Birbalsingh's discussion of Naipaul in *Jahaji* and in *From Pillar to Post*, and also Hassan, *V.S. Naipaul and the West Indies*. The latter is a comparative study of Western and non-Western criticism on V.S. Naipaul's oeuvre.

32 V.S. Naipaul, quoted in Vijay Mishra, '(B)ordering Naipaul,' 220.

33 All parenthetical references to *Butterfly in the Wind* will be cited as *BITW*. All citations are from the original (1990) Peepal Tree Press edition.

34 Naipaul, 'Two Worlds,' 7.

35 The *Ramleela* is a dramatization of the Hindu epic, the *Ramayana*.

36 Walcott, 'The Antilles,' 295.

37 Dash, introduction to *Caribbean Discourse*, by Edouard Glissant, xxxv.

38 See Mahabir, 'Animals from India in the Caribbean.' Mahabir notes that the goat, the cow, and the Rhesus monkey are just a few of the major examples. He also notes that skills such as animal husbandry were carried over from the subcontinent. This has led to cross-breeding with imported Indian species and local or other species imported from elsewhere. A visible product of this cross-breeding is the by now indigenized 'buffalypso.'

39 See Ramchand, 'Coming Out of Repression,' 225. Ramchand, Birbalsingh, and Poynting, who wrote the earliest reviews of Persaud's first *BITW*, refer to it as the first novel by an Indo-Caribbean woman writer.

40 Over a series of email communications, Peepal Tree Press publisher and literary critic Jeremy Poynting provided me with the biographical details of Persaud and Sharlow's life noted in this chapter.

41 See Rampersad, *Finding a Place*, 4.

42 Clifford, *Routes*, 250.

43 See my reading of Ramchandin in Pirbhai, 'An Ethnos of Difference, A Praxis of Inclusion.'

44 Canadian John A. Morton founded a Presbyterian missionary school system in the late 1800s, which offered the children of indenture communities access to education. This often resulted in the child's conversion to Christianity while his/her parents retained their faith. The resultant spiritual and psychic rift between child and parent, younger and older generation, is another common motif in Indo-Caribbean literature that is worth exploring further. For instance, fruitful comparisons could be made between Sharlow's *The Elect* and Mootoo's *Cereus Blooms at Night* in which religious conversion results in patterns of psychological and social dysfunction, which affect both the individual and the community.

45 Birbalsingh, *Jahaji*, 29.

46 Rampersad, *Finding a Place*, 12.

47 Sharlow, *The Elect*, 131.

48 Cyril Dabydeen, *The Wizard Swami*, 57.

49 Ibid., 27.

50 Ibid., 98.

51 Sharlow, *The Elect*, 9.

52 Persaud, *BITW*, 92.

53 The coolie stereotype has followed the indentured labourer across the globe and has remained relatively consistent in its prejudicial connotations, conjuring images of the the indentured labourer as thrifty, a heathen, or of the lowest social rung.

54 Naipaul, 'Two Worlds,' 7.

55 Naipaul, *The Suffrage of Elvira*, 74.

56 Sharlow, *The Elect*, 18.

57 Ibid., 24.

58 Persaud, *BITW*, 93.

59 See James Clifford's discussion of how diasporas define themselves against the local nation-state and nativist/indigenous claims in his seminal study, *Routes*.

60 Mehta, 'Cultural Hegemony,' 131.

61 Persaud, *BITW*, 183.

62 Though these racial tensions are themselves undergoing further critical examination and debate, Brinsley Samaroo echoes other scholars in his suggestion that 'Afro-Indian' tensions came about as a combination of the British Empire's racially divisive infrastructure and racial prejudices, and the pan-African and Indian independence movements. According to Samaroo, 'The visits of Indian missionaries and high commissioners, especially after

1947, and the revival of the Sanatan Dharam Maha Sabha dashed whatever hope there remained of Afro-Indian solidarity' ('Politics and Afro-Indian Relations in Trinidad,' 96).

63 Persaud, *BITW*, 183.
64 Both Kenneth Ramchand and Brinda Mehta touch on the conservative undercurrent in Persaud's *Butterfly in the Wind*, which makes the novel 'symptomatic of the condition it is trying to describe' (Ramchand, 'Coming Out of Repression,' 227).
65 Espinet, 'The Invisible Woman in West Indian Fiction,' 426.
66 Mehta, 'Cultural Hegemony,' 125.
67 See Chatterjee's theorization of Indian nationalist discourse, *The Nation and Its Fragments*.
68 Persaud, *BITW*, 39–40.
69 Niehoff and Niehoff, *East Indians in the West Indies*, 85.
70 Persaud, *BITW*, 34.
71 Brinda Mehta, *Diasporic (Dis)locations*, 18–19.
72 Said, 'Mind of Winter,' 54.
73 Persaud, *BITW*, 105.
74 Ramchand, 'Coming Out of Repression,' 227.
75 Persaud, *BITW*, 174.
76 Ibid., 175.
77 Ibid., 199.
78 Ibid., 201.
79 Ibid., 200–1.
80 Ibid., 202.
81 Ibid., 201.
82 Mehta, 'Cultural Hegeomy,' 126.
83 Sharlow, *The Elect*, 35.
84 Ibid., 73–4.
85 Ibid., 162.
86 See Puri, 'Race, Rape, and Representation.'
87 Sharlow, *The Elect*, 29.
88 Samaroo, 'Politics and Afro-Indian Relations in Trinidad,' 84.
89 Sharlow, *The Elect*, 133.
90 Rastafarians have a strict dietary code known as Ital, in keeping with an environmental sensibility. The dietary restrictions are much like those of Islam, including the rejection of alcohol and meat (especially pork). The concept of Ital is similar to that of the concept of *haram* in Islam, or the deeming of certain foods as unclean or impure. See Fernandez Olmos and Paravini-Gebert, *Creole Religions of the Caribbean*.

91 Sharlow, *The Elect*, 180.
92 Persaud, *BITW*, 175.

7 The Politics of (the English) Language in Malaysia and Singapore

1 Meyer, *Asia: A Concise History*, 59.
2 Ibid., 160.
3 European colonization refers not only to British rule but to competing Dutch, Portuguese, Spanish, French, and English interests. Britain established formal imperial rule in 1819 when Thomas Stamford Raffle acquired Singapore from the sultan of Johore (a period during which the Dutch still held on to Malacca, an important region in the Malaysian peninsula). See Meyer, *Asia: A Concise History*.
4 Arasaratnam, *Indians in Malaysia and Singapore*, 8–9.
5 As Arasaratnam confirms, 'Among Indian Muslims who have been settled for several generations there is a distinct tendency to merge with Malay Muslims.' Ibid., 176.
6 The ethnic make-up of Singapore, for instance, is 76.9 per cent Chinese, 19.7 per cent Malay, 8.8 per cent Indian, and 4.3 per cent Other. See Siddique and PuruShotam, *Singapore's Little India*. The ethnic make-up of the Malaysian peninsula as a whole is as follows: 50 per cent Malay, 37.1 per cent Chinese, 11 per cent South Asian, and 1.5 per cent Other. See Hirshman, *Ethnic and Social Stratification in Peninsular Malaysia*.
7 See Ampalavanar, *The Indian Minority and Political Change in Malaya*.
8 Ibid., 1.
9 Indeed, despite the 'Malayization' of Malaysia, the Chinese continued to dominate business and trade, and Malays themselves continued to suffer economic hardships in the years following independence. After a period of considerable political unrest and racial tension which led to a two-year state. of emergency in 1969, Malaysia came to enjoy considerable economic prosperity and stablilized race relations under the leadership, since 1981, of Prime Minister Mahathir bin Mohammed.
10 Yook, 'Traversing Boundaries,' 277.
11 Here, I am using John Skinner's term to refer to the Empire's permanent linguistic imprint on non-native English speakers. See *The Stepmother Tongue*.
12 Such generalizations are tentatively made in the awareness that Malaysian English literature is itself a relatively new body of writing, particularly in the form of the novel. There are, of course, exceptions even now such as the poet, playwright, and short story writer Ghulam-Sarwar Yousuf. Indeed, a comparative study of Maniam and Yousuf would be an important contribution

to existing criticism of English-language Malaysian literature.

13 Wignesan, 'Religion as Refuge, or Conflict and Non-Change,' 77.

14 Clammer, *Race and State in Independent Singapor*, 12.

15 Ibid., 4. Though the minorities within each 'racial group' are in relative control of their community activities, languages, religious beliefs, and so on, the historic stratification of labour in Singaporean society has resulted in the presence of Chinese and Indian peoples in a fair cross-section of society, the continued elite status of English and Eurasion peoples, and what Clammer refers to as the 'disaffected' status of indigenous Malays in their relatively lower occupational positions.

16 Ibid., 24.

17 See Catherine Lim, 'The Writer Writing in English in Multiethnic Singapore.'

18 Shirley Geok-Lin Lim, *Writing South/East Asia in English*, 115.

19 Ibid., 126. This is equally true of the Malaysian context. See specifically the informative overview of Malaysian English Literature by Yook, 'Traversing Boundaries,' and Vethamani's brief overview in 'Malaysian, Singaporean and Fijian Writers of the Indian Diaspora.'

20 Shirley Geok-Lin, *Writing South/East Asia in English*, 119.

21 Hyland, 'National and International Values,' 431.

22 Wilson, 'An Interview with K.S. Maniam,' 20.

23 In 1957 the Federation of Malaya marked the official last step in the process of decolonization. Malaysia and Singapore were united up until Singapore's split with the Federation of Malaya to form an independent city-state in 1965.

24 Yook, 'Traversing Boundaries,' 277.

25 Manicka, interview.

26 Unfortunuately, Manicka's work as well as that of Satya Colpani (Fiji's first female Indo-Fijian novelist) came to my attention after the bulk of this study had been written. For this reason, it has not been discussed in these chapters. However, as these are relatively recent contributions to the English-language literatures in these regions, I provide them as a reference for future scholarship. Both Manicka and Colpani live abroad. Manicka was born in Malaysia and moved to England where she established her literary career. Colpani mirrors this pattern, though her trajectory is from Fiji to Australia.

27 Singh, 'Staying Close But Breaking Free,' 103.

28 Ibid., 102.

29 All citations from *The Return* are from the first edition published by Heinemann Asia in 1981. There is also a second edition published by Skoob Books in 1996, which offers a more scholarly treatment of the novel with an

introduction by C.W. Watson, Anne Brewster's article 'Linguistic Boundaries' (also found in *A Sense of Exile: Essays in the Literature of the Asia-Pacific Region*), and 'A Note in Preview' by Ooi Boo Eng.

30 All citations from *A Candle or the Sun* are from the first edition published by Serpent's Tail in 1991. All subsequent references to the novel will appear as *COS*.

31 Maniam, *The Return*, 1.

32 Singapore became an independent city-state in 1965, headed by its founder Lee Kuan Yew. It has been governed and dominated by one party, formed in 1954 as PAP (People's Action Party). See Vreland et al., *Area Handbook for Singapore*, 1977.

33 Geok, 'Dissenting Voices,' 285.

34 Ibid., 290.

35 Young, 'K.S. Maniam,' 973.

36 Wilson, 'An Interview with K.S. Maniam,' 23.

37 Maniam, 'Arriving.'

38 Ibid., 9–11.

39 Ibid., 11.

40 Tang Soo Ping provides a wonderful close reading of Maniam's *The Return*. See 'Cultural Crossings,' originally published in *Jurnal Bahasa Jendala Alam* in 1996. The version used here is found on-line.

41 Ngũgĩ wa Thiong'o, 'The Language of African Literature,' 442.

42 Fanon, *Black Skin, White Masks*, 18.

43 Maniam, *The Return*, 4.

44 Ibid., 4.

45 Ibid., 6.

46 Ibid., 15.

47 Ibid., 22.

48 Ibid., 26.

49 Ibid., 76.

50 Ibid., 57.

51 Yook, 'Traversing Boundaries,' 278.

52 Maniam, *The Return*, 75.

53 Singh, 'Staying Close But Breaking Free,' 104.

54 See Maniam's *In a Far Country* (1993). This novel takes its protagonist out of his immediate Tamil community and more fully immerses him in contemporary Malaysian society.

55 Brewster, 'Linguistic Boundaries,' 175.

56 Maniam, 'The Malaysian Novelist,' 169.

57 Ibid., 168.

58 Maniam, *The Return*, 183.
59 Ibid., 184.
60 Ibid., 147.
61 Mishra, '(B)ordering Naipaul,' 226.
62 Le Blond, 'Gopal Baratham,' 103.
63 Siddique and PuruShotam, *Singapore's Little India*, 7.
64 Baratham, *Candle or the Sun*, 39.
65 See Holden, 'Writing Conspiracy.'
66 Lim, 'The Writer Writing in English in Multiethnic Singapore,' 39.
67 As Hyland points out, Baratham's accusation is somewhat problematized given the fact that his novel has been well received in Singapore itself; it has also been officially recognized and 'taught in undergraduate courses at the National University' (National and International Values, 427).
68 Baratham, *COS*, 12.
69 Baratham, interview, 93.
70 Hyland, 'National and International Values,' 429.
71 Baratham, *COS*, 190.
72 Ibid., 45.
73 Ibid., 44–5.
74 Ibid., 16.
75 Ibid., 98.
76 Ibid., 17, 18, 17.
77 Ibid., 152.
78 Ibid., 20.
79 Ibid., 109.
80 Shirley Geok-Lin Lim, *Writing South/East Asia*, 119.
81 Baratham, *COS*, 17.
82 Singh, 'An Approach to Singapore Writing in English,' 12.
83 Ibid., 12.
84 Baratham, *COS*, 58.
85 The notion of the 'sigh of history' is echoed throughout Derek Walcott's oeuvre. It refers to the ruptured sense of identity and history that is, in part, so profoundly represented by the writer's immersion in an imposed language.
86 Rushdie, 'Imaginary Homelands,' 15.

8 From the Ganges to the South Seas

1 Obeyesekere, *Cannibal Talk*, 181.
2 See Stevenson, *The Works of Robert Louis Stevenson*. 32 vols. (New York: Scribner's, 1924).

3 Obeyesekere, *Cannibal Talk*, 153.
4 Keown, introduction to *Postcolonial Pacific Writing*, 1.
5 See Mel Gibson (director), *Apocalypto* (Touchstone Pictures, 2006).
6 Lal, *'Girmit*, History, Memory,' 6–7.
7 Ahmed Ali, 'Indians in Fiji,' 13.
8 See Lal's *Crossing the Kala Pani*. In his historiographic work, Lal offers a richly detailed documentary account, using contracts and records of passage, of the development of indenture in Fiji. He also discusses the new recruitment policies and incentives to bring over 'free passengers' to Fiji in 1920, after the abolition of indenture.
9 Vijay Mishra, *Literature of the Indian Diaspora*, 41.
10 Ibid., 42.
11 Nandan, *The Wounded Sea*, 47.
12 Ibid., *The Wounded Sea*, 96.
13 Satendra Nandan, quoted in Manoa, 'Across the Fence,' 201.
14 Stevenson, *Works*, 24:180.
15 Vijay Mishra, *Literature of the Indian Diaspora*, 41. Mishra notes that the suicide rate among Indo-Fijians is one of the highest in the world.
16 Lal, *'Girmit*, History, Memory,' 23.
17 Manoa, 'Across the Fence,' 205.
18 Satendra Nandan, interview with ABC, 'Fiji's Real Crisis "Just Beginning."' http://www.abc.net.au/7.30/stories/s131085.htm. May 25 2000. Accessed: 18 December 2007.
19 See Naidu, 'The Fiji Indians.'
20 Nandan, *Fiji: Paradise in Pieces*, 97.
21 Ibid., *The Wounded Sea*, 3.
22 Ibid., 123.
23 *Girmitiya*, or the 'agreement people,' refers to the contractual agreement between imperial administrators and contract labourers. Though I find Mishra's theory of *girmitiya* both innovative and useful, I attempt to show some of its limitations in terms of its caste, gender, religious, and other biases.
24 Tiffin, 'History and Development of an Indo-Fijian Literary Tradition,' 66.
25 Vijay Mishra, *Literature of the Indian Diaspora*, 29.
26 Nandan, 'The Ghost,' ll. 38–9, 49–53, p. 152; emphasis added.
27 Nandan, *The Wounded Sea*, 88.
28 Chevla Kanaganayakam, interview with Satendra Nandan, 64.
29 Ibid.
30 Vijay Mishra, *Literature of the Indian Diaspora*, 29.
31 Shameem, 'The Art of Raymond Pillai, Subramani and Prem Banfal,' 44.

32 Lal, '*Girmit*, History, Memory,' 14.
33 Colpani, *Veiled Honour* 12.
34 Itwaru, *Shanti*, 77.
35 See Ramraj, 'Diasporas and Multiculturalism.'
36 Vijay Mishra, *Literature of the Indian Diaspora*, 32.
37 Kanwal, 'Indo-Fijian Poetry in the Colonial and Post-Colonial Eras,' 95.
38 Ibid., 98.
39 Nandan, *The Wounded Sea*, 7.
40 Ibid., 85.
41 Subramani, introduction to *The Indo-Fijian Experience*, xi.
42 Cyril Dabydeen, 'Elephants Make Good Stepladders,' ll. 1–3, 7–10, p. 91.
43 Nandan, *The Wounded Sea*, 18.
44 Vijay Mishra, *Literature of the Indian Diaspora*, 39.
45 Ibid., 40.
46 Harrex, afterword to *Fiji: Paradise in Pieces* by Satendra Nandan, 191.
47 Kanaganayakam, interview with Satendra Nandan, 60.
48 Nandan, *The Wounded Sea*, 161.
49 Ibid., 123.
50 See Lal, 'The Wreck of the *Syria*, 1884.'
51 Nandan, *The Wounded Sea*, 161.
52 Kanaganayakam, interview with Satendra Nandan, 69.
53 Nandan, *The Wounded Sea*, 5.
54 Nandan, *Fiji: Paradise in Pieces*, 98.
55 Mercer, 'Fijians Divided Over Coup Outlook.'

Conclusion

1 See Kuppusamy, 'Facing Malaysia's Racial Issues.'
2 See Mercer, 'Fijians Divided over Coup Outlook.'
3 See Kagande, 'Ugandan-Asian Tensions are Century Old.'

Bibliography

Literary Works

Appanah, Natacha. *Les rochers de poudre d'or.* Paris: Gallimard, 2003.
Baratham, Gopal. *A Candle or the Sun.* London: Serpent's Tail, 1991.
– *City of Forgetting: The Collected Stories of Gopal Baratham.* Ed. Ban Kah Choon. Singapore City: Times Books, 2001.
– *Moonrise, Sunset.* London: Serpent's Tail, 1996.
– *Sayang.* Singapore City: Times Books, 1991.
Beeharry, Deepchand. *Heart and Soul.* Port Louis, Mauritius: Swan, 1983.
– *Never Goodbye.* Port Louis, Mauritius: Editions Nationales, 1965.
– 'Le Nouveau Venu.' In *The Road Ahead,* by Beeharry, 1–24. Port Louis, Mauritius: Ashley Printers, 1976.
– *That Others Might Live.* New Delhi: Orient Paperbacks, 1976.
– *Three Women and a President.* New Delhi: Orient Paperbacks, 1979.
– *A Touch of Happiness.* Port Louis, Mauritius: Editions Nationales, 1966.
Bhagirathee, Jang B. *Chalo Chinidad: 'Let's Go Trinidad': Our Historical Novel, 1900–1950.* Port of Spain, Trinidad: J.B. Publications, 2003.
Budhooram, Kirk. *The Festival.* Washington, DC: Publish America, 2001.
Cary, Joyce. *Mister Johnson.* 1939. New York: Berkeley, 1961.
Cliff, Michelle. *Abeng.* 1984. New York: Plume, 1995.
Colpani, Satya. *Veiled Honour.* Suva, Fiji: Institute of Pacific Studies, University of the South Pacific, 2001.
Coovadia, Imraan. *The Wedding.* London: Picador, 2001.
Dabydeen, Cyril. 'Amerindians.' In *Theatre of the Arts: Wilson Harris and the Caribbean,* ed. Hena Maes-Jelink and Benedicte Ledent, 25–35. New York: Rodopi, 2002.
– *Drums of My Flesh.* Toronto: TSAR, 2005.

– *Imaginary Origins: Selected Poems, 1970–2002.* Leeds, UK: Peepal Tree Press, 2004.

– *The Wizard Swami.* 1985. Leeds, UK: Peepal Tree Press, 2007.

Dabydeen, David. 'Coolie Odyssey.' In *Coolie Odyssey,* 9–13. London: Hansib, 1988.

– *The Counting House.* 1996. Leeds, UK: Peepal Tree, 2005.

– *The Intended.* 1991. London: Minerva, 1992.

Dangor, Achmat. *Kafka's Curse.* 1997. New York: Pantheon, 1999.

– *Waiting For Leila.* Johannesburg: Ravan, 1981.

Danticat, Edwidge. *Breath, Eyes, Memory.* New York: Vintage, 1994.

Das, Mahadai. 'They Came in Ships.' In *India in the Caribbean,* ed. David Dabydeen and Brinsley Samaroo, 288–9. London: Hansib, 1997.

de St Pierre, Jacques Henri Bernardin. *Paul et Virginie.* London: Vernor and Hood, 1796.

Devi, Anand. *Rue la poudrière.* Abidjan: Nouvelles Editions Africaines, 1988.

Dinesen, Isak. *Out of Africa.* 1938. London: Century, 1985.

Espinet, Ramabai. *The Swinging Bridge.* Toronto: HarperCollins, 2003.

Essop, Ahmed. *Haji Musa and the Hindu Fire-Walker.* London: Readers International, 1988.

– *The Third Prophecy.* London: Picador, 2004.

Fernando, Lloyd. *Green is the Colour.* Singapore: Landmark Books, 1993.

– *Scorpion Orchid.* Kuala Lumpur: Heinemann, 1976.

Garcia, Cristina. *Dreaming in Cuban.* New York: Ballantine, 1992.

Goonam, K. *Coolie Doctor – An Autobiography.* Durban: Madiba Publishers, 1991.

Govender, Neela. *Acacia Thorn in My Heart.* Paris: Gaspard Nocturne, 2001.

Haggard, H. Rider. *King Solomon's Mines.* 1885. London: Penguin, 2007.

Hardy, Thomas. *Tess of the D'Urbervilles.* 1891. London: Penguin, 1995.

Harris, Wilson. *The Guyana Quartet.* London: Faber and Faber, 1985.

Hassam, Aziz. *The Lotus People.* Durban: The Institute of Black Research/Madiba Publishers, 2002.

Itwaru, Arnold. *Shanti.* 1988. London: Penguin, 1992.

Jenkins, Edward. *Lutchmee and Dilloo: A Study of West Indian Life.* 1877. Introduction by David Dabydeen. Oxford: Macmillan, 2003.

Jeyaratnam, Philip. *Abraham's Promise.* Singapore: Times Books International, 1995.

– *First Loves.* Singapore: Times Books International, 1987.

– *Raffles Place Ragtime.* Singapore: Times Books International, 1988.

Karodia, Farida. *Against an African Sky and Other Stories.* Toronto: TSAR, 1997.

– *Boundaries.* Johannesburg: Penguin, 2003.

– *Daughters of the Twilight.* London: The Women's Press, 1986.

– *Other Secrets.* London: Penguin, 2000.
– *A Shattering of Silence.* Oxford: Heinemann, 1993.
Kempadoo, Oonya. *Buxton Spice.* 1998. London: McArthur & Company, 1999.
Kempadoo, Peter. *Guyana Boy.* 1960. Leeds, UK: Peepal Tree, 2002.
Khan, Ismith. *The Crucifixion.* Leeds, UK: Peepal Tree, 2008.
– *Jumbie Bird.* 1961. London: Longman, 1987.
– *Obeah Man.* London: Hutchinson, 1964.
Kincaid, Jamaica. *Annie John.* 1985. New York: Noonday Press, 1997.
Kipling, Rudyard. 'The Man Who Would Be King.' 1888. London: Dover, 2004.
Ladoo, Harold Sonny. *No Pain Like This Body.* London: Heinemann, 1972.
Lamming, George. *In the Castle of My Skin.* 1953. New York: Collier, 1975.
Lim, Catherine. *Little Ironies: Stories of Singapore.* Singapore: Heinemann, 1978.
Mahabir, Joy. *Jouvert.* Bloomington, IN: Authorhouse, 2006.
Maharaj, Niala. *Like Heaven.* London: Random House, 2006.
Maniam, K.S. 'Arriving.' In *Arriving and Other Stories,* 7–20. Singapore City:
    Times Books International, 1995. 7–20.
– *Between Lives.* Petaling Jaya, Malaysia: Maya Press, 2003
– *In a Far Country.* London: Skoob, 1993
– *The Return.* Kuala Lumpur: Heinemann, 1981.
Manicka, Rani. *Rice Mother.* New York: Viking, 2003.
– *Touching Earth.* London: Sceptre, 2004.
McDonald, Ian. *The Hummingbird Tree.* London: Heinemann, 1969.
Mittelholzer, Edgar. *Corentyne Thunder.* 1941. London: Heinemann, 1970.
Mohan, Peggy. *Jahajin.* New Delhi: HarperCollins, 2007.
Monar, Rooplall. *Backdam People.* 1985. Leeds, UK: Peepal Tree Press, 1987.
– *High House and Radio.* Leeds, UK: Peepal Tree Press, 1994.
– *Janjhat.* Leeds, UK: Peepal Tree Press, 1989.
– *Koker.* Leeds, UK: Peepal Tree Press, 1987.
Mootoo, Shani. *Cereus Blooms at Night.* Vancouver: Press Gang, 1996.
– *He Drown She in the Sea.* New York: Grove Press, 2005.
Naidoo, Jay. *Coolie Location.* London: SA Writers, 1990.
Naipaul, Shiva. *A Hot Country.* London: Hamilton, 1983.
Naipaul, V.S. *The Enigma of Arrival.* Harmondsworth, Middlesex: Viking, 1987.
– *A House for Mr Biswas.* 1962. New York: Knopf, 1995.
– *The Mimic Men.* Harmondsworth, Middlesex: Penguin, 1969.
– *The Mystic Masseur.* 1957. London: Heinemann, 1971.
– *The Suffrage of Elvira.* London: Andre Deutsch, 1958.
Nandan, Satendra. 'The Ghost.' In *The Indo-Fijian Experience,* ed. Subramani,
    150. St Lucia, Queensland: Queensland University Press, 1979.
– *The Wounded Sea.* Sydney: Simon and Schuster, 1991.

Nazareth, Peter. *The General Is Up.* Toronto: TSAR, 1991.
– *In a Brown Mantle.* 1972. Nairobi: East African Literature Bureau, 1981.
Ngũgĩ wa Thiong'o. *Devil on the Cross.* London: Heinemann, 1982.
– *Weep Not, Child.* 1964. London: Heinemann, 1987.
Persaud, Lakshmi. *Butterfly in the Wind.* 1990. Leeds, UK: Peepal Tree Press, 1996.
– *For the Love of My Name.* Leeds, UK: Peepal Tree Press, 2000.
– *Raise the Lanterns High.* North Charleston, SC: BookSurge, 2007.
– *Sastra.* Leeds, UK: Peepal Tree Press, 1993.
Pillai, Raymond. 'The Celebration.' In *The Indo-Fijian Experience,* ed. Subramani, 91–6.
Pyamootoo, Barlen. *Bénarès.* Paris: Éditions de l'Olivier, 1999.
Ramdin, Ron. *Rama's Voyage.* San Juan, Trinidad: Chakra, 2004.
Rhys, Jean. *Wide Sargasso Sea.* 1966. New York: Norton, 1982.
Rubadiri, David. *No Bride Price.* Nairobi: East African Publishing House, 1967.
Rushdie, Salman. *The Satanic Verses.* London: Viking, 1988.
Sam, Agnes. *Jesus is Indian.* 1989. London: Heinemann, 1994.
Selvon, Sam. A *Brighter Sun.* London: Longman Trade, 1979.
– *The Lonely Londoners.* 1956. Toronto: TSAR, 1991.
Shah, Ryhaan. A *Silent Life.* Leeds, UK: Peepal Tree Press, 2005.
Sharlow. 'Bruit.' In *Jahaji: An Anthology of Indo-Caribbean Fiction,* ed. Frank Birbalsingh, 50–62. Toronto: TSAR, 2000.
– *Colour of Pain.* Longdenville, Trinidad: Sharlow Publishing, 2001.
– *The Elect.* Leeds, U.K.: Peepal Tree Press, 1992.
– *The Promise.* Longdenville, Trinidad: Sharlow, 1995.
– *Requiem for a Village and Apartheid Love.* Port of Spain, Trinidad: Imprint, 1982.
– *When Gods Were Slaves.* 1993. Lincoln, NE: Sirens Publications, 2004.
Shewcharan, Narmala. 'Janjhat: Bhola Ram and the "Going Away Plan."' In *Jahaji: An Anthology of Indo-Caribbean Fiction,* ed. Frank Birbalsingh, 74–88. Toronto: TSAR, 2000.
– *Tomorrow Is Another Day.* Leeds, UK: Peepal Tree Press, 1994.
Shinebourne, Janice. *The Last English Plantation.* Leeds, UK: Peepal Tree Press, 1988.
– *Timepiece.* Leeds, UK: Peepal Tree Press, 1986.
Siddiqi, Jameela. *The Feast of the Nine Virgins.* London: Bogle L'Ouverture, 2001.
– *Bombay Gardens.* www.lulupress.com. 2006.
Stevenson, Robert Louis. *The Works of Robert Louis Stevenson.* 32 vols. New York: C. Scribner's sons, 1925.
Syal, Meera. *Life Isn't All Ha Ha Hee Hee.* New York: Picador, 1999.
Tejani, Behadur. *Day After Tomorrow.* 1971. Nairobi: East African Literature Bureau, 1977.

Vassanji, M.G. *The In-Between World of Vikram Lall.* Toronto: Anchor, 2004.

Walcott, Derek. *Omeros.* 1990. New York: Noonday Press, 1997.

Webber, A.R.F. *Those That Be in Bondage: A Tale of Indian Indentures and Sunlit Western Waters.* 1917. Wellesley, MA: Calaloux Publications, 1988.

Secondary Works

Ahmed, Aijaz. 'Jameson's Rhetoric of Otherness and the "National Allegory."' *Social Text* 15 (1986): 65–88.

Ali, Ahmed. 'Indians in Fiji: An Interpretation.' In *The Indo-Fijian Experience,* ed. Subramani, 3–25. St Lucia, Queensland: Queensland University Press, 1979.

Altnöder, Sonja. *Inhabiting the 'New' South Africa: Ethical Encounters at the Race-Gender Interface in Four Post-Apartheid Novels by Zoë Wicomb, Sindiwe Magona, Nadine Gordimer and Farida Karodia.* Trier: Wissenschaftlicher Verlag, 2008.

Ampalavanar, Rajeswary. *The Indian Minority and Political Change in Malaya: 1945–1957.* Kuala Lumpur: Oxford University Press, 1981.

Anzaldúa, Gloria, and Cherrie Moraga, eds. *This Bridge Called My Back: Writings by Radical Women of Color.* Watertown, MA: Persephone Press, 1981.

Appadurai, Arjun. 'Disjuncture and Difference in the Global Cultural Economy.' In *Colonial Discourse and Post-Colonial Theory,* ed. Williams and Chrisman, 324–39.

Arasaratnam, Sinnappah. *Indians in Malaysia and Singapore.* Bombay: Oxford University Press, 1970.

Attridge, Derek, and Rosemary Jolly, eds. *Writing South Africa: Literature, Apartheid, and Democracy, 1970–1995.* Cambridge: Cambridge University Press, 1998.

Bacchus, M.K. 'The Education of East Indians in Guyana.' In *Indenture and Exile: The Indo-Caribbean Experience,* ed. Birbalsingh, 159–69.

Baratham, Gopal. Interview. In *Interlogue: Studies in Singapore Literature.* ed. Kirpal Singh, 4:80–103. Singapore City: Ethos Books, 2001.

Beeharry, Deepchand. 'Why Do I Write?' In *The Road Ahead,* 1–3. Port Louis, Mauritius: Ashley Printers, 1976.

Benitez-Rojo, Antonio. *The Repeating Island: The Caribbean and the Postmodern Perspective.* Trans. James E. Maraniss. Durham, NC: Duke University Press, 1992.

Benjamin, Joel, et al, eds. *They Came in Ships: An Anthology of Indo-Guyanese Prose and Poetry.* Leeds, UK: Peepal Tree Press, 1998.

Bennett, Bruce, ed. *A Sense of Exile: Essays in Literature of the Asia-Pacific Region.* Nedlands, Australia: Centre for Studies in Australian Literature, 1988.

Bernstein, Michael. *The Tale of the Tribe: Ezra Pound and the Modern Verse Epic.* Princeton, NJ: Princeton University Press, 1980.

Bhabha, Homi K. *The Location of Culture.* London: Routledge, 1994.

Bhana, Surendra, ed. *Essays on Indentured Indians in Natal.* Leeds, UK: Peepal Tree Press, 1990.

Bhautoo-Dewnarain, Nandini. 'Mauritian Writing in English.' *Wasafiri* 30 (1999): 21–4.

Birbalsingh, Frank, ed. *From Pillar to Post: The Indo-Caribbean Diaspora.* Toronto: TSAR, 1997.

– ed. *Indenture and Exile: The Indo-Caribbean Experience.* Toronto: TSAR, 1989.

– ed. *Jahaji: An Anthology of Indo-Caribbean Fiction.* Toronto: TSAR, 2000.

– Review of *The Promise* by Sharlow Mohammed. sharlow.virtualave.net.

Boehmer, Elleke. 'Endings and New Beginnings: South African Fiction in Transition.' In *Writing South Africa: Literature, Apartheid, and Democracy, 1970–1995.* Ed. Attridge and Jolly, 43–56.

Bowman, Larry W. *Mauritius: Democracy and Development in the Indian Ocean.* Boulder, CO: Westview Press, 1991.

Brathwaite, Kamau. *History of the Voice: The Development of Nation Language in Anglophone Caribbean Poetry.* London: New Beacon Books, 1984.

Braziel, Jane Evans, and Anita Mannur. 'Nation, Migration, Globalization: Points of Contention in Diaspora Studies.' In *Theorizing Diaspora,* ed. Braziel and Mannur, 1–22.

– eds. *Theorizing Diaspora.* Malden, MA: Blackwell, 2003.

Brereton, Bridget. 'The Experience of Indentureship: 1845–1917.' In *Calcutta to Caroni: The East Indians in Trinidad,* ed. John La Guerre, 25–38. London: Longman Caribbean, 1974.

Brewster, Anne. 'Linguistic Boundaries: K.S. Maniam's *The Return.*' In *A Sense of Exile: Essays in Literature of the Asia-Pacific Region,* ed. Bennett, 173–80.

Burton, Benedict. *Mauritius: The Problems of a Plural Society.* London: Pall Mall Press, 1965.

Carter, Marina. *Servants, Sirdars and Settlers: Indians in Mauritius, 1834–1874.* Delhi: Oxford University Press, 1995.

Carter, Marina, and Khal Torabully. *Coolitude: An Anthology of the Indian Labour Diaspora.* London: Anthem Press, 2002.

Chatterjee, Partha. *The Nation and Its Fragments: Colonial and Postcolonial Histories.* Princeton: Princeton University Press, 1993.

Chetty, Rajendra. 'Exile and Return in Farida Karodia's *Other Secrets.*' In *Indias Abroad: The Diaspora Writes Back,* ed. Chetty and Piciucco, 143–50.

Chetty, Rajendra, and Pierre Paolo Piciucco, eds. *Indias Abroad: The Diaspora Writes Back.* Johannesburg: STE, 2004.

Clammer, John. *Race and State in Independent Singapore, 1965–1990: The Cultural Politics of Pluralism in a Multiethnic Society.* Aldershot, England: Ashgate, 1998.

Clarke, Colin, et al, eds. *South Asians Overseas: Migration and Ethnicity.* Cambridge: Cambridge University Press, 1990.

Clifford, James. *Routes: Travel and Translation in the Late Twentieth Century.* Cambridge, MA: Harvard University Press, 1997.

– 'Travelling Cultures.' In *Cultural Studies,* ed. Lawrence Grossberg et al. 96–116. New York: Routledge, 1992.

Cohen. Robin. *Global Diasporas: An Introduction.* Seattle: University of Washington Press, 1997.

Crane, Ralph J., and Radhika Mohanran. 'Constructing the Diasporic Body.' In *Shifting Continents/Colliding Cultures: Diaspora Writing of the Indian Subcontinent,* ed. Crane and Mohanran, vii–xv. Atlanta, GA: Rodopi, 2000.

Cudjoe, Selwyn R., ed. *Caribbean Women Writers: Essays from the First International Conference.* Wellesley, MA: Calaloux, 1990.

Dabydeen, David, and Brinsley Samaroo, eds. *India in the Caribbean.* London: Hansib, 1987.

Daly, Vere T. *A Short History of the Guyanese People.* London: Macmillan, 1975.

Dash, Michael. *The Other America: Caribbean Literature in a New World Context.* Charlottesville, VA: University Press of Virginia, 1998.

Davenport, T.R.H. *South Africa: A Modern History.* 1977. 3rd ed. Toronto: University of Toronto Press, 1987.

Deloughery, Elizabeth. '"The Litany of Islands, the Rosary of Archipelagos": Caribbean and Pacific Archipelagraphy.' *ARIEL: A Review of International English Literature* 32.1 (2001): 21–53.

Dorsinville, Roger. *The Rule of François ('Papa Doc') Duvalier in Two Novels by Roger Dorsinville: Realism and Magic Realism in Haiti.* Ed. and Trans. Max Dorsinville. Lewiston, NY: Edwin Mellen Press, 2000.

Dubois, W.E.B. *The Souls of Black Folk.* 1903. New York: Barnes and Noble, 2003.

Elder, Arlene A. 'Indian Writing in East and South Africa: Multiple Approaches to Colonialism and Apartheid.' In *Reworlding,* ed. Nelson, 115–39.

Espinet, Ramabai. Interview. 'A Sense of Constant Dialogue: Writing, Women and Indo-Caribbean Culture.' In *The Other Woman: Women of Colour in Contemporary Canadian Literature,* ed. Makeda Silver, 94–115. Toronto: Sister Vision, 1994.

Fabre, Michel. 'Mauritian Voices: A Panorama of Contemporary Creative Writing in English.' *World Literature Written in English* 19 (1980): 121–43.

Fanon, Frantz. *Black Skin, White Masks.* Trans. Charles Lam Markmann. New York: Grove Press, 1967.

Fernandez Olmos, Margarite, and Lizabeth Paravisini-Gebert. *Creole Religions of the Caribbean: An Introduction From Vodou and Santeria to Obeah and Espiritismo.* New York: New York University Press, 2003.

Figueria, Daurius. 'The Islamic Realities of the Muharram Massacre of 1884.' *Indian Arrival Day* (special commemorative issue) 5.1 (2004): n.p.

Flockemann, Miki. '"Not-Quite Insiders and Not-Quite Outsiders": The "Process of Womanhood" in *Beka Lamb*, *Nervous Conditions*, and *Daughters of the Twilight.*' *Journal of Commonwealth Literature* 27.1 (1992): 37–47.

Foucault, Michel. 'Of Other Spaces.' Trans. Jay Miskowiec. *Diacritics* 16 (1986): 22–7.

Gafoor, Ameena. 'The Depiction of Indo-Caribbean Female Experience by the Regional Woman Writer: Jan Shinebourne's *The Last English Plantation.*' In *The Woman, the Writer and Caribbean Society: Critical Analyses of the Writings of Caribbean Women; Proceedings of the Second International Conference,* ed. Helen Pyne-Timothy, 128–39. Los Angeles: University of California, Centre for African American Studies, 1998.

Geok, Leong Liew. 'Dissenting Voices: Political Engagements in the Singaporean Novel in English.' *World Literature Today* 74.2 (2000): 285–92.

Gilroy, Paul. 1993. 'The Black Atlantic as a Counterculture of Modernity.' In *Theorizing Diaspora,* ed. Braziel and Mannur, 49–80.

Glissant, Edouard. *Caribbean Discourse: Selected Essays.* 1989. Trans. Michael Dash. Charlottesville: University Press of Virginia, 1992.

Gopinath, Gayatri. 'Queer Diasporas: Gender, Sexuality and Migration in Contemporary South Asian Literature and Cultural Production.' PhD diss, Columbia University, 1998. Ann Arbor: UMI, 1998. 9838933.

Gregory, Robert. 'Literary Development in East Africa: The Asian Contribution, 1955–1975.' *Research in African Literatures* 12.4 (1981): 440–59.

Guyana Human Rights Association: *Guyana: A Fraudulent Revolution.* London: Latin American Bureau, 1984.

Hall, Stuart. 'Cultural Identity and Diaspora.' In *Colonial Discourse and Post-Colonial Theory,* ed. Williams and Chrisman, 392–403.

Harrex, Syd. Afterword of *Fiji: Paradise in Pieces,* by Satendra Nandan. Adelaide: Centre for Research in the New Literature in English, 2000.

Hassan, Dolly Zulakha. *V.S. Naipaul and the West Indies.* New York: Peter Lang, 1989.

Henderson, Mae Gwendolyn. 'Speaking in Tongues: Dialogics, Dialectics and the Black Woman Writer's Literary Tradition.' In *Colonial Discourse and Post-Colonial Theory: A Reader,* ed. Patrick Williams and Laura Chrisman, 257–67. New York: Columbia University Press, 1994.

Hirshman, Charles. *Ethnic and Social Stratification in Peninsular Malaysia.* Washington: American Sociological Association, 1975.

Holden, Philip. 'Writing Conspiracy: Race and Rights in Two Singapore Novels.' *Journal of Postcolonial Writing* 42.1 (2006): 58–70.

Huttenback, Robert A. *Gandhi in South Africa: British Imperialism and the Indian Question, 1860–1914*. Ithaca, NY: Cornell University Press, 1971.

Hyland, Peter. 'National and International Values: Singaporean Writing and Its Critics.' In *Nationalism and Internationalism: (Inter)National Dimensions of Literatures in English*, ed. Wolfgang Zach and Ken L. Goodwin, 427–34. Tübingen: Stauffenburg Verlag, 1996.

Ilieva, Emilia. 'Celebrating Nazareth at 60.' *The Sunday Nation*, 10 Dec. 2000: 13.

Issur, Kumari R. 'Le roman mauricien d'aujourd'hui.' *Francofonia: Studi e ricerche sulle letterature di lingua francese* 25.48 (2005): 115–24.

Jameson, Fredric. 'Third World Literature in the Era of Multinational Capitalism.' *Social Text* 15 (fall 1986): 65–88.

Jha, J.C. 'The Indian Heritage in Trinidad.' In *Calcutta to Caroni: The East Indians in Trinidad*, ed. La Guerre, 1–24.

Jorgensen, Jan Jelmert. *Uganda: A Modern History*. New York: St Martin's Press, 1981.

Kakande, John. 'Ugandan-Asian Tensions Are Century Old.' *New Vision*. www.newvision.co.ug. Accessed 13 April 2007.

Kanaganayakam, Chevla. Interview with Satendra Nandan. In *Configurations of Exile. South Asian Writers and Their World*, by Kanaganayakam, 59–71. Toronto: TSAR, 1995.

Kanwal, Jogindar Singh. 'Indo-Fijian Poetry in the Colonial and Post-Colonial Eras.' *SPAN: Journal of the South Pacific Association for Commonwealth Literature and Language Studies* 42–3 (1996): 86–100.

Keown, Michelle. *Postcolonial Pacific Writing: Representations of the Body*. New York: Routledge, 2005.

Khan, Ismith. Interview by Frank Birbalsingh. In *From Pillar to Post*, ed. Birbalsingh, 139–46.

Killam, G.D., ed. *The Writing of East and Central Africa*. London: Heinemann, 1994.

Kiyimba, Abasi. 'The Ghost of Idi Amin in Ugandan Literature.' *Research in African Literatures* 29.1 (1998): 124–38.

Kuper, Hilda. *Indian People in Natal*. Durban: Durban University Press, 1960.

Kuper, Jessica. 'The Goan Community in Kampala.' In *Expulsion of a Minority: Essays on Ugandan Asians*, ed. Michael Twaddle, 53–69. London: Athlone Press, 1975.

Kuppusamy, Baradan. 'Facing Malaysia's Racial Issues.' *Time*. http://www.time.com/time/world/article/0,8599,1687973,00.html. 26 November 2007. Accessed 5 January 2008.

La Guerre, John, ed. *Calcutta to Caroni: The East Indians in Trindad.* London: Longman Caribbean, 1974.

Lal, Brij V. *Crossing the Kala Pani: A Documentary History of Indian Indenture in Fiji.* Canberra: Division of Pacific and Asian History, 1998.

– '*Girmit*, History, Memory.' In *Bittersweet: The Indo-Fijian Experience*, ed. Brij V. Lal, 1–30. Canberra: Pandanus Books, 2004.

– 'The Wreck of the *Syria*, 1884.' In *The Indo-Fijian Experience*, ed. Subramani, 26–40.

Lamming, George. 'The Indian Presence as a Caribbean Reality.' In *Indenture and Exile: The Indo-Caribbean Experience*, ed. Birbalsingh, 45–54.

Latif, Shireen. 'Indo-Fijian Women – Past and Present.' *Manushi* 39 (1987): 2–10.

Lavie, Smadar, and Ted Swedenburg. 'Displacement, Diaspora, and Geographies of Identity.' In *Displacement, Diaspora, and Geographies of Identity*, ed. Lavie and Swedenburg, 1–25. Durham, NC: Duke University Press, 1996.

Le Blond, Max. 'Gopal Baratham.' In *Encylopaedia of Post-Colonial English Literature.* New York: Routledge, 1994.

Lim, Catherine. 'The Writer Writing in English in Multiethnic Singapore: A Cultural Peril, A Cultural Promise.' In *Asian Voices in English*, ed. Mimi Chan and Roy Harris, 33–42. Hong Kong: Hong Kong University Press, 1991.

Lim, Shirley Geok-Lin. *Writing SouthEast/Asia in English: Against the Grain, Focus on Asian English-Language Literature.* London: Skoob, 1994.

Lindfors, Bernth. Interview with Peter Nazareth. In *Mazungumzo: Interviews with East African Writers, Publishers, Editors, and Scholars*, ed. Lindfors, 80–97. Athens, OH: Ohio University Center for International Studies, 1980.

– 'Love in Oppressive Times: South Africa's First Indian Novel.' *Toronto Review* (1997): 66–73.

– 'Sites of Production in African Literature Scholarship.' *ARIEL: A Review of International English Literature* 31.1–2 (2000): 153–71.

Lionnet, Françoise. 'Creolité in the Indian Ocean: Two Models of Cultural Diversity.' *Yale French Studies* 82 (1993): 101–12.

Mahabir, Kumar. 'Animals from India in the Caribbean.' *Indian Arrival Day* 4.1 (May–June, 2003): n.p.

Maniam, K.S. 'The Malaysian Novelist: Detachment or Spiritual Transendence?' In *A Sense of Exile*, ed. Bennett, 167–72.

Manicka, Rani. Interview. http://us.penguingroup.com/static/rguides/us/rice_mother.html. Accessed 6 July 2008.

Manoa, Pio. 'Across the Fence.' In *The Indo-Fijian Experience*, ed. Subramani, 184–207.

Mehta, Brinda. 'The Colonial Curriculum and the Construction of "Coolie-ness" in Lakshmi Persaud's *Sastra* and *Butterfly in the Wind* and Janice Shinebourne's *The Last English Plantation*.' *Journal of Caribbean Literatures* 3.1 (2001): 111–28.

– 'Cultural Hegemony and the Need to Decentre the Brahmanic Stranglehold of Hindu Womanhood in an Indo-Caribbean Context: A Reading of Lakshmi Persaud's *Sastra* and *Butterfly in the Wind*.' *Journal of Commonwealth and Postcolonial Studies* 6.1 (1999): 125–52.

– *Diasporic (Dis)locations: Indo-Caribbean Women Writers Negotiate the Kala Pani.* Kingston, Jamaica: University of the West Indies Press, 2004.

Mercer, Phil. 'Fijians Divided Over Coup Outlook.' http://news.bbc.co.uk/2/hi/asia-pacific/6209620.stm. 5 December 2006. Accessed 21 December 2007.

Meyer, Milton W. *Asia: A Concise History*. Lanham, MD: Rowman and Littlefield, 1997.

Mishra, Sudesh. *Diaspora Criticism*. Edinburgh: Edinburgh University Press, 2006.

Mishra, Vijay. '(B)ordering Naipaul: Indenture History and Diasporic Poetics.' *Diaspora* 5.2 (1996): 189–237.

'The Diasporic Imaginary: Theorizing the Indian Diaspora.' *Textual Practice* 10.3 (1996): 421–48.

– '*Girmit* Ideology Revisited: Fiji Indian Literature.' *Reworlding*, ed. Nelson, 1–12.

– *The Literature of the Indian Diaspora*. New York: Routledge, 2007.

Mohammed, Patricia. 'From Myth to Symbolism: The Definitions of Indian Femininity and Masculinity in Post-Indentureship Trinidad.' In Matikor, ed. Rosanne Kanhai, 62–99. St Augustine, Trinidad: University of West Indies Press, 1999.

Mookherji, S.B. *The Indenture System in Mauritius (1837–1915)*. Calcutta: Firma K.L. Mukhopadhyay, 1962.

Moore, Brian L. *Cultural Power, Resistance, and Pluralism: Colonial Guyana 1838–1900*. Montreal: McGill University Press, 1995.

Morris, H.S. *The Indians in Uganda*. Chicago: University of Chicago Press, 1968.

Mukherjee, Arun. *Postcolonialism: My Living*. Toronto: TSAR, 1998.

– 'Whose Post-Colonialism and Whose Postmodernism?' *World Literature Written in English* 30.2 (1990): 1–9.

Mukherjee, Sirmat, and David Racker. 'Deepchand C. Beeharry (1927–).' In *Writers of the Indian Diaspora: A Bio-Bibliographical Critical Sourcebook*, ed. Nelson, 15–21.

Naidu, Vijay. 'The Fiji Indians: Denial of Citizenship.' In *Global Indian Diaspora: Yesterday, Today and Tomorrow*, ed. K. Mahan Gosine and Jyoti-Barot Motwani, 327–42. New York: Global Organization of People of Indian Origin, 1993.

Naipaul, V.S. *The Overcrowded Barracoon and Other Articles*, 1972. Harmondsworth, Middlesex: Penguin, 1976.

– 'Two Worlds.' The 2001 Nobel Lecture. *World Literature Today* 76.2 (2002): 4–10.

Nair, Supriya. 'Creolization, Orality, and Nation Language in the Caribbean.' In *A Companion to Post-Colonial Studies*, ed. Henry Schwartz and Sangeeta Ray, 236–51. Malden, MA: Blackwell, 2005.

Nandan, Satendra. *Fiji: Paradise in Pieces*. Adelaide: Centre for Research in the New Literature in English, 2000.

Narayan, K. Laxmi. 'Indian Diaspora: A Demographic Perspective.' Occasional Paper no. 3. Hyderabad: Centre for Study of Indian Diaspora, n.d.

Nazareth, Peter. 'The Asian Presence in Two Decades of East African Literature.' *Toronto Review* 13.1 (1994): 17–32.

– *Literature and Society in Modern Africa*. Kampala: East African Literature Bureau, 1972.

– Review of *The Feast of the Nine Virgins*, by Jameela Siddiqi. *World Literature Today* 76.3–4 (2002): 85–6.

– Waiting for Amin: Two Decades of Ugandan Literature.' In *The Writing of East and Central Africa*, ed. Killam, 7–35.

Nelson, Emmanuel S., ed. *Reworlding: The Literature of the Indian Diaspora*. Westport, CT: Greenwood Press, 1992.

– ed. *Writers of the Indian Diaspora: A Bio-Bibliographical Critical Sourcebook*. Westport, CT: Greenwood Press, 1993.

Ngũgĩ wa Thiong'o. 'The Language of African Literature.' In *Colonial Discourse and Post-Colonial Theory*, ed. Williams and Chrisman, 435–55.

Niehoff, Arthur, and Juanita Niehoff. *East Indians in the West Indies*. Milwaukee, WI: Milkwaukee Public Museum, 1960.

North-Coombes, M.D. 'Indentured Labour in the Sugar Industries of Natal and Mauritius.' In *Essays on Indentured Indians in Natal*, ed. Bhana, 12–88.

Northrup, David. *Indentured Labour in the Age of Imperialism, 1834–1922*. Cambridge: Cambridge University Press, 1995.

Obeyesekere, Gananath. *Cannibal Talk – The Man-Eating Myth and Human Sacrifice in the South Seas*. Berkeley and Los Angeles: University of California Press, 2005.

Ocaya-Lakidi, Dent. 'Black Attitudes to the Brown and White Colonizers of East Africa.' In *Expulsion of a Minority: Essays on Ugandan Asians*, ed. Michael Twaddle, 81–97. London: Athlone Press, 1975.

Ormond, Roger. *The Apartheid Handbook: A Guide to South Africa's Everyday Racial Policies*. Harmondsworth, Middlesex: Penguin, 1985.

Parry, J.H., and Philip Sherlock. *A Short History of the West Indies*. 3rd ed. London: Macmillan Press, 1976.

Persaud, Sasenarine. 'I hear a voice, is it mine?' *World Literature Today* 74.3 (2000): 529–39.

Ping, Tang Soo. 'Renegotiating Identity and Belief in K.S. Maniam's *The Return.*' www.asian.child.com/maniam.html, 7 pages. Accessed 2 March 2002.

Pirbhai, Mariam. 'An Ethnos of Difference, A Praxis of Inclusion: The Ethics of Global Citizenship in Shani Mootoo's *Cereus Blooms at Night.*' In *Asian-Canadian Writing Beyond Autoethnography*, ed. Eleanor Ty and Christl Verduyn, 247–65. Waterloo: Wilfrid Laurier Press, 2008.

Pollard, Arthur. 'Beeharry's *That Others Might Live.*' *World Literature Written in English* 18 (1979): 135–8.

Poynting, Jeremy. "The African and the Asian Will Not Mix' (A. Froude). African-Indian Relations in Caribbean Fiction: A Reply.' *Wasafiri* 5 (1986): 15–21.

– 'Anglophone Caribbean Literature: Towards the Millennium.' *The Courier* 174 (1999): 70–2.

– Guyanese Literature (Peepal Tree Press Feature).' http: voiceofguyana. com/2007/06/08/Guyanese-literature-jeremy-poynting-peepal-tree-press. Accessed 17 December 2007.

– '"You Want to Be a Coolie Woman?": Gender and Ethnicity in Indo-Caribbean Women's Writing.' In *Caribbean Women Writers*, ed. Cudjoe, 98–105.

Pratt, Mary Louise. *Imperial Eyes: Travel Writing and Transculturation.* London: Routledge, 1992.

Puri, Shalini. 'Race, Rape, and Representation: Indo-Caribbean Women and Cultural Nationalism.' *Cultural Critique* 36 (1997): 119–64.

Quet, Danielle. 'Mauritian Voices: A Panorama of Contemporary Creative Writing in English (Part Two).' *World Literature Written in English* 23.2 (1984): 303–12.

Radhakrishnan, R. *Diasporic Mediations: Between Home and Location.* Minneapolis: University of Minnesota Press, 1996.

Rajan, Rajeswari Sunder. *Real and Imagined Women: Gender, Culture and Postcolonialism.* London: Routledge, 1993.

Ramchand, Kenneth. 'Coming Out of Repression: Lakshmi Persaud's *Butterfly in the Wind.*' In *Framing the Word: Gender and Genre in Caribbean Women's Writing*, ed. Joan Anim-Addo, 225–38. London: Whiting and Birch, 1996.

Ramdin, Ron. *The Other Middle Passage: Journal of a Voyage from Calcutta to Trinidad, 1858.* London: Hansib, 1994.

Rampersad, Kris. *Finding a Place: IndoTrinidadian Literature.* Kingston, Jamaica: Ian Randle, 2002.

Ramraj, Victor. 'Diasporas and Multiculturalism.' In *New National and Post-Colonial Literatures: An Introduction*, ed. Bruce King, 214–29. Oxford: Clarendon Press, 1998.

– 'Still Arriving: The Assimilationist Indo-Caribbean Experience of
Marginality.' In *Reworlding*, ed. Nelson, 77–86.

Rastoji, Pallavi. 'From South Asia to South Africa: Locating Other Postcolonial
Diasporas.' *Modern Fiction Studies* 51.3 (2005): 536–60.

Rauf, Mohammed A. *Indian Village in Guyana*. Leiden, Netherlands: E.J. Brill,
1974.

Rushdie, Salman. 'Imaginary Homelands.' In *Imaginary Homelands*, ed. Rushdie,
9–21. London: Granta, 1991.

Said, Edward. 'The Mind of Winter: Reflections on Life in Exile.' *Harper's*,
Sept. 1984, 49–55.

– *Orientalism*. 1978. New York: Vintage, 1979.

Samaroo, Brinsley. 'The Indian Connection: The Influence of Indian Thought
and Ideas on East Indians in the Caribbean.' In *India in the Caribbean*, ed.
Dabydeen and Samaroo, 43–60.

– 'Politics and Afro-Indian Relations in Trinidad.' In *Calcutta to Caroni*, ed. La
Guerre, 84–97.

– 'Two Abolitions: African Slavery and East Indian Indentureship.' In *India in
the Caribbean*, ed. Dabydeen and Samaroo, 25–42.

Sarvan, Charles Ponnutharai. 'The Asians in African Literature.' *Journal of
Commonwealth Literature* 11.2 (1976): 160–71.

– 'Ethnicity and Alienation: The African Asian and His Response to Africa.'
Journal of Commonwealth Literature 22.1 (1985): 100–10.

Scheckter, John. 'Peter Nazareth and the Ugandan Expulsion: Pain, Distance,
Narration.' *Research in African Literatures* 27.2 (1996): 83–93.

Seenarine, Moses. 'Indentured Indian Women in Colonial Guyana:
Recruitment, Migration, Labor and Caste.' In *Sojourners to Settlers: The Indian
Immigrants in the Caribbean and the Americas*, ed. Mahin Gosine and Dhinpaul
Narine. www.saxali.com. 24 pages. Accessed 7 January 2002.

– 'The Persistence of Caste and Anti-Caste Resistance in India and the
Diaspora.' In *Sojourners to Settlers: The Indian Immigrants in the Caribbean and the
Americas*, ed. Mahin Gosine and Dhinpaul Narine. www.saxali.com. 24 pages.
Accessed 7 January 2002.

Selvon, Sam. 'Three Into One Can't Go – East Indian, Trinidadian or West
Indian?' *Wasafiri* 5 (1986, special Caribbean issue): 8–11.

Seong, Teoh Boon. 'Singapore-Malaysian Literature in English: Context and
Relevance.' *Southeast Asian Review of English* 11 (1985): 62–80.

Shameem, Shaista. 'The Art of Raymond Pillai, Subramani and Prem Banfal: A
Feminist Critique of the Indo-Fijian Short Story.' *SPAN: Journal of the South
Pacific Association for Commonwealth Literature and Language Studies* 20 (1985):
29–46.

Shepherd, Verene A. 'Indian Indentured Women in the Caribbean: Ethnicity, Class, and Gender.' *Guyana Arts Journal* 1.1 (2004): 68–79.

Shinebourne, Janice. Interview by Frank Birbalsingh. In *From Pillar to Post*, by Birbalsingh, 146–57.

– 'Twin Influences: Guyana in the 1960s and Anglophone Caribbean Literature.' In *Caribbean Women Writers: Essays from the First International Conference*, ed. Cudjoe, 142–4.

Siddiqi, Jameela. 'Uganda: A Personal viewpoint on the Expulsion, 30 Years.' http://libr.org/isc/articles/15–Siddiqi-1.html. Downloaded 13 April 2007.

Siddique, Sharon, and Nirmala PuruShotam. *Singapore's Little India: Past, Present and Future*. Pasir Panjang, Singapore: Institute of Southeast Asian Studies, 1982.

Simatei, Tirop Peter. *The Novel and the Politics of Nation Building in East Africa*. Bayreuth, Germany: Bayreuth University, 2001.

– 'La question asiatique: Peter Nazareth et Moyez Vassanji, deux romanciers en exil.' In *Litteratures anglophones de l'est de l'afrique d'Addis Ababa á Harare*. 2003. http://www.adpf.asso.fr/librairie/derniers/pdf/nl152.pdf. Accessed 14 May 2007.

Singh, Kelvin. 'East Indians in the Larger Society.' In *Calcutta to Caroni*, ed. La Guerre, 39–68.

Singh, Kirpal. 'An Approach to Singapore Writing in English.' *ARIEL: A Review of International English Literature* 15.2 (1984): 5–24.

'Staying Close But Breaking Free: Indian Writers in Singapore.' In *Reworlding*, ed. Nelson, 99–104.

Skinner, John. *The Stepmother Tongue: An Introduction to New Anglophone Fiction*. New York: St Martin's Press, 1998.

Smith, Angela. 'Mauritian Literature in English.' In *The Writing of East and Central Africa*, ed. G.D. Killam, 70–81.

South Africa Census. 2001. http://www.statssa.gov.za/census01/html/RSAPrimary.pdf.

Sowell, Thomas. *Migrations and Cultures: A World View*. New York: Basic Books, 1996.

Spivak, Gayatri. 'Can the Subaltern Speak?' In *Colonial Discourse and Post-Colonial Theory*, ed. Williams and Chrisman, 66–111.

Subramani, ed. *The Indo-Fijian Experience*. St Lucia, Queensland: Queensland University Press, 1979.

Suleri, Sara. 'Woman Skin Deep: Feminism and the Postcolonial Condition.' In *Colonial Discourse and Post-Colonial Theory*, ed. Williams and Chrisman, 244–56.

Swan, Maureen. 'Indentured Indians and Accommodation and Resistance, 1890–1913.' In *Essays on Indentured Indians in Natal*, ed. Bhana, 117–36.

Tiffin, Helen. 'History and Community Involvement in Indo-Fijian and
Indo-Trinidadian Writing.' In *Reworlding*, ed. Nelson, 87–98.
– 'History and Development of an Indo-Fijian Literary Tradition.' *SPAN:
Journal of the South Pacific Association for Commonwealth Literature and Language
Studies* 10 (1980): 63–8.
Tinker, Hugh. 'Indians Abroad: Emigration, Restriction, and Rejection.' In
Expulsion of a Minority: Essays on Ugandan Asians, ed. Twaddle, 15–30.
– *A New System of Slavery: The Export of Indian Labour Overseas, 1830–1920*.
Oxford: Oxford University Press, 1974.
– 'The Origins of Indian Migration to the West Indies.' In *Indenture and Exile*,
ed. Birbalsingh, 63–72
Twaddle, Michael. 'East African Asians through a Hundred Years.' In *South
Asians Overseas: Migration and Ethnicity*, ed. Clarke et al., 149–63.
– ed. *Expulsion of a Minority: Essays on Ugandan Asians*. London: Athlone Press
for the Institute of Commonwealth Studies, 1975.
– 'Was the Expulsion Inevitable?' In *Expulsion of a Minority: Essays on Ugandan
Asians*, ed. Twaddle, 1–14.
Vassanji, M.G. Introduction to *A Meeting of Streams: South Asian Canadian
Literature*, ed. Vassanji, 1–6. Toronto: TSAR, 1985.
Versi, Anver. 'Not at Home, At Home.' *New African* (April 1994): 39–40.
Vethamani, Malachi Edwin. 'Malaysian, Singaporean and Fijian Writers of the
Diaspora.' *World Literature Today* 21 (1995): 52–3.
Vreland, Nena, et al. *Area Handbook for Singapore*. Washington: Library of
Congress, 1977.
Walcott, Derek. 'The Antilles: Fragments of Epic Memory.' *The Georgia Review*
44.1 (1995): 294–306.
Wicomb, Zoe. 'Shame and Identity: The Case of the Coloured in South Africa.'
In *Writing South Africa*, ed. Attridge and Jolly, 91–107.
Wignesan, T. 'Religion as Refuge, or Conflict and Non-Change: The Case of the
Malaysian Writer in English.' *Journal of Commonwealth Literature* 16.1 (1981):
76–86.
Williams, N.D. (Wyck). Review of *Corentyne Thunder*, by Edgar Mittelholzer.
http://www.guyanacaribbeanpolitics.com/books/corentyne_thunder.html.
Posted 11 January 2005. Accessed: 18 June 2007.
Williams, Patrick, and Laura Chrisman, eds. *Colonial Discourse and Post-Colonial
Theory: A Reader*. New York: Columbia University Press, 1994.
Wilson, Bernard. 'An Interview with K.S. Maniam.' *World Literature Written in
English* 33.2 – 34.1 (1993–4): 17–24.
Yook, Wong Ming. 'Traversing Boundaries: Journeys into Malaysian Fiction in
English.' *World Literature Today* 74.2 (2000): 277–82.

Young, Margaret. 'K.S. Maniam.' In *Encyclopaedia of Post-Colonial English Literature*. New York: Routledge, 1994.

Young, Robert. *Colonial Desire: Hybridity in Theory, Culture and Race*. London: Routledge, 1995.

Index

150–1; East Indian (as term),
101–2; in *The Elect*, 150–1; and
English language, 46; in Fiji,
183–5; in Guyana, 102–3, 109,
216n11; *In a Brown Mantle*, 90–1;
Indian (as term), 14; indigenous
peoples, 101, 179–80; interracial
relationships, 73, 75–6, 86, 92; and
literature, 197–8; in Malaysia,
224n9; native paramountcy, 23–4,
90–1, 181–5; non-white solidarity,
72; racial categories, 211n9; in *The
Return*, 168; segregation, 127, 129;
in Singapore, 160, 171, 225n15;
South Asian (as term), 15; in the
South Seas, 179–81; in *That Others
Might Live*, 63–4; in *Tomorrow Is
Another Day*, 122–5; West Indian
(as term), 101
Ramayana: and Deepchand Beeharry,
54; and Derek Walcott, 111; and
Edward Jenkins, 104; and *girmit*
ideology, 186–9; influence of, 19;
and Lakshmi Persaud, 135, 149;
as literary source, 27; and V.S.
Naipaul, 130; and women, 26,
147. *See also* Hindu epics
Ramdin, Ron: *The Other Middle
Passage*, 221n28; *Rama's Voyage*,
133, 204n14
Ramlella, 111. *See also* Hindu epics;
Ramayana
Rampersad, Kris, 139
Ramraj, Victor, 130, 190
rape, 86
Rastafarians, 223n90
Rastoji, Pallavi, 71–2
recruitment, 15
religion: *baitka*, 210n72; belief
systems, 146–7; in *Butterfly in the

Wind, 145–7; dietary codes,
223n90; and education, 222n44;
in *The Elect*, 137–8, 149–50, 152–3;
in Indo-Caribbean society, 107–8;
in Indo-Trinidadian literature,
139–42; Islam, 82, 158; and
Malaysia, 160; Muslim-Hindu
relations, 141–2; Muslims, 7,
107–8; religious archetypes, 150;
religious identification, 9; and
satire, 196–7; Vedic traditions, 18.
See also Hindu epics
·relocation, as theme, 77
reserving land, 182–3
Return, The, 22, 26, 36, 164–70.
See also Malaysia; Maniam, K.S.
return, site of, 12
Réunion (island), 44
Rhys, Jean: *The Wide Sargasso Sea*,
220n8
rootlessness, 130, 134
Rubadiri, David: *No Bride Price*, 73,
213n36
Rushdie, Salman, 12, 79, 177, 185;
Satanic Verses, 75

Said, Edward, 146
Sam, Agnes: 'And They Christened
It Indenture,' 22, 71; *Jesus is
Indian*, 70–1; 'The Well-Loved
Woman,' 76
Samaroo, Brinsley, 107, 222–3n62
Sanatan Dharam Maha Sabha, 143,
222–3n62
scrupulous subjectivity, 146–7
sea. *See* water imagery
segregation, 127, 129. *See also* race
self-censorship, 171
Selvon, Sam: on ethnic self-assertion,
101–2; on labelling, 99, 101;